Nationalism and Jewish Identity in Morocco

A History of a Minority Community

Kristin Hissong

I.B.TAURIS
LONDON • NEW YORK • OXFORD • NEW DELHI • SYDNEY

I.B. TAURIS
Bloomsbury Publishing Plc
50 Bedford Square, London, WC1B 3DP, UK
1385 Broadway, New York, NY 10018, USA
29 Earlsfort Terrace, Dublin 2, Ireland

BLOOMSBURY, I.B. TAURIS and the I.B. Tauris logo are trademarks of Bloomsbury Publishing Plc

First published in Great Britain 2021
This paperback edition published in 2022

Copyright © Kristin Hissong, 2021

Kristin Hissong has asserted her right under the Copyright, Designs and Patents Act, 1988, to be identified as Author of this work.

For legal purposes the Acknowledgments on p. vi constitute an extension of this copyright page.

Cover series design: Adriana Brioso
Cover image © FADEL SENNA/AFP/Getty Images

All rights reserved. No part of this publication may be reproduced or transmitted in any form or by any means, electronic or mechanical, including photocopying, recording, or any information storage or retrieval system, without prior permission in writing from the publishers.

Bloomsbury Publishing Plc does not have any control over, or responsibility for, any third-party websites referred to or in this book. All internet addresses given in this book were correct at the time of going to press. The author and publisher regret any inconvenience caused if addresses have changed or sites have ceased to exist, but can accept no responsibility for any such changes.

A catalogue record for this book is available from the British Library.

A catalog record for this book is available from the Library of Congress.

ISBN: HB: 978-1-8386-0738-8
PB: 978-0-7556-3936-6
ePDF: 978-1-8386-0739-5
eBook: 978-1-8386-0740-1

Typeset by Deanta Global Publishing Services, Chennai, India

To find out more about our authors and books visit www.bloomsbury.com and sign up for our newsletters.

Nationalism and Jewish Identity in Morocco

Contents

Acknowledgments	vi
Introduction	1
Part I Nationalism Foundations and Theory	13
1 What, When, and Who Is the Nation?	15
Part II Jewish Morocco Historical Background	47
2 Precolonial Moroccan Heterogeneity	49
3 Competing Narratives: French Assimilation and Political Zionism	58
4 Development and Transformation of Nationalism in Morocco	88
Part III Jewish Moroccan Voices	119
5 Zohra, Yaakov, and Michel	121
6 Is Jewish Morocco Exceptional?	158
Notes	175
Bibliography	211
Index	235

Acknowledgments

I am so grateful to Professor Clemens Sedmak without whom this book would lack focus and energy. To the many compassionate and generous colleagues, especially Dr. Vanessa Paloma and Younes Laghrari, who aided me in my fieldwork in Morocco and the friends I met there who showed me so much of Morocco beyond this research project: thank you for making the research possible and the country come alive. Finally, thank you to the interview participants who welcomed me into your homes and lives and patiently and ardently shared your stories.

Introduction

One of the first things I like to do when traveling to a new place is to visit the street vendor selling periodicals to get a feel for what is going on and being discussed and read in my new locale. Though a student of Moroccan Jewry since 2007, I was pleasantly surprised to see the cover story of the Moroccan historical periodical *Zamane* when I arrived in Rabat in May 2013: *Maroc, Terre Juive*. The issue contained several pieces written by leading Moroccan scholars of the field including Jamaa Baïda, Mohammed Hatimi, and Ruth Grosrichard and discussed Jewish history in Morocco, their experience during the Second World War, Zionism in Morocco, and the current situation. In a 2018 visit, I found Morocco's Jewish heritage to be discussed as a nostalgic boast of tolerance and diversity, though few young people knew where the mellah is or why the Jews left. I found this to be the case in Casablanca, Rabat, and Marrakech, though Fez may be the exception where young Muslim Moroccans were eager to show me the Jewish cemetery and recently renovated synagogue. From this general lack of historical awareness, it is unsurprising to discover that Moroccan museums and the Moroccan Tourist Office generally preach a mixed past of Roman, Berber, and Arab presence while omitting Moroccan Jewish heritage. Public institutions like this reflect deeper judgments of power and authority and are often representations of how those in power see themselves or want to be seen. The omission of Moroccan Jews is then a self-fulfilling void; the absence of knowledge in the majority public conscience is reflected in the public institutions and vice versa.

An example raised in this issue of *Zamane* demonstrates both the void and the changing ways in which it may begin to be filled. The content of Grosrichard's piece in particular reveals the omission of Moroccan Jews in state institutions when discussing "the editing of Moroccan high school history books, from which uncomfortable yet very important facts about the war have been completely excised, such as the topic of Nazi anti-Semitism and the extermination of six million of Europe's Jews."[1] However, the fact that this piece among others is featured in the popular periodical with wide Moroccan readership reveals great opportunity for the history of Jews to be known and recognized for their place in historic and modern Morocco.

This is one initiative that Casablanca's Jewish Museum hopes to correct by supplementing school curriculum and textbooks with a fuller version of Moroccan history, one that includes its long Jewish presence. It is precisely because of the small numbers of the current Jewish population of Morocco that this work is important so that it is not diluted entirely. There are more than 200 Jewish cemeteries, synagogues, and music (among other contributions) in Morocco that must be preserved and recorded as a significant piece of Moroccan history. The recent inclusion of Moroccan Jewish experiences in *Zamane* reveals the ways in which Morocco's Jewish past can be a show of pride for modern Moroccans regardless of religious affiliation. For instance, among its opening remarks, the contribution, "Moroccan Judaism, a Millennial Presence", states,

> In the Arab and Muslim world, marked by the Israeli-Palestinian conflict an absurd anti-Judaism . . . Morocco is an exception. The country's constitution recognizes the Jewish contribution to the Moroccan identity. A Jewish community, although reduced, continues to live in Morocco.[2]

This point of pride is held by the Moroccan Jews that I spoke with who felt that their place there, and the fact that Morocco did not fall to chaos in the Arab Spring revolutions of many of its neighbors, reflects a uniquely Moroccan, liberal spirit of their state. In the current political climate that so often pits Muslim against Jew or Arab against Israel, the theory around memory capability (discussed in depth in Chapter 6) suggests an exciting new theory and practice for heterogeneous communities. We see this in Morocco where memory capability allows for not only safe residence by the Jewish minority but even boastful pride of the Muslim population for their country's Jewish heritage and continued coexistence.

The multiple fieldwork trips and adventures that amount to the proceeding text present a picture of urban Jewish life during the Protectorate years and the continued presence of Moroccan Jews in their birthplace. Since the first time I began to get interested in this topic in 2007, my research interests and curiosities evolved into three main questions.

1. How was the Jewish minority present, supported, and active (or not) in the development of various nationalisms?
2. In such a case where multiple nationalisms existed simultaneously, why did Moroccan nationalism come to exclude its historic and sizable Jewish brethren?

3. What does it say of the nation-state and its Jewish minority that there remains a decreased but enduring Jewish community?

The first question will be explored across the three primary nationalist narratives through existing literature, archived periodicals and colonial archives, and participant interviews that elucidate the Jewish presence, engagement with, and sentiment toward these developments. The second question will be explained in two veins: first, through the rise of pan-Arabism and the solidarity and narrative building capacity of Islam to unite the blad al-siba and the blad al-Makzhan and Arab and Amazigh through religious networks that excluded the Jews; second, as a result of the Jews' close relationship with the Protectorate administration or, at the very least, the Alliance Israélite Universelle (AIU), the necessarily anti-Protectorate Moroccan nationalist narrative for independence came to exclude those who were so closely aligned with the Protectorate. The third question will be addressed primarily through memory capability with further discussion through the solar system diaspora approach. Memory, so vital to identity on individual and collective levels, is a powerful tool in the remembering and forgetting that creates a national unit. Where reference points are forbidden to reflect the full heterogeneity of a community, minorities may struggle to identify with the nation-state. In Morocco, Jews have the freedom and opportunity to remember rightly and the intangible and actual infrastructure to retain their religious and national identities and communities within the state; this memory capability explains the continued Jewish presence in Morocco and has hopeful implications for the well-being and peaceful coexistence of diverse nation-states beyond the place and time of Protectorate Morocco.

In today's tense political climate where religion is often wielded as the motivation for extremism and violence, the quotidian, majority voices of those among a religious group are passed over in the media and press for the polar extremes of fundamentalism or secularism, terrorism or leftist liberalism, etc. Though an increasingly globalized world facilitates the movement of people and ideas, it has not so easily accommodated religious tolerance and communication between diverse groups. What is needed is greater attention to the majority, everyday voices who aspire toward peace and well-being. In Protectorate Morocco, the same extremes can be identified at the furthest poles of the three primary narratives; however, what is presented in this book is a collection of the scholarly and of the everyday voices to stand as a reference point for the story of Moroccan Jewry and as an example of the complex, interrelated cooperation of Muslim and Jewish communities before 1948.

Remembering Morocco's Jewish past and present honors, protects, renders justice, and keeps it, in a sense, alive.

Whose Voices are Included?

In the years since independence, "Moroccan, French, British, Spanish, and American scholars have built a considerable body of literature on the topic" of Protectorate-era Morocco calling upon "surveys, memoirs, and monographs representing a variety of viewpoints and perspectives."[3] This body of literature not only shares each author's input toward the field but also reflects the time in which it was written, such as with more historic texts of the colonial era. Others focus more on the Jewish religious tradition and others on the Moroccan monarchy. Yet a thorough reading and understanding of the field at large offers us the opportunity to mold a historical reconstruction in which we see the evolution of Protectorate studies; this process also highlights gaps in the literature that demand better investigation and representation.

One such key source is that of French scholar Charles-André Julien whose personal connection to the Protectorate period and training as a journalist resulted in two major works documenting mid-twentieth-century Morocco.[4] His work continues to influence the way scholars address the development of Moroccan nationalism into different phases: as prewar and postwar phases interrupted by the "stasis of the war years"[5] and referred to by Julien as the "parenthesis theory."[6] Also addressing the Vichy regime in the Maghreb and Morocco in particular are the Christine Levisse-Touze sources[7] and those of William Hoisington.[8] Levisse-Touze details Vichy politics and France's desire to keep its colonial sphere alive while Hoisington looks more broadly at the résident général of the time, Charles Noguès, and how Protectorate policy operated in the wartime years.

Several scholars address various regions and sections of the Jewish population.[9] Laskier provides a detailed history and influence of the AIU[10] on Morocco's Jews while Baïda's insight is valuable for his focus on the Jewish press during the interwar period as well as reasons for emigration. These sources, along with Boum's attention to the southern Moroccan Jews and Jewish memory, are valuable when addressing the Jewish presence and role in the development of conflicting nationalist narratives during the Protectorate. Miller's more recent work on Moroccan Jewish history (and Moroccan history in general)[11] is a refreshing survey of the pre-Protectorate period through postindependence concerned with minority spaces in Moroccan cities and the life of Jews as the sultan's dhimmi[12] subjects. Rivet's recent update[13] to Julien's colonial history benefits from its temporal distance from the subject; whereas Julien's anti-colonial rhetoric colors his account's portrayal of the Protectorate, Rivet draws upon recently made available archival material[14] to present various narratives and discuss the 'parenthesis theory' put forward by Julien. The recent collaboration led by the Moroccan scholar Mohammed Kably,[15] published by the Royal Institute for Research on the History of Morocco in Rabat, produces an overarching history spanning from prehistory to the present day. Its material on the period of 1939 to 1956, which presents a "pluralistic and inclusive nature of the nationalist movement that ultimately embraced every element in Moroccan society,"[16] may be indicative of the tone its Moroccan authors wish to suggest; however, it is an impressively thorough and comprehensive source. Daniel Schroeter is a prolific expert on the history of Moroccan Jews, and Jonathan Wyrtzen's dissertation referenced herein has since become a successful book touching on Berber, Jewish, and gendered experiences in the making of modern Morocco. Emily Gottreich's latest publication covering pre-Islamic to postcolonial Morocco is notable for its treatment of Malikism and Sharifism and the impact of Islamic doctrine and jurisdiction on Berber and Jewish Moroccans.

Scope and Contribution

The book is organized into three parts. Part I focuses on the theories of nationalism and identity in order to lay the foundation for our vignettes later in Chapter 5; Part II tells the history of Moroccan Jews as a minority community from the pre-Protectorate period up to its end in 1956 to show how the status of Moroccan Jews has changed from a protected *dhimmi* to a citizen of an independent Morocco in the space of fifty years; Part III presents interviews with Moroccan Jews and explores their experiences as exceptional or valid for transnational lessons. The main questions addressed herein include, first, how was Morocco's Jewish minority present, supported, and active (or not) in the development of these nationalisms? Second, in such a case where multiple nationalisms existed simultaneously, why did Moroccan nationalism come to exclude its historic and sizable Jewish brethren? Third, what does it say of the nation-state and its Jewish minority that there remains a decreased, but enduring, Jewish community? From these three main questions the nature of identity, multiethnic nation-states and nationalist narratives, and memory are examined.

In order to contribute both empirically and theoretically to the fields of Moroccan Jewish history, the development of nationalist narratives, and the transnational implications of memory capability, this book draws upon a triangulation of the existing secondary scholarly literature, archived periodicals and colonial documents, and semi-structured interviews with Moroccan Jews who lived during the Protectorate and remain in Morocco today. The composite of these sources provides a full and thorough reconstruction of Protectorate Morocco with increased credibility and validity of the analysis through cross-checking sources and accounts for the highest methodological integrity. Particularly poignant following the above discussion of the complexity of identity and narrative, this is a fitting method insofar as it allows the three perspectives to compliment one another and highlight points of contention to give a robust reconstruction of events and experiences during the Protectorate.

As an analytical framework, this book designs French cultural-linguistic assimilation, Political Zionism, and Moroccan nationalism as three primary nationalist narratives to track and map fluid and dynamic identity and narrative. Because the Moroccan nationalist narrative took on an Arab-Islamic identity with influence coming from the region's pan-Arab narratives, I use the identity trait 'Arab' to refer to Moroccan Muslims, though "many of these people were not, in fact, ethnic Arabs; a large proportion . . . were Berbers."[17] Similarly, labeling Moroccan Jews under their religious identity trait is an oversimplification of the linguistic, cultural, and ethnic diversity among them; this diversity will be explored in more detail in Chapters 3 and 4. Nevertheless, proving the hypothesis of fluidity and dynamism, the semi-structured interview method allows for the vibrantly complex stories of individual nuances to shine so that no participant is restricted to one label.

Consulting the existing literature gives a historical overview that informs the reader of the period on which it focuses as well as some indication of the climate in which the author is writing. A thorough understanding and awareness of this literature aids in the historical reconstruction while also highlighting voids in the literature that can be complimented or supplemented by archival material and personal testimony. Toward this end, I gathered archived periodicals in Rabat from the National Library of the Kingdom of Morocco and the Hassan Archive of the Royal Palace[18] as well as the King Abdul-Aziz Al Saoud Foundation for Islamic Studies and Human Sciences and the Foundation for Moroccan Jewish Heritage in Casablanca.[19] In France, I gathered colonial diplomatic archives in Nantes and Paris.[20] The periodicals and colonial archives discovered and explored add detail to the historical reconstruction and reveal the attitudes and opinions of the Protectorate administration officials and their 'protectees.'

For greater depth and detail beyond those preserved in written sources, I wished to ascertain whether a general group consciousness existed while simultaneously allowing for the complexities of identity affiliations and the nuance of personal experience. In order to do so, I interviewed Moroccan Jews from a variety of backgrounds and status though, purposefully, limiting myself to those in urban settings[21] and not from the mountains or countryside.[22] Because Morocco's Jewish population is severely decimated with an estimated number of 3,000–4,000 Jews remaining[23][24] in contrast to well over 200,000 during the Protectorate period, I endeavored to collect the stories and experiences of a generation of Jews who, though not exposed to the Holocaust in the same ways as Jews on the European continent, carry with them unique and personal remembrances and experiences of this era. Their experience provides an interesting platform through which to analyze the complexity and plurality of identity and narrative, the Jewish presence and role in the development of nationalist narratives, especially Moroccan nationalism, and the transnational implications of memory capability. This qualitative approach contributes to the nuance and specificity of the historical reconstruction while adding personal meaning and experience of historical events that may not be present in the official historical narrative.

One type of source that this book will not draw upon is the personal memoir, neither of Moroccan nor of European authorship. Lawrence is right to point out that "relying on nationalist memoirs is problematic because they were written after the movement for independence had begun, when elites were engaged in the project of constructing nationalist history."[25] He is referring here to nationalist movement leader Allal al-Fassi whose memoir stresses the presence of nationalist consciousness both before and after the coming of Islam to Morocco. Certainly, the memoir's reader cannot divorce a reading of this text from the political project of nation building that al-Fassi was engaged with before and during its writing. This is not to say the text lacks historical value; rather, it is to say that one must highlight and address the nuances in order to escape the retroactive 'white-wash' that national rhetoric can bring.[26] That is, the terms, labels, and theories that can be applied in light of a world of nation-states should not be applied to the past for risk of ignoring its specific time, place, and people.

Although contributing a written record of an outsider perspective, many scholars[27] criticize the value of the European travel memoir, often referred to as 'travel narrative,' where Morocco is presented through "clichés and caricatured profiles."[28] Popular travel narratives of Réné Caillié (1799–1838), John Davidson (1839), Charles de Foucauld (1884), de La Porte Des Vaux (1952), Flamand (1952, 1959), and Goldberg (1983) are well known and frequently cited in the colonial historiography of Morocco but require serious deconstructing to strip away the stereotypes and biases upon which past scholarly and popular work has been built. This colonial lens has led a group of Moroccan historians to call for a reappraisal of colonial Moroccan historiography on the grounds that European sources are mere reflections of their European authors' interests and preoccupations.[29] When the accepted historiography reenacts the European colonial powers subordinating the internal, domestic accounts, one can understand the frustration of Moroccan scholars. Because the interpretation is affected from the perspectives of European travel narratives, even the "native interpretation of history is not as independent as it claims to be from the colonial texts"[30] with 'indigenous' historians appropriating elements or idioms of the travel narrative sources. These narratives require contextualized analysis within the ideology of the French colonial presence in Morocco. Boum allows that such clichés and caricatures, albeit distortions, are not "systematically incorrect or inappropriate" just as they are also neither systematically true nor accurate; they can be "pregnant with historical significance."[31] However, peeling away the layers of inherent prejudice or political motive from the travel memoirs' authors is not a priority from the perspective of this book.

In order to provide sufficient background to fully explore the research questions, the structure allows for theoretical and historical background before delving into the stories of the interview participants. Chapter 2 focuses on the theoretical explanations of identity and narrative in order to discuss what and when is the nation. From an understanding of individual and collective identity as plural, dynamic, social, and fluid, theories of nationhood and national identity are explored with particular emphasis on the role of memory in constructing individual and national identity. Discussing the various predominant theories of nationhood, I develop a hybrid view of ethno-symbolism and modernism wherein the nation is a construction of rediscovered, reinterpreted, and regenerated symbols and myths to fit its modern circumstances and motives: adaptive ethno-symbolism. In this discussion, notions of ethnicity, culture, and race are deconstructed in order to clarify the language of studying the nation and the transition of identity to ideology is examined in order to understand nationalism as a political narrative.

In order to approach the first question (how was the Jewish minority present, supported, and active (or not) in the development of these nationalisms?),

Chapter 3 embarks on a pre-Protectorate view of Moroccan heterogeneity before the arrival of European colonial influence. This inclusion is necessary to understand the Moroccan Jewish dhimmi status and the various types of Jewish-Muslim relationships before the Protectorate. Different perspectives on the advantages and disadvantages of dhimmi life are discussed so as not to inaccurately glorify the state of Jewish-Muslim cohabitation; however, the various forms of cooperation and economic interaction suggest a favorable status quo of pre-Protectorate coexistence that recognized the long Moroccan Jewish heritage. Next, Chapter 3 introduces the coming of European influence, in particular France, with its protégé opportunities. These changes rearranged Moroccan urban society and began the transition of Jews from indigenous subjects to associationists to the Protectorate regime. This chapter lays the foundation for the proceeding discussion of the implications of the Protectorate treaty and the period of growing nationalist narratives it would foster.

Chapter 4 introduces the first two primary nationalist narratives, French cultural-linguistic assimilation and Political Zionism, and the role of the Protectorate in bringing Western liberal ideals of autonomy and self-determination that furthered the development and reception of nationalism. Drawing upon archived periodicals and colonial diplomatic archives, it is clear that the Protectorate officials aimed to further the administration's civilizing mission with pacification policies while also providing the essential infrastructure and institutions that would enable nation building. This chapter evaluates the construction of French identity among Moroccan Jewish communities with particular emphasis on the role of the AIU as well as the arrival of Political Zionism and its divisive effect. In order to explore the Political Zionist narrative in Morocco, a brief background of the narrative as well as the concept of orientalism is given before addressing both French assimilation and Political Zionism in the Protectorate context. As a key turning point of immense significance, the Vichy period of the Second World War is also examined before turning to the development of the Moroccan nationalist narrative.

Having presented two of the three primary narratives in question, Chapter 5 then turns to the development and transformation of nationalism in Morocco from calls for reform to demands for independence. From the first meetings of educated Muslim Moroccans in the early 1920s to the eventual exile of many of their leaders in 1937, the movement grew both in size and demands. Wanting primarily to reform the Protectorate administration and hold France accountable to the 1912 Treaty of Fez which established the Protectorate in Morocco, early reformists sought to work within the framework of the Protectorate. This chapter uses extensive archived periodicals and colonial diplomatic archives to trace the development of the movement in the press and the Residency; these sources give great insight to the changing attitudes that prevailed and were distributed to the literate elite. In its transition from calls for reform to demands for independence, the 1930 Berber Dahir, the Second World War, and the sultan's 1947 Tangier speech are given specific attention as turning points in the development of an Arab-Islamic Moroccan nationalism. Having detailed this third primary narrative, the chapter then turns to the extent of Jewish inclusion in the movement and their role or presence in its development.

From the detailed historical reconstruction and archival insight of preceding chapters, Chapter 6 approaches Protectorate Moroccan Jewish identity across the three primary narratives with the presentation of interview participant findings. With the exploration of the nationalist narratives in Chapters 4 and 5 and the primary data in Chapter 6, the second research question (in such a case where multiple nationalisms existed simultaneously, why did Moroccan nationalism come to exclude its historic and sizable Jewish brethren?) is addressed. After a brief note on methodology, I present three in-depth vignettes of participant data that highlight the participants' memories and personalities. This primary data confirms the theoretical framework of plural identity and narrative and challenges the limitations of designing Moroccan Jewish identity across three primary narratives in their fluid, dynamic negotiations. Following these in-depth vignettes, Chapter 6 analyses the participant findings across four key markers: education, religion, language, and political involvement.

In addition to the presentation and analysis of the primary data, Chapter 6 revisits the theoretical discourse presented in Chapter 2 in light of the triangulated sources presented in the intervening discussion. Cutting across identity, narrative, and nationhood, memory is found to be the omnipresent, essential common aspect. Its frequency and powerful presence is therefore identified to be an innovative concept with transnational implications where the opportunity to remember rightly can lead to the achievement of well-being in heterogeneous nations and nation-states. Sen's capability approach is examined as a way of framing the powerful implications of memory and remembering. After first providing background on the capability approach, Chapter 6 presents the possibility of memory capability to achieve well-being using the participant interviews to illustrate its applicability.

Lastly, following a reflection on the case study of Morocco and the methodology applied in Chapter 6, Chapter 7 examines the unique qualities of Protectorate Morocco and its Jewish population and addresses the third research question: What does it say of the nation-state and its Jewish minority that there remains a decreased, but enduring, Jewish community? As it remains one of only few countries of the Middle East and North Africa (MENA) region to have a continuous Jewish presence following the great 'exodus' of Jews from the region beginning in the late 1940s, Morocco is unique. Its deep national identity that, through the malleable construction of memory, can include its Jewish minority is a unique feature among its neighbors who underwent more violent transitions to independence and harbored more extreme pan-Arab sentiment than country-specific pride in the decolonization process. Because Jews have been able, and have chosen to, remain, Morocco forms a sort of solar system diaspora[32] where the homeland-exile dichotomy of Jewish return is challenged in that there is more than one ancestral homeland due to the long Jewish heritage in Morocco.

To examine and evaluate these unique features, Jewish experience in other Arab countries, in particular the case of Egyptian Jewry in the colonial period, is briefly addressed. This comparison notes several similarities such as the historic longevity of Jews in their respective lands, the disruption of indigenous relations due to the colonial presence, and the irrevocable consequences of the establishment of the State of Israel. However, significant contrasting elements pervade such as the state's attitude toward the Political Zionist narrative in its early years and Jewish aliyah (emigration to Israel), the distinct country-specific tone of Morocco's nationalist narrative, and the ability of Moroccan Jews to continue to call Morocco home during the decolonization process and in the following years. Examining this brief parallel furthers the need for transnational-reaching theoretical implications of narrative and memory.

Egypt's close geographical proximity to Israel heightens the need and the potential for memory to serve as an opportunity to achieve peaceful well-being by acknowledging diversity and creating common space for its diverse citizens. Chapter 7 concludes with a discussion of memory capability and the significance of remembering for future well-being finding the role of memory and memory capability to be essential to identity construction and maintenance as well as reconciling heterogeneous societies that share nation-states toward stable coexistence. The freedom to remember rightly and retain reference points of memories that reflect the state's diverse groups may reconcile the tension between dominant ethnic group states and the challenge of new global structures and universal human rights; by allowing minority groups their freedom to remember and acknowledging their memories in the state's common spaces, members of minority groups have their place in the state and dominant ethnic groups may recognize themselves as living alongside others as fellows rather than rulers. In this sense, ethnicity need not be eradicated but rather put to use through "trans-ethnic networks of national and supranational governance."[33] Memory capability presents a way forward toward such a new configuration where the opportunity to remember is a capability toward well-being and peaceful heterogeneous coexistence.

This book contributes both empirically and theoretically to the fields of Moroccan Jewish history, the development of nationalist narratives, and memory studies. I support the notion of the plurality and socially bound construction of identity and reinforce the importance of narrative and memory in individual, collective, and national identity. I claim that adaptive ethno-symbolism provides the best theoretical model for the nation-state where premodern symbols and myths are readapted beyond their original significance for the nation-state's modern setting, institutions, and societies. While identity's fluidity and dynamism defies the strict division of Moroccan Jews into three distinct categories, the three broad spheres of French cultural-linguistic assimilation, Political Zionism, and Arab-Islamic Moroccan nationalism during the Protectorate years are reinforced by the participant interviews.

This book provides unique participant data of an ever-diminishing population and proposes a new theoretical approach to well-being in the form of memory capability. Because of its location and demographic, Morocco is often torn between Africa and the Middle East, the Arab world and Europe, and Jewish and Muslim research disciplines. This lack of defined field makes Morocco the ideal case study for an interdisciplinary study and an example of memory capability at work for its ability to give diverse perspectives a common space in a heterogeneous nation-state. In the modern political climate where Jewish and Arab are so often opposing identities and narratives, this book preserves stories of a generation of Jewish-Muslim cooperation and cohabitation that predates this dichotomy and offers an approach toward overcoming its current divide.

Part I

Nationalism Foundations and Theory

1

What, When, and Who Is the Nation?

In working toward defining the nation, objective and subjective criteria that form the basis of individual identities and collective identities may include "religion, language, or race . . . self-awareness, solidarity, self-defined, or other-defined, etc."[1] To this list, the concepts of state, nation, and ethnic group are equally important and their distinctions often subtle. While some ethnic groups transformed into nations in the modern era, others, due to "territorial dispersion, lack of political ambition or low level of self-consciousness did not."[2] Furthermore, where many ethnic groups achieved nationhood, not all achieved modern nation-statehood, one timely mention being the Scottish people. In the last several decades, scholarly literature in the field of identity, ethnicity, and nationalism has continued to expand.[3] As a result, various theories of the nation and nationalism exist, to be discussed in detail in Chapter 2, and much work has been focused on developing normative approaches toward these entities of state, nation, and ethnic group. To fully understand these concepts and their demographic, cultural, political, and economic consequences, it is first necessary to explore the discourse regarding individual and collective identity.

Though identity as an academic metric has been debated and challenged by some,[4] identity and the social norms which inform it continue to pervade the arts and humanities and social sciences. For instance, the disciplines of economy, sociology, anthropology, and history study the way in which social norms inform behavior, motivate action, shape culture, and connect previous and future generations. When approaching a study of the nation and nationalism, one cannot overlook its component parts: the institutions and actors of which it is comprised. Therefore, to deconstruct the nation into its many collectives, one must address the individuals that make up those collectives. Many scholars approach their study of identity in its societal setting where identity is formed, influenced, shaped, and acted out in social mediation.[5] Extending upon this notion, Avishai Margalit and Josheph Raz introduced the idea of encompassing groups of belonging in which Charles Taylor, and later David Brown, would build with work on the importance of recognition.[6] In acknowledging the powerful presence that society has in shaping both individual and collective identities, these scholars and many of their contemporaries continue to work on the plurality of identity.[7] National identity is one of the characteristics that construct plural identity. Leading works on the nation and nationalism debate whether or not the national connection is a modern phenomenon, though most acknowledge that the present world organization of nation-state borders is a modern construction.[8] Drawing upon the existing literature and applying it to the case of French Protectorate Morocco, the work herein tests and bridges theories of identity, nationhood, and nationalism.

Illustrating its relevance and significance, scholarly interest in the study of identity spans across not only the arts and humanities and social science disciplines but also studies of genetic and ancestry biological studies and psychology. The relationship between deoxyribonucleic acid (DNA) and culture, for instance, raises multidisciplinary and interdisciplinary questions about how societies are connected and why humans behave the way they behave and think the way they think. A recent account attempting to explore these questions is Kenneally's *Invisible History of the Human Race*[9] which examines the connections of individual and collective identity between and across generations, reviewing events of the past with the aid of DNA evidence and the sequencing of the human genome. The scientific precision with which these genetic indicators may be forecasted is fashionable of late; perhaps this is due to the new certainty it can confer on ancestral heritage and health risks when linking past, present, and future or perhaps because modern technology has created a society wherein one desires to track each detail of human existence in a mobile application. Nevertheless, a linguist and journalist herself, Kenneally acknowledges that genetic material takes on meaning only in the story of the people who embody it. The suggestion that one's identity is shaped by one's genetic inheritance overlooks the complex plurality and context-dependent fluidity of identity.

Indeed, beyond genetic inheritance, identity is constructed and maintained in one's social context: "It is not the attribute that makes the group, but the group and group-differences that make the attribute significant."[10] Economist and philosopher Amartya Sen, whose capability approach will be drawn upon in detail in Chapter 6, furthers the socially shaped plurality of identity adding the factor of an individual's ability and freedom for reasoning and choice in one's identity. The focus on genetic makeup overlooks the many intangibles that are passed down between generations and among encompassing groups of belonging such as memory and narrative. What is passed down is not only economic and political infrastructure or roads, railways, and utilities but also types of intangible infrastructure "brought about by human resources" such as cultural values and education.[11] In heterogeneous societies where various influences and people coexist, such as nearly all nation-states, studies of identity cannot be complete without deep understanding of the memories, narratives, and human capabilities[12] present from those who live the identities in question.

Further escalating interest in nationalist identity and narrative is the notion of the right to self-determination and universal human rights that has spread in its discourse and application since the conclusion of each world war, respectively, and continued to grow in the civil rights and anti-colonial struggles in the decades following. In this rhetoric, nations are "encouraged to look to their future" rather than the past, to "treasure cultural diversity (past and present) rather than homogeneity, to recognize the autonomy claims of minorities," and be open to foreign influences.[13] In an increasingly globalized world, these issues remain relevant with new studies appearing in citizenship, border, and migration studies. The universality of self-determination, human rights, and future-oriented solidarity undermines the glue of indigenous legitimacy and emotive power that nationalism theorists claim ethnic groups bring to the narrative. States where a dominant ethnic group holds the demographic or politico-economic power provide exciting case studies for how dominant ethnic groups can negotiate or circumvent "new global structures and values."[14]

Self-assigned or state-applied identity labels and language do not help to account for the diversity of nations or members of nation-states. If one refers to the 'Arab people,' this term does not reflect the varying "ethnicity, religion, nationalism, and race that produces the entire range of human passions"[15] among this label. The Israeli-Arab conflict since the creation of the modern State of Israel has led to an opposing dichotomy of Jewish and Arab identities that ignores those among the 'Arab people' who would identify as Jews. Though scholarly literature addresses his history, "Many who have studied the modern history of the Middle East and North Africa have been caught in the western European mode of interpretation, which focuses on the familiar trajectory of modern Jewish history: from emancipation to assimilation, from anti-Semitism to Zionism."[16] As a result, non-Western or non-Ashkenazi Jews become grouped under the term 'Mizrahi' (oriental), and their history is then shaped by the influence of the West and the State of Israel. The Maghreb (generally considered to encompass Morocco, Algeria, Tunisia, and Libya, though frequently used interchangeably with the term 'North Africa'), and Morocco in particular, highlights the coming together of multiple identities and narratives. Located geographically and demographically between Africa and the Middle East and, equally, the Arab world and Europe, Morocco's internal diversity is no less significant. Though the Morocco of 1956, and the years leading to independence in this year, came to construct and develop a nationalist narrative that centered on Arab-Islamic notions of its past and present, Morocco is a suitable case for comparative religious studies with its heterogeneous Berber, Jewish, Muslim, and colonial influences.

In order to explore the complexities of nation and other kindred concepts like ethnicity, culture, and national identity in Protectorate Morocco, it is necessary to first understand the foundation of the terms and ideologies at play. While the ideas of nation-state and nationalism have come to be viewed by many in the West as an omnipresent, inherent attribute of humanity, it is only in hindsight that these labels can be applied to pre-eighteenth-century and non-Western societies with their modern meaning. The purpose of this chapter is to address the foundations of the concepts of identity, nationhood, memory, and ethnicity in order to begin to understand how these concepts affect the development of the nation-state and the contrasting narratives its citizens share with the state.

Inherent in the conceptualization of various forms of collective identity (national, ethnic, etc.) is the individual identities that comprise these collectives. With that in mind, it is necessary to remember identity, narrative, and the role of memory throughout the discussion of nation, ethnicity, and national identity; in doing so, attempts toward a normative approach for nations and nationalism will include a transparent path regarding the application of terms and meanings. This understanding of the historical and ideological roots of these terms will be crucial in the discussion and analysis of Jewish and Arab ethnicity in the development of nationalist narratives during the French Protectorate and will provide unique and thorough perspective upon which to reflect when meeting interview participants in Chapter 6.

Individual identity does not develop in a vacuum but is rather linked to society and social relations producing socially shaped identity. Indeed, identity is a "complex, evolving, multilayered, and situational relationship between an individual and the group, or groups, to which he or she relates."[17] Identity formation comes from both self-perception and societal influence that may arise frequently through the negation of other. This highlights the role of society in the development of an individual identity in the way that each individual is shaped by, and for, the society: "Society expects from each of its members a certain kind of behavior, imposing innumerable and various rules, all of which tend to 'normalize' its members, to make them behave, to exclude spontaneous action or outstanding achievement."[18] This includes forms of discontent that are recognized as important motivators for ethnic, collective action alongside, or in combination with, other facilitating factors such as mobilizing resources.[19]

If identity is understood as the outcome of exclusionary practices in which the 'inside' is threatened by the 'outside,' the role of the outsider is equally influential and important in the shaping of the insider's identity. This is a daily process of operating within a society; through a matter of symbols and appearances we see "people with names that sound like mine, with the same colour skin, with the same affinities, even the same infirmities, it is possible for me to feel that that gathering represents me" and a continual process of identifying, or not, is taking place.[20] Tajfel defines social identity as "that part of an individual's self-concept which derives from his knowledge of his membership of a social group (or groups) together with the value and emotional significance attached to that membership."[21] This social view of individual identity stresses that it is one's belonging to collectives that informs self-perception and, further, action. This outward identity theory, in which individual identities are socially influenced, allows for both personal and social self-perceptions but argues that personal self-perception is highly informed by social norms and belonging where one perceives herself in terms of relevant group memberships. Honneth's work on identity formation explains this personal to social connection in terms of self-confidence, self-respect, and self-esteem.[22] These modes of self-perception and recognition are acquired and maintained in relation to the other so that personal identity recognition is dependent on the establishment of relationships.

This theory of recognition,[23] situated in greater discussion of critical theory and social justice, fits in outward identity and, for the purpose of exploring identity as a metric of analysis and practice, aids in examining the relationship between identity and belonging. These social relationships are referred to by Margalit and Raz as "encompassing groups."[24] Encompassing groups share many characteristics: common culture, mutual recognition, membership based on belonging rather than achievement, and group-related symbols to enable mutual recognition;[25] these characteristics will resonate in the discussion of nationhood to follow. The group characteristics are not fixed but "in flux in relation to other socio-economic and political processes and situations, rather than a distinct unit with an essential identity."[26]

Taylor questions the link between recognition and identity to the extent that recognition, and the possibility of misrecognition or lacking recognition, can be destructive to identity. Challenging the view of individualized identity where one's unique selfhood is authentic, an ideal that will emerge again when examining Rousseau and Herder, he labels this a modern phenomenon that came with the late eighteenth century.[27] To the extent that identity is dialogical, it is socially molded; however, the ideal of authenticity undermines socially derived identity in that it calls on the individual to discover her own way of being and this necessitates inward identity. Discovering one's identity does not imply that it happens in isolation, rather that the individual negotiates identity dialogically both internally and with others. Taylor offers an example: "If some of the things I value most are accessible to me only in relation to the person I love, then (the person I love) becomes part of my identity."[28] In this sense, inward identity is shaped by relationships, too, but it is the internal negotiation and owning of authenticity that molds and motivates the individual. This modern phenomenon of turning inward is not merely a liberal egoism, but, for Taylor, a way toward well-being and human goodness.[29]

It is important to note, however, that identity is not necessarily an inert or fixed trait, but rather one's self-image may change and flux with its spatial and historical setting. For instance, "the Christian subject of a Christian emperor may become a member of the Muslim umma and perhaps transform into a citizen of the People's Democratic Republic."[30] Several scholars agree upon this plural approach[31] that identity is dynamic and plural depending on context. Individuals and collectives alike may have several affiliations simultaneously, any of which may at any one time be foremost in their minds, depending on the context.[32] This hierarchy assumes that humans lead segmented lives consisting of different identity affiliations of which national identity is usually one. Hierarchy is determined by the temporal context:

> For long periods of time these different attachments would not make incompatible demands on a person, so that a man might have no problem about feeling himself to be the son of an Irishman, the husband of a German woman, a member of the mining community, a worker, a supporter of Barnsley Football Club, a liberal, a primitive Methodist, a patriotic Englishman, possibly a Republican, and a supporter of the British Empire. It was only when one of these loyalties conflicted directly another or others that a problem of choosing between them arose.[33]

This plurality underscores another conflict in classifying identity, that is, the struggle in the attempt to define an individual between what he is (labels) and who he is (thoughts, actions, relationships). All definitions "being determinations or interpretations of what man is, of qualities, therefore, which he could possibly share with other living beings, whereas his specific difference would be found in a determination of what kind of a who he is."³⁴ This distinction demonstrates how even individuals among homogeneous groups can come to see themselves in contrast to the other and highlights diversity and nuance among collectives.

Accepting this theory of pluralism is not to presume that "people's particularistic and subjective concerns—about gender, ethnicity, or any other form of affinity—should be downplayed in favor of the great universalisms."³⁵ The universality is not that people do not identify personally and with individualized nuance but that identities are composed of plural affiliations. The task then remains to understand the priority and ordering that is given to the multiple affiliations of one's identity. Maalouf admits, "In every age there have been people who considered that an individual had one overriding affiliation so much more important in every circumstance to all others that it might legitimately be called his identity."³⁶ Whether this is one's nation or religion, for example, this view insists that a base, fundamental allegiance will overcome regardless of plural affiliations. In looking at various conflicts being fought throughout the world, however, one can see that context matters in determining which allegiances are asserted: "Where people feel their faith is threatened, it is their religious affiliation that is asserted. But if their mother tongue or their ethnic group is in danger, then they fight ferociously against their own coreligionists."³⁷

The recognition that identities are robustly plural and that these multiple affiliations may coexist simultaneously negates the solitarist approach that sees humans as members of exactly one group only.³⁸ This approach is not only reductive and shortsighted; it ignores the existence of choice and reasoning in identity formation and fuels a narrative of national exceptionalism that views its nation and its people above all others. Disputing the notion of a fundamental, core identity affiliation, the constructivist approach echoes that identities are socially constructed and not immutably fixed from birth; this allows for multiple and dynamic negotiation of identity affiliations but is lacking when it comes to understanding shifts in, or mobilization of, identity. Cooper raises the question of why politicians seeking to transform categories of people into unitary and exclusive groups are often successful through the chant of identity politics: What is at work that takes the multiple identity affiliations of an individual and allows her to strongly exert just one? I contend that a fluid hierarchy, with an emphasis on context, is a more complete extension of dynamism. Whereas dynamism allows for identity affiliations to change and the hierarchy to rearrange, it implies a shift from affiliation x to affiliation y. Fluidity is applied herein to represent the nonlinear, subtle, or gradual shifts among plural affiliations that may create new categories all together instead of moving among preexisting ones. The situationalist approach, which suggests that communal identities are shaped by the context within which communities find themselves, helps to express fluidity. When under threat from an outside other, the collective reacts defensively so as to react to "the identity of the dominant other, and so as to provide a suitable basis for emotional, and often physical, defence"[39] according to the situation.

While one discovers certain elements of her identity from a young age in the community around her, identity is not a one-time discovery but is rather built upon and altered through a person's lifetime. What determines an individual's affiliation to a community is not a solitary experience; rather, it depends on the community's exclusion or inclusion of certain traits and characteristics. Identity formation is not happening in a vacuum, but it is a continuous process of back-and-forth between the individual and her community. Here, Maalouf's expression is fitting, "He is not himself from the outset; nor does he just grow aware of what he is; he becomes what he is. He acquires it step by step."[40] This is not to undermine the significance of the communitarian aspect in identity formation; however, an element of choice is still present in whether one affiliates with the community and how.

A person makes choices about the hierarchy of her allegiances through context so that it is a constant renegotiating, or balancing act, between establishing one's allegiances and then weighing the relative importance of these allegiances. Sen insists, "Both tasks demand reasoning and choice. The importance of a particular identity will depend on the social context."[41] While not all allegiances will be contrasting, some may be or may be perceived to be. Whereas some traits like language are indisputably plural (a person can speak multiple languages without tension), others are less so (one cannot be Jewish, Muslim, and Christian simultaneously).[42] However, it is not always the case that to assert one allegiance will be to deny another, but rather that an individual will have to decide on the relative hierarchy of different affiliations.

Although identities are in some measure created, sustained, and made relevant in political narrative by ethnic groups and by the state, this is not to take for granted the relationship between individual and collective identity. Many factors may influence individuals' social realities, but which factors form a substantive base for the construction and mobilization of ethnic identities[43] and what is the flow of information between individual and collective? Certainly, relations between groups contending for resources do not exist in a sociopolitical vacuum and, as a result, both domestic and international factors play a role in shaping a collective's narrative and goals. Because identity involves both sameness and otherness, it is inherently linked to "social narratives that inform dimensions of time, space, and relationality."[44]

If identities are fixed, this allows no room to evaluate changing power relations or simply events in time that inform and constitute identity over time. Human existence in society takes narrative form where identity is the hierarchy of plural identity traits informed by, and simultaneously informing, narrative. Narrative and context are conditions of society and social being and one's self comes to being within the context of time, place, and power that are constantly in flux.[45] Therefore, a guiding force in the negotiation of one's hierarchy of identity affiliations is narrative in that it "guides social action as it is mediated through social and political institutions."[46] By this definition an individual's identity narrative informs and influences social action that operates in the time and place of its surrounding institutions that, in turn, influence the identity narrative. This reciprocal relationship is compatible with different theories of nation and nationalism; regardless of contrasting views on the primordial, immemorial, or invented and modern nature of the nation-state, the back-and-forth between individuals and institutions through narrative is the self-fulfilling motor of the nation.

The study of identity and narrative is innately linked to memory. The organization of memories is essential to the establishment of identity narrative because remembering is needed to inform the individual of her past, which in turn influences the present, and the constant negotiation of past and present informs the future. Because memory is comprised of assigned meaning and emotion in addition to knowledge of the past, the putting together of memories in the sequence of one's life results in a self-constructed, socially informed narrative. The ability to remember (moreover, the ability to do so freely) and the way in which individuals reconstruct narrative selectively from their arsenal of memories toward an imagined future will be discussed later and reflected upon further in Chapter 6 in regard to well-being and nation building.

Deeply influenced by the ideas of the Enlightenment prevalent in eighteenth-century Europe, the concept of nationhood is rooted in the notion of a law of Nature, which humans can understand through reason. If applied to the organization of society, humans can achieve an "ease and happiness" that governs the universe.[47] If this law is intended to be universal, then that is to say that every individual has something in common with one's fellow human being. The doctrine that all people are created equal with rights to life, liberty, and the pursuit of happiness may be a popular statement of Western political doctrine, but it articulates the notion that as a collection of individuals, the nation by extension should secure, through reason, the welfare of its members. A nation can act as a "school of human expression" that fulfills a deep need in human beings, the need to belong to an encompassing group that provides them with a complete form of life.[48]

Drawing from nationalism's founding fathers, Rousseau[49] and Herder,[50] who stressed the need for individuals to immerse themselves in natural communities like nations, Smith compiles an understanding of the nation to be "a territorialized human community whose members share common myths and memories, a distinct public culture and common laws and customs, and nationalism as an ideological movement for the attainment and maintenance of autonomy, unity, and identity for a human community."[51] While abstaining from a formal definition of the term, Gellner offers two approaches toward this end: "Two men are of the same nation if and only if they share the same culture, where culture in turn means a system of ideas and signs and associations and ways of behaving and communicating," and "Two men are of the same nation if and only if they recognize each other as belonging to the same nation."[52] These frameworks imply that a group of people become a nation if and when the group recognizes itself as an entity of shared membership, possessing shared attributes, loyalties, and solidarities and owing to one another mutual rights and duties. The mutual recognition of these individuals transforms them into a nation and, simultaneously, separates them from those who do not fall within this recognized encompassing group of belonging.

Anderson argues that the nation is a collectively imagined cultural construct that results from its members receiving the same type of education, absorbing the same media, and "sharing the same mental map of the nation."[53] Anderson goes on to define the nation as an imagined political community both inherently limited and sovereign and by this reasoning the nation is but a construct that is similar everywhere yet varies in its use of different cultural symbols. These views on the foundation and formation of the nation raise questions about the interactive nature of the relationship between the nation and its members. The factors which result in a group of individuals internalizing their own membership as a unit certainly require some common basis to unify a collective identity that comprises the nation.

I structure the five main schools of thought which have arisen in the last century of literature regarding the issue of what and when is the nation as follows: primordialists, perennialists, ethno-symbolists, modernists, and postmodernists. The details that separate these main theories are concerned with the origins of the nation, what comprises the nation, and the function of the nation. The fact that there are multiple theories struggling for a normative approach is indicative of the unique specificities of historical and present-day cases. After considering each of these theories later, I propose a synthetic model inspired by Smith's archaeological model,[54] an adaptive ethno-symbolism that allows for a balance between acknowledging the influence of an ethnic past while recognizing the modern impact and malleability of nationalist rhetoric and activity. This varies from the traditional perennialist or ethno-symbolist approach addressed later in that it concerns the selectivity of modern actors who pick and choose from an ethno-symbolist past in order to craft the modern nation. As will become apparent in Chapter 6 through the primary data of Protectorate Morocco, each case of nationhood has its "inner worlds of subjective meaning," but this does not mean that "we cannot, or should not, try to advance and test theories."[55] With that in mind, I shall visit each of the predominant theories in order to demonstrate and justify the path taken in regard to the case study of French Protectorate Morocco.

Primordialists[56] view the nation as being prehistorical or, that is, immemorial, having emerged organically in all times and places with an instinctive kinship. Whereas modernists see the nation as a "modern and constantly changing construction ex nihilo," primordialists view the nation as an "unchanging communal essence."[57] Primordialism is used to explain ties deriving from birth such as a particular family, community, religious, or language group.[58] The perennialist view[59] recognizes that the nation is a "deposit of the ages" with stratified layers of "social, political and cultural experiences and traditions laid down by successive generations of an identifiable community."[60] In this view the nation is the outcome of its members and their past experiences; that is, the ethnic past explains the national present, wherein modernization cannot be understood without relating it to commonly known shared pasts. For perennialists, communities are built up similar to the metaphor of layers of the earth where one stage cannot be explained without the knowledge of the other. While nations are not ex nihilo as modernists believe, they are not continuous or ubiquitous as primordialists uphold; therefore, they are perennial drawing from shared past in modern circumstances with an accumulation of the past deposits.[61]

Many place ethno-symbolism in line with modernism because they share the belief that nationalism is "an innovation, and not simply an updated version of something far older";[62] however, ethno-symbolists link with perennialists as well in that they place past myth, symbol, and memory as significant in forming the nation. Ethno-symbolists critique both modernists and perennialists of neglecting subjective elements of nationhood and nation building such as collective passion and attachment of the people. For ethno-symbolists, the nation cannot be created ex nihilo but rather must draw upon "pre-existing repertoires of ethnic symbols, myths, and memories if they are to mobilize . . . the sources of national identities are to be sought in popular sentiments and culture" not through invention.[63] Though these resonating and embedded myths, symbols, and memories are drawn from the past, they are reinterpreted and refashioned by each generation in the modern era.

For early scholars of nation and nationalism, modernization signified "a breakdown of the traditional order and the establishment of a new type of society with new values and new relationships."[64] In this view, the emergence of nations was due to the demands of modern society whose economic and social development (in the late eighteenth-century West) generated nationalism that produced the modern nation, "the only reliable basis and framework for the growing modern society."[65] For modernists then, the nation is "socially and politically determined by purely modern conditions."[66] For Gellner, industry needs the culture and the state, the culture needs the state, and the state needs the "homogeneous cultural branding of its flock."[67] Because each state presides over, maintains, and is identified with one kind of culture and communication (resulting from a centralized educational system), culture shapes the state institutions which, in turn, act in a collaborative and interactive manner of nationalist indoctrination.

Whereas passion and attachment matter for ethno-symbolists, modernists put the key segment of the group on elites or the ruling class who, in competition with each other, use the nation in an instrumental manner where myth and heritage are invented in a top-down manner. For instance, the kind of culture and communication that Gellner references is illustrated clearly in the created image of France where history curriculum was prescribed for all pupils in every French school, both in France and in the colonies. Toward the imagined community of the French nation, pupils learned by repetition of "our ancestors, the Gauls,"[68] a phrase echoed by participant interviews in Chapter 6.

Gellner describes the transition of an agrarian to industrial state alongside the existence and prominence of low and high cultures where a man's education is his "most precious investment" as it "confers his identity on him."[69] He continues to explain that employability, dignity, security, and self-respect are direct results of one's education and that "some organism must ensure that this literate and unified culture is indeed being effectively produced . . . only the state can do this."[70] This link of shared responsibility between state and culture is a product of the age of nationalism. For Gellner, industrial mass societies require cultural homogeneity within units that are large enough to be viable, that is, large enough to support the costs of supplying standardized and universal education.[71] Meadwell supports the modernist theory as well; he maintains that of course there can be social life without nationalism, but that human life in industrial society requires nationalism.[72]

While Kedourie maintains that nationalism precedes the nation, Gellner counters that nationalism engenders the nation. Hastings and Hobsbawm agree that "nationalism is not the awakening of nations to self-consciousness: it invents nations where they do not exist. Nations do not make states and nationalisms, but the other way round."[73] The verb 'invent' links to Hobsbawm's terminology of invented tradition where historical references are not those that have "actually been preserved in popular memory," but rather those that have "been selected, written, pictured, popularised and institutionalised by those whose function it is to do so."[74] The tension present in this 'which came first' debate is similarly present between nationalism and homogeneity. Here, too, Gellner disagrees with Kedourie: "It is not so much that nationalism as a sentiment, as a political aspiration, has imposed homogeneity. Rather, homogeneity is a requirement of the modern state, and it is this inescapable imperative that eventually appears on the surface as nationalism."[75]

Most recently in the nation and nationalism debate is the postmodernist approach that views nations as being composed of "discrete elements" whose "cultures possess a variety of ingredients with different flavours and provenances."[76] The gastronomy metaphor here extends to the ingredients that make up the nation where the ingredients are culturally determined such as history, symbols, myths, and languages. Postmodernists deconstruct the power of nation to be a recited narrative or discourse to be interpreted like a recipe. Postmodernists and modernists agree that nations are products of modernity and are created in modernity so the present shapes and filters the past (not the other way around). Orwell's famous *Nineteen Eighty-Four* quotation fits this aptly: "Who controls the past controls the future: who controls the present controls the past."[77]

While I do not dispute the modernist claim that nations are products of modernity and shaped by modern institutions, the presence of premodern myths, symbols, and memories put to use in the modern nation deny its ex nihilo creation. Additionally, modernists and postmodernists both leave out the "complex interplay between creators, the social context in which they act, and the ethnic heritages of their societies."[78] The adage nothing comes from nothing seems appropriate here; however, it is difficult to make the case for the kind of continuity that the primordialists argue exists. While perennialists and ethno-symbolists both give weight to the ability of the past myths, symbols, and memories to influence the modern nation, perennialists ignore the importance of collective attachment and passions. The geology metaphor that sees different stages of the nation across time as different layers of earth is interesting in that it shows the ability of elements to appear in different eras; however, it does not account for the potential seepage between layers or the possibility that one layer, upon combining with another, may form something utterly new that does not appear to be a composite of the former two. This explanation fails to convey the active dynamism that comes from popular participation in, and interaction with, a world of nation-states.

Upon considering each theory's strengths and limitations, I accept that the nation is a modern social formation but contend that it draws from preexisting cultural identity including myths, symbols, and memories. This approach labeled herein as adaptive ethno-symbolism combines the notions of both ethno-symbolism and modernism; however, it presents an alternative when it comes to the questions of when and what is the nation: accepting that the rise of nations must be studied in the context of their specific modern conditions, even when shaped by the past, is much like excavating the past to reconstruct it to relate to later periods including the present. In this sense, "The nationalist is the archaeologist who seeks to provide a suitable and dignified past from which to lend authority to the modern nation and place it in a certain time and space thereby giving it roots."[79] In this view, nationalists are not social engineers or chefs as in the postmodernist gastronomy metaphor but rather political archaeologists whose activities consist of rediscovering, reinterpreting, and regenerating the nation. Whereas the primordialists' nation is an artichoke with the immemorial heart at the middle, perennialists' nation is layers of geological stages, and postmodernists' nation is a compilation of ingredients, the adaptive ethno-symbolism nation is a repository from which nationalists can select relevant myths, symbols, and memories in order to link past to future and vice versa. The meaning and use of the rediscovered, reinterpreted, and regenerated material may be manipulated and applied in ways completely foreign to its original reality and in this sense may be part of inventing the nation but the myths, symbols, and memories do not appear ex nihilo. This is certainly relevant in the postcolonial era where fledgling nations present a mélange of myths, symbols, songs, and so on in order to form the nation. In Protectorate-era Morocco, Moroccan nationalism took inspiration from Arab nationalism in the surrounding regions, but the French language and Berber heritage sustained great influence.

National identity is one affiliation that nearly all individuals in the modern world of nation-states share. Nevertheless, it is not inherently placed above others or recognized as real, important, and worth defending but is rather contingent on content and fluid.[80] Members of a nation and nation-state will have other communities of loyalty, but the national affiliation seems particularly vulnerable to "flare up extremely quickly in times of war or some real or imagined threat and can then become overwhelmingly and irrationally strong, to subside in altered circumstances almost as quickly as it has been inflamed."[81] This is because collective narrative, as an extension and transmitter of identity, is similarly plural, fluid, and emotional and cannot be simplified to a binary understanding. In a binary understanding, for example, ethnicity could serve as a basis for excluding others who share their culture but not ethnicity or could serve as a basis for including people who share ethnicity but not culture.[82][83] Eriksen elaborates with this example:

> It's I against my brother, my brother and I against our cousins; my cousins, my brother and myself against our more distant relatives, etc. In a modern multi-ethnic society, segmentary oppositions could be expressed thus by a member of the X's in country N: "It's I against my family, my extended lineage and myself against the rest of the X's; further, it's all of us X's against the other people and the state of N; but it's all of us citizens of N against the people of the country M."[84]

Because identity affiliations are plural and fluid, it follows that collective identities should not be reduced to a binary understanding of exclusion versus inclusion.[85] Just as individual identity is crafted through a constant interaction with the other, so too is the story of a national identity made up of its relations with other nations in a binary 'us' versus other fashion. The national consciousness as a social construct draws upon what its people perceive to be their distinctive characteristics, and this process necessarily entails an inclusion and exclusion of traits:

> Unsurprisingly, the preferred traits are characteristically favorable. We are intelligent and witty, open-minded and brave. But these are comparative characteristics. It is a daunting conceptual feat to maintain the view that we score so well on them without thinking that by comparison our neighbors are stupid and humorless, bigoted and cowardly.[86]

The exclusion of other individuals or groups from one's conceptualization of her nation inherently disregards the claim that all humans are created equal and portrays rather that only those within a specific categorization qualify. This attitude of exceptionalism leads to animosity and jingoism but need not be the norm if attention is given to the construction and understanding of national memory. The connection between individual and collective identity is bridged through narrative, which, in turn, cannot be formed, internalized, nor maintained without memory. Memory and remembering bridges past and present and individual and collective and is integral to nation building and the present and future of nation-states. National memory will include some inclusion and exclusion (remembering and forgetting) as well; however, its malleability can be manipulated for acceptance and heterogeneous coexistence instead of exceptionalism.

Since knowledge cannot be recollected without the invocation of memory, it holds that the history of the study of memory is long and vast. Indeed, Augustine's *Confessions* relies on memory for his inquiry into the nature of self-knowledge and innate knowledge of God.[87] Memory for Augustine is not only the ability to remember or the act of remembering but also the repository of all experiences and knowledge. Centuries later, Locke reiterated the necessity of memory for knowledge and highlighted its place in constructing identity. For him, without the capacity to remember and the reliability of memory, one could not construct a self nor communicate with others.[88] These texts travel across generations and remain relevant; just as the individual draws from her repository and selects from the suitable memories to construct identity, so can the adaptive ethno-symbolist draw from the repository to construct the nation-state.

A more modern scholar of memory, Halbwachs developed the sociology of memory wherein civil society forms associations that tell stories about who they are and what matters to them, for instance, the family.[89] In this sense, collectives, comprised of and constructed by memory, tell individuals who they are and what matters so the sense of the past informs the present. Memories, according to Halbwachs, are built, developed, and sustained in society and its shared experiences. Halbwachs's view of social ties fits with Durkheim in that humans express themselves most fruitfully and live most fully through group associations. For Halbwachs, this means civil society; however, the notion fits with the aforementioned encompassing groups of belonging. A modern communitarian critique of liberalism reinforces the importance of social institutions for individual identity—that individual choices and actions gain significance and meaning within, and from, society.[90]

Supporting this notion is Lichtenberg's *Flourishing Argument* which maintains that not only do humans need to belong to a group beyond their immediate family but, moreover, they flourish when they do.[91] This view is often presented by advocates of global humanism to counter the claim that individuals need nations and, by extension, nationalism in order to flourish. Rather, individuals flourish as a result of their group membership which may take the form of many different, and potentially simultaneous, collectives. For the scope of this book, where plural national narratives and affiliations are seen to cause conflict of identity and belonging and create a push-pull sense of allegiance, the thesis concerning the importance of group membership to human flourishing is supported.

Memory has been a growing field of interdisciplinary study in the last thirty years; from cultural studies to medical and psychological studies, the applicability of memory to diverse fields demonstrates its centrality in human life and society. Assmann proposes possible reasons for its recent popularity including "the breakdown of the so-called 'grand narratives' at the end of the cold war that had provided frameworks for the interpretation of the past and future orientation," the postcolonial situation which led to study of indigenous histories and cultures, "the post-traumatic situation after the Holocaust and the two World Wars" which motivated 'never forget' testimonials, or perhaps new digital technology that makes capturing a moment easier but preserving its significance less of a priority.[92] While the study of memory, its role in politics and its implications for well-being, is a fairly recent phenomenon, the notions of common origin, shared past, and duty to remember are certainly not.

In fact, some of the clearest examples come in the form of religious communities that certainly predate the era of nation-states. In Judaism, in particular, the Jewish calendar is based around "figures of memory."[93] One need only consider festivals, rites, images, and commemorations as the repeated remembrance of a long history in order to understand the central place of memory in Judaism. An Israeli philosopher who focuses on morality and the human condition as well as a range of political and societal issues, Margalit demonstrates the place of memory in Judaism with the example of the obligation of Jews to remember their Exodus from Egypt; this shared memory "goes beyond the experience of anyone alive" as it is a "memory of memory"[94] yet is nevertheless an obligation of gratitude to God for delivering one's ancestors from slavery. Memory in Judaism serves as a constant reminder for this debt of gratitude, a duty to remember not foreign to Christianity and Islam wherein all of humanity owes God for having been created in His image.

In Islam, though human beings are endowed with, and responsible to carry, the Trust with God in their time on earth, humans are forgetful and heedless and may stray from the right path. In remembering, Muslims bring back together that which was in a dispersed state. This same enduring utilization of memory is similarly honored and manipulated for the maintenance of national identity; for instance, the modern State of Israel where memory is shaping not only the national identity narrative but also a religious imperative.[95] From Deuteronomy and Isaiah to Herzl and Netanyahu, the command to remember runs throughout the Jewish nation across the globe and the Israeli nation-state for those who belong within its national identity.[96] The significance of capturing Holocaust survivors' stories is important in order to guard against future horrendous acts but is also used to maintain solidarity and defense against any threat to the nation. The naming of the Holocaust Museum of Israel, Yad Vashem, connects the tragedy of the Holocaust to Isaiah in which the eunuchs who leave no trace will be remembered and honored.[97] Connecting the Holocaust Museum to the religious scripture illustrates the importance of having a national depository for the names of the Holocaust victims; in remembering their names, the visitor is fortified to 'never forget.'

The intersection of memory and ethics displays the way in which memory can be manipulated to reshape past events and its ability to be commissioned for future agendas. For instance, Assmann's focus on cultural memory and remembering, in particular in the context of memory in Germany after the Second World War, makes the distinction of memory and argument and calls for communities of remembrance to maintain and cultivate memories as common and inclusive.[98] By examining the ways in which individuals participate in a collective construction of the past, Assmann draws attention to the tension between personal experience and collective remembrance and advocates "giving memory a common space."[99] If this can be done, memories can be contextualized and understood in an appropriate framework. Assman's ethics of remembering are reinforced in Volf's invocations to remember rightly,[100] in a way that heals one's identity, allows one to learn from the past, and enables humankind to prevent the "banality of evil."[101]

Margalit views memories as a source of knowledge; however, complicated by different empirical understandings of knowledge, he addresses the imprecision that neurologists or cognitive psychologists raise wherein memories are contextual, embedded, and fragmentary. As a result, the question of the reliability of memory as a source of knowledge remains. While I do not challenge the contextual,[102] embedded, fragmentary[103] nature of memory, I propose an alternate view be taken that considers memory as an important source of knowledge simply because it matters to individuals and society and informs present and future obligations (which in turn reshape the past): "Memory has power . . . when people come together in political life and transform representations of the past into matters of urgent importance in the present."[104] This transformation is achieved through narrative that provides memories with form and structure. Assmann states its importance simply, "as human beings we have to rely on (memories), because they are what makes human beings human."[105] Indeed, in the participant interviews conducted and presented herein, memory is powerful, influential, and essential in the recollection of past events and the way in which they present them in the present.

Any study into the identity of individuals and nations naturally asks, "Who are we?" The previous passage devoted to identity formation explores the ways in which we come to know who we are: both inward and outward, identity formation is contextual and social. Relations in society comprise humanity and the interrelatedness of humans across time and space is communicated through knowledge of the past. Just as identity is socially informed, "our personal memories include much more than what we, as individuals, have ourselves experienced."[106] Therefore, the plural encompassing groups of belonging in which individuals operate influence memory. Because human beings organize themselves socially and belonging entails some type of acknowledgment and reciprocation, each 'we' is constructed through narratives that mark boundaries and reveal circles of inclusion and exclusion. The formation of these narratives is not possible without memory and, as will be illustrated in Chapter 6 throughout participant stories, "to acknowledge the concept of collective memory is to acknowledge the concept of some collective identity."[107] Varying dimensions of memory interact in different ways so that one's family, nation-state, and culture, for instance, will incorporate the same, and different, memories in various ways.

Memory and remembering of the past bind together and communicate within communities of belonging whether they are cultural, ethnic, religion, or nation-state. Indeed, far before literature concerning nation-states and nationalism, philosophers examined the ideas of knowledge of the ultimate true reality, but "if in the search for this knowledge we never know what we are looking for, how can we tell when we have found the thing we are in search of?"[108] Plato[109] and Augustine come to similar conclusions: that at some point in the past, we knew what we were looking for and somehow came to forget it.[110] The search for knowledge is therefore not possible without remembering, putting back together the pieces of past knowledge from the 'storehouse,' so that "we can recall and recollect that which we once knew."[111]

The notion of multiple memories comprising the collective is an extension of the plural characteristics and affiliations that comprise the individual. As a member of a collective, one is related to the group through memory of people from its previous generation. "They in turn are related to the memory of people from the generation that preceded them, and so on"[112] so that the collective is both shaped by and actively shaping its memories. Just as identity's hierarchical affiliations are fluid and unequal in the emotional response and commitment they elicit, so do relations between the 'us' and 'them' vary. Furthermore, because identity and experiences are mediated by memory, individuals and collectives alike may be different over time as they reconstruct memory to serve different needs. Speaking of the nation as a collective does not negate its individual citizens' plural affiliations. For example, though religion continues to be an important component of cultural identity for many nation-states, it cannot be said that religious affiliation will always override national, ethnic, linguistic, or other cultural affiliations.[113] Durkheim's view of social solidarity supports this; that is, people feel connected through similar experiences, education, kinship, and so on.[114] If social cohesion and solidarity is based upon dependence and reliance among individuals, a nation is one such type of interdependent social formation. Margalit applies the terms thick and thin to help explain one's varying relations within communities of belonging: insofar as we hold our family and immediate circles of relations "near and dear," these are thick relations that are "short on geography and long on memory."[115] Insofar as we relate to strangers or humanity in general, these are thin relations that are conversely long on geography and short on memory. Whereas memory is the cement that keeps thick relations together, thin relations lack deep roots and are more frequently and easily overturned.[116] The continuity in the interplay between "the being I was" and "the one I am now" or between the "past and present of my group" reinforces the bond among the collective and makes the past a "principle of action for the present."[117]

Assman insists that "to move from individual and social memory to political and cultural memory" is to move from memories "grounded in lived experience" to mediated memories "founded on the more durable carriers of external symbols and material representations" such as education and collective participation.[118] This is fitting with the modernist view that the nation is constructed by and for the fulfillment of its institutions. Institutions cannot inherently have memories but rather, they are made with the use of symbols, rites, and myths. This selection, and exclusion, leads to a collection of individuals and a gathering of collectives that necessitates self-awareness of its existence; as a result, the nation can be said to be a product of both remembering and forgetting. Ricoeur claimed that every narrative inscribes forgetting into remembering in the sense that in reconstructing any story or being requires some element of selectivity.[119] Narratives of identities are "conferred a posteriori" and therefore remembering (and forgetting) is an essential aspect of the work of "identity-shaping recollection"[120] individually and collectively alike. For instance, if one recalls her entire personal history in order to establish her personal identity, she will have a fragmented collection of "islands of remembered events floating in a sea of forgotten ones."[121] The resulting reconstruction of personal identity is not dissimilar to the theory of nation building taken in this book where events, myths, and symbols of the past are selected in the modern era to reinvent and bond together the people into a cohesive entity in the modern nation-state. The contrast and threat of the other frequently legitimizes the central political authority of the nation on behalf of its members and further solidifies one's national identity affiliation. Kedourie explains, "Only if man is conscious of his individuality in his present conduct can he be sure of not violating it in his next act."[122] The continuous cycle of surveying the other maintains consciousness of unique selfhood.

Memory informs and constructs the narrative that bridges time and space. To answer the question, "Who are you?" one reaches to the past to connect it to the present with the help of memory. This "reflexive mobilizing of self-identity" is exemplified succinctly by Volf:

> I am what I remember that I have experienced. The more that happens to me and the more of it I remember, the richer my identity. Inversely, the less that happens to me and the less of it I remember the poorer my identity. From this perspective not to remember something that happened to me is to lose a chunk of myself.[123]

By extension, then, the nation is a sum of its memories as an "accumulated wisdom of the ages"[124] that undergoes the same selective process of remembering and forgetting when constructing its identity. Nation building recalls what is significant to the nation and this complex interchange between retention and forgetting results in national memory. The ability to retrieve knowledge, as Plato believed,[125] permits individuals to connect the past, apply it to present, and shape the future; "Because memories shape identities, they also give identities richness . . . without the ability to retain and access past events and knowledge, cultures would be impoverished and could not even develop."[126] By evoking past in the present, the past is given new life and application. Appeals for public commemoration are common in the aftermath of tragedy just as studies of

Holocaust survivors collect and record memories in order to "serve as a shield against death."[127]

This connection between memory and morality and justice will be considered in more depth in Chapter 6 in terms of memory capability; however, the charge that forgetfulness can be insulting and dangerous implies the power and necessity of remembering that connects past to not only present but also future. In this sense, memory can serve both to legitimize violence and conflict and to prevent and warn against such acts depending on how it is wielded by nations. Putting back together knowledge from the past, nations reconstruct memories with the emotion and trauma that come with it. For instance, "those who suffer from repressed traumatic memories might overreact to events in the present."[128] Margalit gives the example of Madeleine Albright's 'overreaction' to Milosevic due to her memories of being a Jewish girl during the Second World War or the case of de Gaulle France attempting to override memories of the Vichy period by reconstructing memories of the glory of the Republic.[129]

In addition to bridging individual to collective identity and past to present, memory's integral role in narrative is capable of justifying action and solidarity among nations. Margalit chronicles the ways in which "even the most brutal regime seeks legitimacy" with "mythmakers, epic poets, and chroniclers of the royal court" involved in providing legitimacy for "regimes whose entitlement to govern is anchored in events of the past."[130] As a result, memory is not only knowledge from the past but also, in remembering it and manipulating it for present use, belief about the past. While common memory is compiled of aggregate memories of all the people who remember and experienced a certain event, shared memory is distinct in that it requires communication; a shared memory "integrates and calibrates the different perspectives of those who remember the episode."[131] It is shared memory in particular that creates and builds narratives.

In premodern communities where knowledge was communicated and transmitted orally, remembering was the essential bridge between generations. Passed down memory was passed down knowledge and belief. To make sense of this distinction with thick and thin relations then, those who share thick relations are more likely to have shared memory as a result of shared institutions, monuments, and street names, whereas those who share in thin relations may have aggregate memories of an event resulting in common memory but lack the communication that strengthens and unites. Thick relations may transform a kind of flashbulb memory into shared memory by conferring upon it significance and connection. Assmann adds a further level of distinction when defining cultural memory. First, that cultural memory (shared memory) directs behavior and experience in society because it is repeated over generations and, second, that cultural memory is characterized by its distance from the everyday and, in this sense, transcends temporal limitations.[132] What one remembers about her personal past affects, and is affected by, the community in the sense that the "second-hand material will be folded into whatever firsthand material there may be through a process of narrativization, that is, a quite spontaneous process of transforming memory into narrative."[133] The channels by which one becomes related to a shared event (rituals, observance, recitation) and, therefore, shared memory, are the same channels of narrative that give a nation a national identity. Memory collects and preserves the knowledge from which the nation derives an "awareness of its unity and peculiarity."[134] From this knowledge, national identity is reconstructed within its own context by relating memories of the past into modern appropriation and transformation.

The ways in which memories are appropriated and transformed in modern nation-states is ambiguous as remembering and forgetting may be invoked to guard against future injustice or to mobilize solidarity in defense of itself. Identities, individual and collective, are "formed and re-formed through narrative in history"[135] and this keeps memory active and dynamic. Nora's well-known Leiux de memoire[136] accounts for the need for archives, marked anniversaries, and organized commemorations in order to initiate members to the nation and maintain the communal narrative. These tangible reference points enable and validate individuals' and collectives' memories within the greater nation and provide proof of belonging and participation.[137] Memory's role in national narrative is both the glue that holds its solidarity and the shield that defends the nation from opposing narratives. Nora's discussion of memory reads similarly to a modernist view of the nation-state: "Moments of history are plucked out of the flow of history, then returned to it—no longer quite alive but not yet entirely dead, like shells left on the shore when the sea of living memory has receded."[138] These moments are selectively chosen for, and reproduced in, the nation linking both past to present and ensuring thick relations among citizens.

Empirical struggles of memory concern the ontological tension between history and shared memory. Critical historians may be reluctant to rely on memory, preferring instead to look for alternative sources that connect a past event to its understanding of the present. History yearns to secure the event which the memory is about while shared memory is located in between this conception of history and myth. If the community believes the myth as a literal truth or adheres to the myth as a literal truth, "as if it were a plain historical narrative,"[139] then the community is shaped by it and it is significant in the national identity.

The triangulated approach of this research utilizing secondary literature, archived periodicals and colonial documents, and semi-structured interviews is designed to locate and secure identity narratives in their historical context thereby allowing for stories about the past that are held by communities of thick relations with shared memory. It is not memory versus history but rather complementary findings designed to enrich and unveil the complexity of identity. Memory provides a meeting place for the complex, oft-overlapping terms of ethnicity, culture, religion, and nation to come together; a community of memory with thick relations to its living and dead commemorates the past and revivifies its present connections through shared memory. This builds upon, and is reinforced by, Halbwachs's work on collective memory where the individual does not remember alone but rather as a member of groups.[140]

The community of memory shapes the nation, giving it a common origin and shared past that is acquired, recalled, recognized, and localized socially as members of the nation. Transnational communities of belonging, such as religion or language, exemplify the plurality of shared memory. Transforming memory's ability to preserve identity, early Zionist settlers sought to rewrite Jewish history by reshaping Jewish memory.[141] For Moroccan Jews, the balance of Moroccan memory and Jewish memory coexists just as identity's plural characteristics coexist. It is when remembering becomes incompatible that the identity hierarchy shifts and allegiances, including nationality, may realign.

In the post–Cold War era, with the increased frequency of complex and integrated societies, political scientists embracing modernization theory believed that greater political and economic interaction among peoples, as well as the growth of communication networks, would break down peoples' identities with ethnic kindred and replace them with loyalties to their larger, national communities.[142] The continued eruption of conflicts centered on ethnicity has discredited this notion and led to various theoretical explanations. Gurr discusses one such view wherein ethnic identities are primordial, perhaps genetically based, and therefore more fundamental and persistent than loyalties to larger social units.[143] Smith distances himself from strictly primordial theories but insists that nations have roots in premodern ethnic communities which he calls ethnies. Ethnies (units of population with common ancestry myths and historical memories, elements of shared culture, and some link with a historic territory) are distinct from Smith's concept of the nation (human population which shares myths and memories, a mass public culture, a designated homeland, economic unity and equal rights and duties for all members) in that ethnies "have been able continuously to sustain a royal dynasty or a succession of dynasties recruited from the ranks of one ethnic group" embedding an ethnic core that gives national identity its force.[144]

A contrary view is that ethnic identities are no more salient than any other kind of identity; they become significant when they are invoked by entrepreneurial political leaders in the instrumental pursuit of material and political benefits for a group or region. Gellner maintains that "mankind has always been organized in groups, of all kinds of shapes and sizes, sometimes sharply defined and sometimes loose, sometimes neatly nested and sometimes overlapping or intertwined" but that will (voluntary adherence, loyalty, solidarity) and fear (coercion, compulsion) are the two most present and crucial components.[145] The purposeful invoking of fear by political leaders to rally a collective's solidarity is now common; when competition and inequality among groups in heterogeneous societies are great, the potential for ethnic identities to strengthen, and conflicts to erupt, increases.[146]

Ethnicity and ethnic consciousness arise from a group's possession of a particular trait (culture, religion, race, etc.) and the various intertwined characterizations these subcategories include. For instance, one's language carries with it cultural connotations, religious values affect social and political values and behavior, and common genetic background may contribute to feelings of collective kinship. Fishman connects the ideas of kinship and ethnicity through terms of solidarity. He states,

> Kinship is the basis of one's felt bond to one's own kind. It is the basis of one's solidarity with them in terms of stress. It is the basis of one's right to presume upon them in times of need. It is the basis of one's dependency, sociability, and intimacy with them as a matter of course.[147]

Schildkrout also invokes this notion of kinship: "The minimal definition of an ethnic unit . . . is the idea of common provenance, recruitment primarily through kinship, and a notion of distinctiveness whether or not this consists of a unique inventory of cultural traits."[148]

From this reasoning, it can be expected that communities possessing distinct but common attributes will develop corresponding group consciousness. Brown recognizes that cultural affinities are only one of several bases for political affiliation but ethnicity, which people rarely seem to perceive themselves as choosing, appears to offer a more "all-embracing and emotionally satisfying way of defining an individual's identity."[149] Horowitz relates an ascriptive versus voluntary affiliation view of ethnic identity. He surmises that ethnic identity is established at birth for most group members, though the extent to which this is so varies: "Ethnicity is based on a myth of collective ancestry, which usually carries with it traits believed to be innate."[150] Some notion of ascription, however diluted, and affinity deriving from it may be inseparable from the concept of ethnicity but the element of reasoning and choice is still present.

Horowitz goes on to highlight the familial concept of ethnicity. For instance, the idea of common ancestry makes it possible for ethnic groups to think in terms of family resemblances, traits held in common, on a supposedly genetic basis, or cultural feature acquired in early childhood, wherein harmonious relations among groups are referred to as brotherhood.[151] Fishman concludes this as well, that ethnicity is simultaneously "suffused with overtones of familial duty and laden with depths of familial emotion."[152] The familial link highlights the point that ethnicity is not felt without social reproduction and the classification of different categories of people. Depending on the sociopolitical context, ethnicity can become relevant to individuals or not in the same way that nationalism can. It is with this in mind that Eriksen categorizes ethnicity as an ideology that, like nationalism, is manifest through political organization.[153]

It is clear in these overlapping views toward definitions and struggles for a normative approach that the nation is made of many components; herein lies the difficulty in defining it. When scholars address the concept of nationhood, the concepts of ethnicity, race, culture, language, and religion are nearly always intertwined. Ethnicity, race, and nation, for instance, share a common core which Fenton refers to as descent and culture: "There is not a single unitary phenomenon 'ethnicity' but rather an array of private and public identities which coalesce around ideas of descent and culture."[154] Descent and culture may entail myths about the past, beliefs about culture, language, dress, and custom—characteristics necessary for nation building and maintaining. As noted earlier, context is significant in identity choice and reason; the challenge remains to understand the condition under which ethnicity becomes important and decisive in national ideology. The distinction between ethnicity and nationalism is that nationalism "entails the ideological justification of a state, actual or potential" whereas ethnicity is not attached to a state building project (though it may become manifest as nationalism).[155]

In order to establish a clear definition of ethnicity, one must address the categories of which an ethnic group is comprised and the key words that often appear when discussing ethnicity. For example, whereas race implies the idea that local groups are divisions of humankind with physical or visible traits as markers of difference and inequality, ethnicity's point of difference is culture and the cultural markers of social boundaries, not necessarily physical appearance.[156] The concept of race gained attention and popularity as a scientific classification following Darwinian evolutionism and this theory, accompanied by the increased frequency of self-determination movements and migrations of people, came to 'scientifically' defend the racist division of people into groups such as Aryans and Semites.[157] Also frequent in discussion of ethnicity are the indicators of language and religion. Brubaker illustrates the simultaneously uniting and dividing categories of language and religion where both categories are forms of cultural and political identification that sort people into distinct communities. Both categories are frequently central to most ethnic and national identifications and can serve as a form of ethnic or national socialization.[158] Consistent with the theory of plural and fluid identities, Brubaker insists that neither language nor religion is primordial or fixed—an important note to keep in mind for the discussion of the Jewish people who are often described as an ethnic, religious, or national group.

Conversi demonstrates the continued complexity of these terms in his attempt to clarify: "By ethnicity we refer to a belief in putative descent. Ethnicity is thus similar to race. Culture is instead an open project . . . [but] since culture is necessarily based on tradition and continuity, it is often confused with ethnicity."[159] A key distinction from Weber is helpful: common descent is a key element of ethnic identity but it is the belief in common origin, not any objective common ancestry that is socially persuasive.[160] This brings back into question the freedom of reasoning and choice; it is not necessarily significant to share in common descent but rather the belief in it that matters. To conceptualize the nation then, one can refer to descent and culture communities with one distinct addition: that nations are, or should be if they aspire to be nation-states, associated with a state and political platform. If an ethnic group is a group of people with shared culture and language, a nation is a collective of one or more ethnic groups that possess or claim the right to autonomy as a people, and a nation-state is a territorial entity that provides the space for the realization of the nationalist ideology.

In this view the state has a positive role in the shaping of identities. This is particularly strong in states that have a strong majority who identify as an ethnic collective because its status as a majority is enhanced or at least preserved by state institutions. The form of national identity which the state seeks to inculcate influences the development of ethnic consciousness where the attachment of the majority to the state is expressed through nationalism and, as a result, the ethnic consciousness of minority groups is transformed either to assimilation or to solidification of its other. In states where ethnic affiliations offer a basis for identity and the state is capable of intervening in society sufficiently enough to influence cultural attributes, political options, and security, it "would seem feasible to look towards a focus on the character of the state as the basis for an understanding of how and why ethnic consciousness develops and becomes politicized."[161] For instance, "National attributions of 'Arab' . . . are never entirely accurate . . . until the rise of Arab nationalism in the nineteenth and twentieth centuries the term 'Arab' commonly designated a Bedouin or a peasant" but this identity was reclaimed and redefined in the Arab nationalist movements.[162] The connection between the nation and the individuals of which it is comprised is a successful ideology that not only legitimizes social order but also frames "the articulation of important, perceived needs and wishes of its adherents."[163]

Where this can become complicated and potentially violent is within a heterogeneous nation-state where multiple ethnic groups are in competition or see others as potential threats toward their group's success. Where ethnic groups belong to distinct and separate encompassing groups of belonging, members of the group see themselves connected as co-ethnics, and advances made by one group are often at the expense of another so that competition creates or reinforces prejudices between groups and varying social attitudes or types of mobilization may be viewed as a group threat.[164] When faced with a perceived threat, individuals must choose to identify and fight or to dis-identify in order to escape the prejudices toward the group.[165] This ties back to the aforementioned push-pull element of belonging and nationalist narrative where context informs self-identity toward or away from the identity affiliation under threat.

Horowitz maintains that strong ethnic allegiances permeate organizations, activities, and roles to which they are formally unrelated, especially in deeply divided societies.[166] The permeating character of ethnic affiliations, by spreading to multiple sectors of social life, imparts a pervasive quality to ethnic conflict and raises sharply the states of ethnic politics. In severely divided societies, ethnicity finds its way into a myriad of issues (development plans, educational controversies, trade union affairs, land policy, business policy, tax policy), and issues that elsewhere would be relegated to the category of routine administration assume a central place on the political agenda of ethnically divided societies.[167] Ethnicity offers political leaders the promise of secure support as demonstrated by Sir Neville Henderson, British high commissioner to Egypt, in 1926:

> In itself, nevertheless, a little xenophobia is not a bad thing, as it inclines the foreigner to acquiesce more readily in the predomination of British control and

influence as their only real safeguard . . . that is surely the ideal position: that the Egyptian should regard us as his friend and protector against the rapacious foreign cuckoo and that the foreigner should consider us to be his only safeguard against the injustice and discrimination of the Egyptian fanatic.[168]

Yet leaders cannot call into play an identity that is not founded on judgments of relative likeness or difference. If the perceived context changes so as to reactivate some higher or lower level of group or subgroup identity formerly regarded as highly salient, changes in identity may happen quickly.[169] That said, Horowitz is quick to reiterate that wholly new ethnic groups do not come into being overnight: "There can be no 'big bang' theory of ethnogenesis. . . . Group boundaries must be underpinned by a suitable apparatus of myth and legend, which cannot be generated spontaneously."[170] Rather, historical ethnic identities are "revived and redeveloped"[171] when modern context creates new manifestations of old challenges so that there is generation or regeneration of ethnic identities in the modern world. This will be revisited in Chapter 5 when addressing the Arab-Islamic character of the burgeoning Moroccan nationalist narrative.

Though contrasting theories, as detailed earlier, have different views of the origins of nations, the ideas of nation-state and its political ideological expression in the form of nationalism are generally agreed to have emerged from eighteenth- and nineteenth-century Western Europe and the Americas.[172] Indeed, increased ethnic heterogeneity in some countries due to the movement of peoples across and among territorial borders both challenged and motivated the state and nationalist mobilization. It is from this setting that "the principle of national sovereignty first developed, with its emphasis on representative institutions, a centralized administration, fixed borders, compulsory military service and a public jurisdiction," and these features, in general, have come to characterize the nation-state.[173] The model of the nation-state as the supreme political unit has spread throughout the twentieth and twenty-first centuries. The collapse of the multinational empires of central and Eastern Europe and the Russian Revolution further revealed the geographical dissemination of nationalist movements.[174] The Wilsonian popularity of self-determination became one more message passed through imperial assimilation channels, and henceforth, nationalist ideology was used against its European founding fathers in justifying decolonization movements.

When many thinkers spoke of national hegemony, cultural unity was held as a condition for the realization of a set of specific political ideals. "Rousseau believed it was impossible without cultural unity. This unity was sometimes achieved by establishing states around groups which already enjoyed such unity. However, it was quite often achieved by assimilating culturally distinct populations."[175] While nationalism holds that nations (understood here as a group or collective) and states (the physical borders or boundaries of a territory) were "destined for each other (and) that either without the other is incomplete," neither exist at all times in all circumstances.[176][177] If its members do not identify with the state, its authority is undermined thereby promulgating an interactive relationship wherein the collective nation has enacted some form of self-determination toward statehood but the state, in turn, is responsible for developing and maintaining the collective sense of identity. The ideology of nationalism derives its mobilizing force from the ability to organize and make sense of the experiences of its followers:[178] the ideology could not be sustained without the followers who mold it and are molded by it. Therefore, the nation-state is a physical space with which the majority of its members identify to the extent of seeing it as their own, and nationalism is its ideological movement for attaining and maintaining the nation-state.

As a political theory, nationalism is a broad ideology wherein each nation should have its nation-state; however, it is in particularist terms that the ideology sees success.[179] For this reason, nationalist ideology must be tailored to a distinct society in order to be successful. It is not just that nations strive to become states; it is also that modern states, in order to survive, strive to create national allegiances to their own measure. While nationalism, with its roots in self-determination and liberation, is often seen as a universal kind of ideology emphasizing equality and human rights, it contradicts itself in particularist application which must, in defining its citizenry, exclude membership to anyone outside. This explains why the multiethnic or plural state is the rule rather than the norm; however, it is common that cultural plurality slowly fades either through assimilation, emigration, or further attempts at self-determination from the minority groups present.[180] In particularist terms, it is not that each nation should have its nation-state but rather that my nation should have my nation-state. In this sense, nationalism can "function as a glue, bringing together people previously separate, or as a solvent, undoing links between previously united groups."[181]

Indeed, nationalism can be "aggressive and expansionist" as well as "peacekeeping and culturally integrating."[182] In this sense, there are a multitude of functions which nationalism can serve: "For some, it helps modernization; for others, it helps maintain traditional identities."[183] In both instances, the ideological power of nationalism is often expressed in official identification of enemies whether they are enemy nation-states or enemy ideologies. However, the diversity with which it is exercised demonstrates the malleability of nationalist narratives, built through selective remembering and forgetting. It follows that this malleability is just as susceptible to transnational well-being and peace as mobilization for aggression or war.

Because nationalism is the political expression of a nation into statehood, it must transform the nation from a purely cultural and social collective to an economic and political one; national collectivity may exist in a private sphere concerning cultural, language, religion, and so on without the desire for sovereignty and expression of self-determination. However, when that collective creates and directs its ideology toward the achievement of statehood, its nationalism becomes public both within the nation (to educate, build solidarity, and establish social norms) and outside the nation (international actors that support or attack the nation's efforts toward statehood). Among the modernist theory there is the distinction between statist nationalism[184] and cultural nationalism.[185] For statist nationalism, the national culture is the means and the values of the state are the aims, whereas for cultural nationalism, the culture is the aim and the state is the means.[186] Statist nationalism dictates that sovereign political units should strive for not only political but also cultural unity. According to cultural nationalism, cultural groups should strive for states of their own. Therefore, to realize their state, "even dominant ethnic groups must turn a latent, private sense of ethnicity into a public manifest one, if only to ensure the national loyalty of their members against claims of other groups."[187] In this spirit, nationalism has the ability to legitimize and direct ethnic collectivity.

The transition from identity to ideology can be viewed through the lens of narrative which in turn is constructed through belonging and memory. I contend that a person makes choices about the hierarchy of her allegiances through context so that it is a constant two-step balancing act between establishing one's allegiances and weighing the relative importance of these allegiances. Identity is personal and defies categorization through personal nuance and experience, whereas belonging implies some sort of reciprocal acknowledgment from within the community of belonging. Just as with identity, so too can belonging be plural and dynamic; the key difference is a matter of self-ascription versus social categorization. While outside the realm of its inception, twentieth-century Protectorate Morocco provides a complex case study of the abstract allegiances of ethnicity and national identity. Being at once identified by their religion, ethnicity, and nationality, Jews of Arab states experienced additional identity questions brought on by colonial presence as well as the introduction of

Political Zionism, a narrative born by, and largely for, Ashkenazim, that further complicated one's allegiances.

The preceding discussion of identity, nation, memory, ethnicity, and nationalism presents a plural and fluid approach to identity where identity allegiances are multiple and capable of change over time and space. The nation is a collective constructed of myths and symbols that are selected to build social cohesion and culture that may include shared features in overlapping terms such as race, language, religion, and, significant in the case of Jewish and Arab Moroccan national identity, ethnicity. Before focusing on the state of identity and nationalist narratives in Protectorate Morocco, Chapter 3 will first provide a brief historical background of Muslim-Jewish relationships and status in pre-Protectorate Morocco.

Part II

Jewish Morocco Historical Background

2

Precolonial Moroccan Heterogeneity

Following a history of crusades and Western persecution under Christianity, it can be argued that Islam provided a preferable experience for the Jews. Historically, the Islamic world is often portrayed as a safe haven for Jews, where "the sons of Judah were free to raise their heads, and did not need to look out with fear and humiliation."[1] In more modern times, especially following the establishment of the State of Israel, the favorable view of Jews under Islam has been interpreted and manipulated to different aims where Jewish and Arab come across as opposing identity affiliations. This chapter explores the pre-Protectorate setting of Jews in Morocco in order to understand the changes and complexities that French, Jewish, Arab, and Moroccan identity narratives underwent during the Protectorate.

Throughout the areas of Muslim rule, Jews and Christians were classified as dhimmi. This classification placed Jews and Christians in a secondary status but, in labeling them, gave them a codified legal protection and place in Muslim society. Contrasting views of the dhimmi existence reveal the various perspectives of this secondary status. One view is that the Jewish existence under Islam was preferable to that of their life under Christian rule, but it is important to consider that this does not mean that there were not incidents of the contrary in either realm. Cohen's view is that "the Jews were one of several minorities in Islam, not the sole minority, as in (Christian) Europe. And because Muslim society was diverse and pluralistic, the minorities were far less noticeable."[2] In Morocco, Jews were "perceived primarily as dhimmis, humbled, but protected subjects. As long as the Jew conforms to this role, he arouses little interest."[3]

A contrasting view is one of oppression and dehumanization. Ye'or describes dhimmi status as such:

> Twelve centuries of humiliation impressed upon the individual and collective psychologies of the oppressed groups a common form of alienation—the dhimmi syndrome. On the individual level it was characterized by a profound dehumanization. The individual, resigned to a passive existence, developed

a feeling of helplessness and vulnerability, the consequence of a condition of permanent insecurity, servility, and ignorance.[4]

While Cohen does not go so far as to account for the status of individual happiness or feelings, it is difficult to reconcile the two descriptions and the inconsistencies spread through each author's examples. Cohen provides a story of Moroccan Jewry which supports his mosaic theory of society under Islam. With specific reference to Sefrou, Morocco, he highlights the coexisting identities of Jewish and Moroccan:

> The Jews were at once Sefrouis like any others and resoundingly themselves . . . [not] a set-apart pariah community, deviant and self-contained. . . . Moroccan to the core and Jewish to the same core, they were heritors of a tradition double and indivisible and in no way marginal.[5]

Cohen proposes that one reason for this ability to have plural identities is because the Jews, as dhimmis, have a scripturally allocated place within the Koran and Islamic society. Because contexts are distinguished with elaborate precision (marriage, diet, worship, education, etc.) society is separated but predictably proscribed in its separation. Ye'or gives a very different experience of Moroccan Jewry through the reflection of a French writer: "One is amazed that under such a tyranny a people could preserve intact the faith which earned it this martyrdom. One can still imagine the hatred that inspires the conquerors faced with the resistance of these wretches and the frequent massacres that decimated them."[6]

One key distinction that may account for the disparity between these two contrasting views may be the portrayal of Jewish dhimmi: in comparison to Jews in Christendom, Cohen maintains that Jews in Islamic ruled areas fared comparatively better, whereas Ye'or, focusing solely on Jews in Islamic ruled areas vehemently, claims otherwise. The scholarly literature focusing on pre-Protectorate Morocco confirms Cohen's view. Certainly precolonial Morocco was not without its regional and religious tensions; however, Jews were considered to be "native to the country, pre-dating the arrival of Islam, as evidenced by their involvement in nearly every realm of Moroccan life."[7] Precolonial Morocco was a heterogeneous society that coexisted upon local and regional levels with a range of sociopolitical circumstances. One explanation for this comes from a powerful individualistic element of Moroccan society with a weak or nonexistent corporate element.[8] Eickelman agrees,

> [In] Morocco persons are conceived as the fundamental units of social structure, rather than their attributes or statuses as members of groups. It is the culturally

accepted means by which persons contract and maintain bonds and obligations with one another which constitute the relatively stable elements of the cultural order.⁹

Deshen supports this claim and finds its roots in Islam—that is, "the prominence of the element of enthusiastic inspiration relative to the element of ordered, formal, and restrained religiosity" leads to the emphasis on the weight of individuals as against that of impersonal institutions.¹⁰

Similar to Jews in medieval Egypt, Iran, and Yemen, Moroccan Jews lived in imperial cities, smaller trading and administrative centers, mountain villages, and oasis towns, and these circumstances naturally grouped communities as opposed to territory-wide affiliations. Therefore, while Jews were classified throughout Morocco as dhimmi, their local and regional sociopolitical relationships were often more highly prioritized than a feeling of collectivity as a national minority group. This feeling was compounded by internal distinctions among Moroccan Jewry between the toshavim and megorashim.¹¹ With legends claiming origins as far back as the time of King Solomon, Jewish toshavim communities in Morocco have an ancient and long-standing tradition that predates the arrival of Islam to the Maghreb. The fact that Jews did not constitute a homogeneous or even monolithic ethnic and religious bloc continued into the eighteenth and nineteenth centuries when the toshavim-megorashim distinction was replaced by a distinction between the merchant elite and the popular masses. The arrival of European colonial influence would further divide Moroccan Jews with protégé economic, administrative, and educational privileges.

Deshen provides an example of these community-specific solidarities and prejudices. In a Sefrou woman's letter concerning the selection of a bride for her son, the woman objects to "one who is sly like the Fez women."¹² Though the Fez and Sefrou communities maintained friendly contact with each other and in times of trouble regularly sought refuge among those of the other,¹³ this example demonstrates the strong feelings of local patriotism and prejudice toward neighboring communities. In fact, Brown insists that the widespread mobility of the Jews "did not diminish emotional ties of individual to their home towns."¹⁴ While people were categorized according to religion, they were also arranged according to city so that the "People of Salé, Fez, Marrakesh, etc." had particular characteristics regardless of religion.¹⁵ Indeed, as will be seen in Chapter 6, one interview participant continues to self-identify with the family's Tétouan roots as a source of pride and status. As a result of these regional fragmentations, the interpretations and implementation of the original text known as the Pact of

'Umar[16] was constantly fluctuating and "changing political, economic, social, and environmental conditions (e.g., drought, epidemics, and other calamities)" shaped the foundations and features of Muslim-Jewish relations.[17]

A key aspect of Jewish-Muslim relations can be seen through the types of protection that were exchanged for services or taxes. Under normal circumstances, Jews in Morocco had little need for protection; in fact, they "lived with their Muslim neighbors in peace, if not tranquility, and went about their activities unharmed."[18] In rural areas, a more tribal patron-client relationship existed, wherein Jews depended upon a network of patrons to provide security along trading routes. In many of these accounts,[19] the Jewish client and Muslim patron are portrayed as having a relationship of mutual dependence, respect, and friendship where Jews were needed by Muslims for economic survival and Muslims were needed by Jews for personal security.[20] In urban areas, Jews were dependent on the sultan for protection. In order to limit the exposure of Jews to insurgents and thereby expose their own impotence, the sultan enclosed Jewish communities within the confines of mellah[21] walls. The first mellah was built in Fez in the fourteenth century with others following in Tétouan, Rabat, and Salé in the early nineteenth century.[22] While this may have been partially motivated by the desire to isolate and ostracize the Jews, it also aimed at their physical protection since an attack on the Jews of the cities close to the sultan was an affront to his sovereignty.[23] Jews were therefore the only group in Morocco whose status was based exclusively on the personal protection guaranteed by the sultan himself.

The ritual of the jizya tax-paying ceremony, the tax due to the sultan in exchange for their security as dhimmis, demonstrated the subordination but also protected privilege that is present in the dhimmi relationship. While "both Jew and Muslim agreed that the payment of the [tax] was a corollary of a fundamental condition predicated on a disparity of power," the Jews could justify the tax for their security in return.[24] These two types of protective ties complemented each other: whereas sultanic protection tended to be communal in nature, tribal patron-client protection tended to be individual. Hart maintains that the keynote of Jewish behavior was that of "safety in humility; conversely, for a powerful man to have 'his own' Jew was considered a sign of prestige."[25] Because the Jews stood entirely outside the political system, and because their occupational services were much in demand, many informants said that to kill or even to molest a Jew was an infinitely worse offense than to kill a fellow tribesman.[26] In the urban areas where Jewish residential areas were gathered into the mellah, rabbis oversaw the transfer of land between Jews, acting on behalf of a Muslim authority.[27] Cooperation is also evident in business where economic concerns outweighed considerations of religious identity. Holden demonstrates this through the example of butchers and meat markets where he claims the "intensity of interfaith interaction" existed before the arrival of European commercial schemes.[28]

The arrival of Europeans introduced commercial and tax incentives that disrupted the existing order of business. Jewish and Muslim notables alike were eager to take advantage of the economic opportunities that came with the European expansion.[29] This is evidenced, as Holden's in-depth study on butchers' rights demonstrates, by the protected legal status French officials granted Jewish butchers, as well as other professions, through becoming protégés. This introduced market competition that increased butchers' sales and profits; for example, "If a Jewish butcher, perhaps a protégé who was exempt from the taxes of both the [Moroccan government] and the exacting Jewish Council, undercut competitors, then Muslim consumers purchased his meat."[30] This status allowed protégés to function outside the Moroccan legal system and evade tax requirements, thereby fracturing established relations between the sultan and his subjects. From the reign of Mawlay Hassan I (1873–94) until the beginning of the Protectorate in 1912, European capitulation privileges increased among rich Jewish subjects as well as wealthy urban Muslims.

Thus, the means by which Jews could escape dhimmi status were not the legal changes implemented by the Moroccan sultan, but rather, becoming subjects of foreign powers, or protégés, of foreign nations represented in Morocco. Among some of the Muslim religious leaders, foreign trade was seen as a cause of weakness because the foreign merchants seemed to be enhancing the status of Jews.[31] Beyond economics, a wedge was driven in language and culture as Gallicization infiltrated the protégés and frayed links between Muslim and Jewish neighbors.[32] In 1862, another form of European interventionism began with the creation of the AIU. Promising to bring moral progress and emancipation of Jews living in the Muslim world through French language and culture, the AIU operated, unofficially, as a branch of the French assimilation narrative. This European wedge created or exacerbated divisions and unequally distributed privileges that would develop in the Protectorate era and alter Jewish-Muslim relations as they were in pre-Protectorate Morocco.

Lacking a defined Christian minority in the pre-Protectorate era, Moroccan Jews and Muslims naturally grew in relation to, and interaction with, each other. Just as Jews were informed and molded by the surrounding non-Jewish majority,[33] so too was Muslim identity reified through its Jewish minority.

Larhmaid claims that the Muslim identity of the sultans was best expressed through the fact that they had Jewish subjects; indeed, "having Jewish subjects accentuated Muslim identity and gave it value."[34] The lower status of the Jews was evidence of the superiority of Islam and therefore helped to legitimize the Islamic dominance of the state. It is in this setting that local communities developed relationships of functional interdependence that reinforced simultaneously the authority of Islam and value of Moroccan Jews. While these relationships were formed around the distinction between Jew and Muslim, they gave no sign of incompatibility between Jewish and Moroccan or Jewish and Arab. It was not until the influence of French colonialism that these divisions were highlighted and set as opposing terms. Along with institutions and infrastructure, colonialism brought additional aspects of modernity with social and economic consequences. Expanding the economy into imperial markets and engendering social changes and divisions, Morocco also received Western liberal ideals such as nationalism and capitalism.

During the time of the Protectorate, in the transition from Sultanate to nation-state, Moroccan Jews were subject to competing political narratives in three primary forms: French cultural-linguistic assimilation, Political Zionism, and Arab-Islamic Moroccan nationalism. Each narrative, as it coexisted and interacted with the others during the Protectorate period, constituted a push-pull competition for Jewish allegiance. This interaction coupled with the natural awareness of, and reaction to, events on the ground made for an often plural and conflicted involvement in each national narrative. French language, education, and culture held the attraction of French citizenship and economic advantage; Political Zionism catered to both political nationalism and, for some, religious messianism; and Moroccan nationalists represented an appeal to the watan, homeland, calling on the Jews status as subjects of the sultan as equal citizens.

During the 1930s, Moroccan Jewish national identity came to be more significantly addressed than during the precolonial period of dhimmi and protégé status. With the perceived threat of Political Zionist expansion to the Maghreb and the perceived attraction to French assimilation, Moroccan nationalists took care to assert Morocco's ancient Jewish past and generations of dhimmi protection. However, with growing tension in Palestine and the anti-Semitic legislation to come with Vichy France, Jews experienced a simultaneous disenchantment with France and an increasingly hostile Morocco that required distinctions to be drawn between Jewish faith and Political Zionist sympathies. In order to examine the three primary nationalist narratives and the context which would lead to their simultaneous, competing influences, and various successes, a brief historical background is included to set the scene in which these narratives came to develop.[35]

From the French conquest of Algeria in 1830 to the beginning of Protectorate rule in Morocco by 1912, Moroccan sovereignty was challenged by European intervention at an increasingly accelerated pace. During this time, North African Jews would come to achieve "equality within their Islamic states and special privileges through their connection to the outside forces that were penetrating their world"[36] that would simultaneously undermine their connection to their respective nation-states. In the first decade of the twentieth century, France succeeded in removing Italy, Britain, and Germany from the arena of colonial rivalry. France agreed with Italy that the latter should have free rein in Libya while the Italians had to forfeit claims in the expansion of colonial rule in Morocco.

The Entente Cordiale of 1904 between Britain and France resulted in a French decision to renounce claims to Egypt and, in return, received a British promise to abandon imperial motives in Morocco. Spain agreed with France in 1904 to share spheres of influence in Morocco, therefore defining the geographical boundaries of French and Spanish territorial influence. French troops landed in 1907 in Casablanca and subdued most of the surrounding city while, from the east, troops under French commander Hubert Lyautey's command occupied the Moroccan-Algerian border town of Oujda. Under the destabilizing pressure of this foreign military threat, a Moroccan civil war broke out between Moulay Abd al-Aziz and his brother Moulay Abd al-Hafidh, who claimed leadership of a jihad to try to defend the country's sovereignty. Hafidh defeated his brother's forces in 1908, and was recognized as the sultan in 1910 by the international signatories who had created the 1906 Act of Algeciras.[37] In 1911, a Franco-German agreement was signed which gave Germany two strips of territory in the French Congo with access to the Congo River and, in return, Germany agreed to a French Protectorate over much of Morocco.

Before this Franco-German agreement, a conference held in Algeciras, Spain (1906), attended by the European powers, granted the French (and Spanish) considerable power over the Moroccan economy, enabling them to intervene in the country's internal reforms more than Britain had done previously.[38] During this crucial meeting, an international control body was established, dominated by the French, who had the power to intervene in the economic life of the country, a special port police force to ensure security for European interests, and a state bank dominated by representatives of the consortium headed by the Bank of Paris. It became the sole financial agent of the Moroccan government and was to negotiate all future loans, rendering the Makhzan (the Moroccan elite then in power in the region and clustered around the sultan) subordinate to the Paris banking establishment. As a result, Moroccan sovereignty was already facing enormous economic, military, and political challenges by 1906.[39] With the consent of its European neighbors and increasing economic and military control in the Maghreb, France was ready to add Morocco to the countries under its colonial sphere of control.

France continued to benefit from political events in 1912 when the Moroccan sultan, Moulay Abd al-Hafidh, signed the Treaty of Fez. On March 30, 1912, he consented to French plans to place troops throughout the French zone, granted the French full police and military power for the restoration of public order and Morocco's air and land defenses, and agreed that the French government would be represented before the Makhzan by a commissaire résident général. For his part, the commissaire résident général, the French commander Hubert Lyautey, consented to "respect Islamic institutions and traditions as well as the Sultan's dignity."[40] Thus, the central elements of the traditional system remained but were reduced to a role of secondary importance under the Protectorate regime. On November 27, 1912, Morocco was further divided when France and Spain signed an agreement formalizing their division of Morocco into territorial spheres of influence. The vast majority of the country came under the jurisdiction of a French Protectorate while northern Morocco, Tangier excluded, became a Spanish zone.[41]

To impose controls on the population, the French created a bureaucratic state apparatus including ministries governing education, health, commerce, agriculture, industry, antiquities, interior, and indigenous affairs. The colonial vision of the first résident général, Lyautey, was to modernize the country, mainly to the economic benefit of the French, without obliterating traditional culture. A core feature of this associationist policy, therefore, was to "retain an indigenous partner, the Sultan and the Palace administration, in which the trappings of traditional government could be preserved in a reinvented neo-makzhan to legitimize the French role in the nation-building project."[42]

By the nature of the Protectorate treaty, the French could unify and modernize the country under the nominal authority of the sultan while simultaneously dividing the country politically, administratively, and juridically. Colonization generated the physical conditions necessary for the emergence of a unified modern nation-state by creating what amounted to a national transportation and communications infrastructure (including the dramatic expansion of roads, railroads, ports, telegraph-telephone, and post) that strengthened connections between city and countryside. In this partnership, the French agreed to 'protect' the position of the Moroccan 'protectee,' the sultan, and to establish the conditions necessary to modernize the Islamic kingdom. The stated purpose of the Protectorate, according to the treaty, was to "establish a stable regime founded on internal order and general security that will permit the introduction of reforms and will assure the economic development of the country."[43] This was the first time in more than 1,300 years that an external, Christian power came to impose central governmental control.

Opinions of European intervention among Moroccan Jews were far from uniform; however, the new element of French rule greatly altered the existing Jewish-Muslim relations. Indeed, under the French Protectorate the Jewish elite became increasingly linked to the European powers with some of the most important Jewish families becoming protégés or even consular agents of European or American states. In a sense, just as they historically emblematized dhimmis of the sultans, they now became simultaneously like dhimmis of European states, which offered their protection and jurisdiction in accordance with treaty arrangements often imposed on Morocco by the threat of force. The Moroccan sultan's control over the Jewish quarters diminished as a result.[44] Thus, for Moroccan Jews in contact with foreign consulates, Europe and European Jewry, especially French, had now become significant arbiters of their welfare. The resulting plural identities that emerged due to indigenous, religious, and foreign influence led to the development of contrasting national narratives. Two of the three primary narratives to which Moroccan Jews were drawn to belong, including the allure of French cultural-linguistic assimilation and the solidarity of Political Zionism (particularly in light of the eventual Vichy regime), are examined in the following chapter.

3

Competing Narratives
French Assimilation and Political Zionism

The previous chapter detailed the intertwined nature of Jewish and Muslim history in Morocco, explaining the notion of the Christian visitor as foreigner. By demonstrating the compatibility of Jewish, Arab, and Moroccan identity traits, it is clear that not one of these identities is inherently opposed to another. This is not to say that precolonial Morocco was a utopian heterogeneous population without conflict, but rather to demonstrate that Jews were considered to be indigenous to the country, predating the arrival of Islam, and were deeply embedded in both urban and rural spheres of Moroccan life. Precolonial Morocco was indeed a heterogeneous society but one that coexisted upon local and regional levels with power exchanges including protection and profits. It would take time, new methods of mass communication,[1] and a sequence of internal and external events to bring about the popular support that would eventually merge the blad al-Makhzan (land of the government, predominantly urban) and blad al-siba (the territory outside government control, predominantly rural).[23] This transition, as well as reactions to the changes brought by the French administration and Political Zionist agencies, is evident in the colonial archival reports and archived periodicals from this time. It is this heterogeneous nature and division of powers that the French colonial powers exploited in order to legitimate and prolong their own influence during the Protectorate period.

The extent to which the colonial project was calculated and measured is evident in the colonial archives. One such example is the participation of Morocco in the International Colonial Exposition of Paris in 1931 where, in order to demonstrate the value of pacification policies, the colonial officers needed to show what Morocco was like before their arrival.[4] Pacification policies, which emerged at the advent of the Protectorate period, enabled important economic and political changes for the Jews in particular. The essential infrastructure of roads, harbors, railways, and so on created simultaneously with political, administrative, and financial structure increased the ease of transporting both ideas and people and the blad al-Makzhan was quickly subjugated.[5] This subjugation permeated the urban Jewish communities as well; in fact, one of Sefrou's most renowned rabbis observed that, with the stabilization of French presence, the self-confidence of the Jews increased.[6] Laskier connects this phenomenon to the Berbers being disarmed, a ruling administrative unit known as the Bureau of Indigenous Affairs emerging for every rural region, Jews becoming community suppliers for French soldiers, and in a short period roads being built, a modern rail system established, and new transportation facilities being put to use. These changes in quick succession enabled the Jews to extend their business activities with relative ease.[7]

The history of Morocco's forty-four year colonial period pivoted in the early 1930s. Pacification during the Protectorate proved to be disadvantageous to the Muslims, particularly for intellectuals. The new system alienated the educated who, in turn, would group into nationalist factions, first asking for reform and a greater participatory role in the administrative apparatus. Convinced that they were marginal participants, their calls for reform developed into demands for a total break with the system. This transition will be examined in depth in Chapter 5 and is illustrated most evidently with the issuance of the Berber Dahir in 1930 which, according to Muslim leaders, aimed to Christianize Morocco's Berber population.[8] Immediately thereafter, Arabic newspapers featured articles attacking French policy in Morocco, interpreting the attack on their "Berber brothers" as a threat against the Muslim religion as a whole. One such article in the newspaper Al-Adel reported that France was no longer the Protectorate within which reform could be made but rather the enemy of Islam:

> It is a duty for everyone who can stand up to France, the enemy of Islam, and oppose it with evidence, documentation, and protests to kings, princes, to just men, and to just states: to come to the aid of their Berber brothers at last, to defend the patrimony of the Muslim religion, and its sacred traditions and rights.[9]

By November 1930, the French were being criticized for the violation of religious conventions, separating the great Muslim Berber people from Muslim law and society,[10] and demands grew for the abrogation of the Berber Dahir.[11]

For the next twenty-six years, until Moroccan independence in 1956, the Moroccan nationalists actively contested France's near-monopoly of control over the Protectorate state, defending Moroccan sovereignty by constructing a rival definition of the Moroccan nation, unified since the founding of the

Idrissid dynasty in the late eighth century, by Islamization and Arabization. While the outbreak of protest against this decree in 1930 was only the first of many developmental stages in the mobilization of a Moroccan nationalist movement, I uphold that this key turning point was crucial in creating a lasting precedent for how Muslim and Arab identity could be used to frame and mobilize anti-colonial protest in defense of national sovereignty. The consequences of this event can be viewed as a mirror with which to gauge the development of other nationalist narratives. In order to investigate the development of French assimilation-driven nationalism among the Jews as well as the growth in popularity of Political Zionism, this chapter will trace the development of both through the systematic lens of identity and narrative. This chapter will address research question one in particular; that is, how the Jewish minority was present, supported, and active in the development of French cultural-linguistic assimilation and Political Zionism. From this foundation, Chapter 5 will address this question as well in illuminating the identity and narrative of the Jews in the development of an Arab-Islamic Moroccan nationalism.

As addressed in Chapter 3, Moroccan Jews had been exposed to the economic advantages of French or other European powers through the privileges of protégé status. French Jews gained civil rights including citizenship in 1790, a time when European Jews came to be accepted and included in modern secular European societies and viewed themselves in terms of the Enlightenment discourse.[12] No longer did Jews see themselves as "part of the same trans-national identity in which being Jewish transcended any type of national affiliation"[13] but rather primarily as citizens of the nation-state in which they were born. With the coming of colonialism and France's civilizing mission, citizenship was a component of the governing institutions that would be enforced beyond France's borders. For instance, before establishing the Protectorate in Morocco, France colonized neighboring Algeria in 1830. With this colonial status, Algerian Jews were considered subjects of France, and after 1870 with the issuance of the Crémieux Decree,[14] Algerian Jews were made French citizens so long as they accepted French civil law. For Jews, this meant sacrificing the right to be governed by rabbinical courts under Jewish communal law in return for French citizenship.[15] In response, a growing number of Moroccan Jews went to Algeria, became subjects of France after a short stay, and then returned to Morocco with newfound rights.[16] The desire to do so may be attributed to the lure of political and economic privileges but also demonstrates the growing bond between the French and Moroccan Jews.

Unlike in Europe where 'emancipation' led to integration and assimilation into society, the granting of French citizenship to Jews and not their Muslim peers only served to further divide Jewish-Muslim solidarity among North African communities. The Crémieux Decree was an early turning point in Moroccan Jewish identity; a willingness to cross borders to gain citizenship to a nation-state abroad indicates that the privileges of French citizenship were attractive enough to actively pursue or the status of Jews in Morocco was difficult enough to encourage its pursuit. This pursuit demonstrates the significance of social norms influencing the desire for membership; the lure of improved educational and economic opportunities was enticing enough to motivate identity shifting among the urban Jewish communities. Furthering the outward identity claim is the fact that once a few connected (former protégé Jews) members of the community were successful in achieving French citizenship, many more aspired to do so as well. More than social pressure and influence, archived periodicals from the decades that followed the 1870 Crémieux Decree suggest practical legal and economic motivation deepened with the arrival of the AIU.[17] Though French citizenship would not be offered to Moroccan Jews, *L'Avenir Illustre* published that to remain Jewish would be the best chance for becoming Frenchmen.[18]

Within the first six months of the Protectorate, in September 1912, Albert Saguès of the Casablanca Boys' School secured a meeting with Résident Général Lyautey to discuss the matter of citizenship for Moroccan Jews. Lyautey, however, "was particularly angry at efforts undertaken recently by Casablancan Jews to obtain Spanish citizenship (for he could not understand why any Jew would seek citizenship from a country that persecuted and expelled him)."[19] When Saguès and the Casablanca community assured Lyautey that they preferred French citizenship, and rumors circulated in the major cities that a decree had been negotiated that would naturalize Moroccan Jews,[20] Lyautey responded that if the Protectorate were to establish the option, the Protectorate administration would carefully screen individual candidates once they "proved to be thoroughly assimilated to French culture."[21] This introduces the notion of culture and assimilation to the legal and economic incentives that motivated Moroccan Jews to pursue French citizenship.

Moroccan Jews were ultimately unsuccessful in obtaining French citizenship en bloc; however, the fact that they had the forum in which to debate or request doing so demonstrates that they had acquired a kind of leverage with the French Protectorate leaders regarding their legal status in Morocco. For instance, in 1922, during a visit to Fez by the president of the French Republic, Alexandre Millerand, the community council demanded that Jews be permitted to move outside the mellah and purchase land in the Muslim quarter (just as Muslims purchased land in the Jewish quarter), that they be able to open retail stores in the Muslim quarter, and that Jewish testimony in judicial matters involving Muslim courts be received like a Muslim's testimony.[22] It would seem that, for the Jews, to maintain good relations with the Protectorate administration was the best option to assure that they were treated well.

The feeling of exploiting leverage was mutual: it proved to be in the Protectorate's interest to exploit Morocco's heterogeneity. In undermining the unity of a Muslim-Arab majority and highlighting Jewish religious and ethnic diversity, France was able to utilize a malleable colonial narrative of control. Kosansky provides this example through Jewish pilgrimages to demonstrate the benefit to the Protectorate administration:

> Through the end of the Protectorate period, annual Jewish pilgrimages were venues for colonial officials to demonstrate their protection of, control over, and affection for the Jewish community. In return, representatives of the Moroccan Jewish community offered declarations of loyalty to the French project.[23]

This highlights the purposeful intent of the French in their relationship with the Jews; "Seen from the perspective of the Maghreb, the assumptions are reversed; the Jews did not necessarily choose to identify with Europe. Rather, Europe, in effect, chose them."[24] Restructuring and uprooting the Jews from their pre-Protectorate societies and designing French cultural-linguistic assimilation as a path to higher status and economic opportunity laid the groundwork for the arrival of the AIU schools. The educational progress of the Jews before and after 1912, the social consequences of the cultural and educational diversity among Muslims and Jews, the policies of the colonial system, and the activities of the AIU in all aspects of communal and educational activities deepened the already existing divisions between the two for France's gain.[25] More than social status and administrative benefits, the opportunities of a French education motivated Moroccan Jewish parents to send their children to the AIU schools and created a self-fulfilling colonial project with generations of culturally and linguistically French pupils.

The intervention of European and American Jewish associations was part of the process of change that Moroccan Jewish communities underwent from the nineteenth century onward. Of crucial importance in this regard was the philanthropic assistance provided to the impoverished populations of overcrowded mellahs. Extremely influential was the establishment of a network of schools throughout most of the country by the French Jewish organization,

AIU. The first schools in the Maghreb predated the Protectorate period by forty years and were created in order to aid Jews and Judaism in three ways: first, by working toward the emancipation and moral progress of the Jews. Although not stating explicitly that education was the basic motivation behind emancipation and moral progress, the first aim defined the educational sphere. Moral progress signified the need to combat disease, poverty, ignorance, and to acculturate the Jews in the tradition of French secular education. For that purpose, the AIU established schools that served as vehicles for the Jews to absorb the concepts of the French national slogan of equality, fraternity, and liberty. The instrument to transmit ideas from France was the language, which, in the eyes of the AIU, constituted the most important and effective instrument for the dissemination of modern civilization.

The second goal was to lend support to all those who were seen to suffer because of their Jewish faith. It referred to the need for allocating the necessary funds to help Jews in distress around the world, and more importantly, to inform European leaders and their diplomatic representatives in countries where Jews were harassed, to urge that action be taken. Along this line of thought, the third goal was to awaken Europe to the Jewish problem. It called for encouraging all proper publications to bring an end to Jewish sufferings. Whereas the second category called for quiet negotiations and diplomatic action, the third stressed the utilization of AIU and other periodicals to influence public opinion.[26]

The arrival of the AIU demonstrates the diversity among Moroccan Jews in rural versus urban areas and among the cities in general. For instance,

> In the economically developing communities, the Jews were more eager to welcome the schools, for it meant giving their youths modern education that could provide them with ample employment opportunities. . . . Unlike Tétouan and the key coastal towns, the political situation in Fez, Meknès, or Sefrou was far less stable in view of political unrest and European reluctance to open consulates. Therefore, the AIU found it impossible during its first years of activities to become established in these communities.[27]

In Meknès the orthodox Jewish community rejected the AIU with much criticism, whereas in Tétouan and Mogador the schools were welcomed from the beginning. Nevertheless, by the eve of the Protectorate, fifteen communities were endowed with a total of twenty-seven AIU schools, twelve of them with schools for both boys and girls.[28]

Due to the French education style and curriculum introduced in the AIU schools, traditional Moroccan Jewish culture began to change. Such changes affected not only the minds and mentality of the people and generations who learned the French language, French history, and Enlightenment thought but also social relations in the mellahs and long-established and previously unchallenged hierarchies. Within a year of signing the Treaty of Fez in 1912, the AIU schools were supported politically by the Protectorate administration. Given the importance of the commercial treaties, the creation of European banks, post offices, and commercial houses, the AIU schools fortified their role in the colonial project as the most important agent for the preparation of an educated Jewish elite to confront the new realities and economic developments. At its inception the AIU was not in any official sense an organ of French colonialism and received no Protectorate funding. Not until 1924, when the AIU, by an arrangement with the Protectorate government, took primary responsibility for educating Morocco's Jewish children, did the AIU teachers become de facto employees of the state. By this point, they could already demonstrate their success: six months into the Protectorate, in September 1912, French troops were welcomed in Marrakech by the students of the AIU who greeted them in French while waving French flags.

By absorbing French language and culture in Morocco before the Protectorate period, AIU families and students were prepared to live, work, and benefit from the French system. For instance, "A contingent of secretaries, employees, bookkeepers and interpreters. . . . At the beginning of this century, at a time when the destiny of Morocco still stood in the balance, the Alliance school formed in Marrakech a veritable small French post."[29] Evolués, as modern Jews educated in the AIU schools came to be called, absorbed more than language and French history lessons as they were surrounded by French culture, and this challenged the traditional social order within their own communities and with regard to their relations with Muslims.

With these privileges, they rejected dhimmi status under Moroccan law. To enjoy a status similar to that of their coreligionists in Algeria (French citizenship) became their goal. It is interesting to note that although they embraced French European culture, this did not correlate directly to sympathy with another European Jewish movement, Political Zionism. In fact, the AIU was only one, though the largest, of French organizations establishing branches in Morocco. During the mid-1930s, the International League against Anti-Semitism (LICA),[30] an organization founded in Paris, came to Fez, Rabat, Casablanca, Meknès, Mogador, Marrakech, Oujda, and Tangier as well as the League for the Rights of Man and Citizen and the French Socialist Party.[31] LICA was founded and led by Bernard Lecache, the French-born son of Ukrainian Jewish immigrants, in order to raise awareness about "hatred of Jews and to mobilize Jews and non-Jews to take action against racial and ethnic discrimination."[32] The rise of anti-Semitism in the French Algerian Press led to the establishment of branches first in Algeria, and later in Tunisia and Morocco. Lecache attempted to foster strong relationships with Muslim leaders in North Africa with their shared Semitic heritage and a common enemy in the form of anti-Semitism. His proposed "Judeo-Arab rapprochement towards Palestine" located the roots of Political Zionism in the "intolerance and racial persecution in some parts of Europe,"[33] and called for Jewish and Muslim solidarity. Nonetheless, LICA failed to be able to "place Muslims in municipal jobs or improve living conditions for the Muslim population," and, eventually, Lecache was sent to the Vichy internment camps in Algeria.[34] Notably, the evolués were not interested in the Muslim-Arab nationalists who aimed to improve the social condition of Moroccans through independence from the Protectorate. Though a push had been made for the instruction of literary Arabic in the AIU curriculum with the intent of establishing closer relations with the students' Muslim peers and obtaining employable skills in the Protectorate offices of indigenous affairs, only Tétouan introduced the subject in 1937.[35] French nationality and assimilation remained the primary goal of AIU graduates until the Second World War.[36]

The tenuous position of Morocco's Jews was particularly evident in the legal realm, where they faced a complex overlap of jurisdictions that delineated vastly different rights to different nationalities. Caught between national identities, Moroccan Jews were left to navigate the colonial system. Wyrtzen highlights this complexity through an inheritance case where the son of the deceased claimed the inheritance should be divided according to rabbinic law as opposed to French law despite the fact that his grandfather had become a French citizen. In this case of a Moroccan Jew fighting to maintain his status as a subject of the sultan (thereby opting for rabbinical interpretation) and not opting for French citizenship privileges simply because his grandfather had, he maintained his Moroccan nationality.[37]

Cases more frequently featured Moroccan Jews fighting to confirm French nationality, usually with more advantageous rights. The complexities of national identity amid a colonial regime are evident in the case of Abraham Benoliel, for instance, who, as a Moroccan subject with one brother, naturalized to Portugal and one as a French protégé fought among rabbinic, Portuguese, and French laws to sort the different provisions of inheritance rights for the male and female members of his family.[38] These legal complications point to the ways in which Jews were differentiated in the Protectorate period from Arab or Berber Muslim

Moroccans as well as Europeans (Jewish and non-Jewish alike). Gottreich's recent publication delves deeper into the ways that Islamic jurisprudence and religious courts played into this notion of parallel pick and choose systems.[39]

By having access to many different jurisdictions, legal matters were frequently manipulated to reach the most favorable outcome for the case at hand. The Protectorate regime's success in preserving minority groups' outsider positions is clear not only in legal jurisdiction but in military participation as well. Though Jews across North Africa flocked to volunteer and give their support to the war,[40] they were not allowed to enlist or participate due to their status as subjects of the sultan.[41] By denying Jews the opportunity to fight in either world war while Muslim Moroccan colonial troops were allowed, France kept the Moroccan Jewish population at a sometimes privileged, sometimes nominal, but always distinct distance.

Despite a campaign launched by three Moroccan Jewish professionals in October 1939 where over 1,300 Jewish volunteers signed up for French military service, the French Ministry of National Defense sent a memorandum to the commanders in North Africa reaffirming that non-naturalized Jews would not be directly incorporated into the French military.[42] The Protectorate believed that Jews were only volunteering "with the explicit hope of being granted French citizenship" welcoming the Francophile sentiment but not allowing enlistment. By June 1940, however, this became unimportant as France fell to Germany and Vichy's takeover attempted to define French national identity in ethnic terms. On August 27, 1940, the 1938 Marchandeau Law, which protected racial or religious groups from attacks through the press, was abrogated, allowing anti-Semitism in the French press. In October, the Statut des Juifs (Status of Jews) was enacted, creating a second-class category of citizenship that more or less mirrored the Nuremberg Laws thereby enforcing a system of racial classification that defined a Jew as an individual with three Jewish grandparents (or two if one's spouse was also Jewish) and banned them from public posts in the government, military, and the media.[43] "Disgraced at their rapid loss of honor, pride, and confidence," the Jews became the scapegoat and anti-Semitism became state policy.[44]

In French North Africa, the Statut des Juifs was implemented unevenly, depending on local circumstances. It was put into effect most swiftly and comprehensively in Algeria highlighting the difference between Morocco as Protectorate and Algeria as colony. Just four days after the Statut des Juifs was passed in France, the Crémieux Decree was abrogated in Algeria, immediately depriving more than 105,000 Algerian Jews of their French citizenship and leaving them stateless but still subject to French civil code.[45] In many respects,

Vichy rule only exposed a colonial apartheid already in place in which economic, political, and legal rights were tied to one's ethnic status. In Morocco, where the Statut des Juifs had to be negotiated with the sultan, it took until October 31, 1940, for a decree to be issued.[46] The administration's refusal to issue a Crémieux Decree for Morocco's Jews and its insistence on preserving their status as subjects of the sultan left them slightly more protected and under the leverage of Mohammed V. As 'Commander of the Faithful' the sultan exercised his agency to protect the Jews as dhimmi in addition to those who had converted to Islam but would have been subject to the racial definition used in Europe nonetheless.

Accompanying the sultan's efforts to minimize the Vichy threat to Morocco's Jews, the palace took this opportunity to restore the traditional social order, reminding Jews of their proper place as dhimmi in Moroccan society, protected but second-tier to Muslims. Though he was not able entirely to protect his subjects, the "symbolic influence of his office" maintained significance in the eyes of the Protectorate administration, and he was able to demand two concessions to the October 31, 1940, anti-Jewish statute: first, that Jews in Morocco be defined by religious choice, not by race or parentage (in the case of converts for instance), and second, that prohibitions against Jewish professions and quotas on Jewish students would not apply to exclusively Jewish institutions such as religious school and communal charities.[47]

During the summer of 1941, Vichy France increased anti-Semitic pressure in France and North Africa when the head of the General Commission for Jewish Questions, Xavier Vallat, called for a census of all Jews and their property. In Morocco, it took until August to negotiate and publish four decrees about the new laws which banned Jews from more professions and ordered a census in which all non-Moroccan and Moroccan Jews were told to declare their Jewish identity according to "the law, their civil status, their family situation, their profession, and the state of their property."[48] Officials tried to process the census data based on region, professions, and the commercial and industrial situation to determine the economic impact of a full application of the Statut des Juifs. Consistent with the ambiguity of nation-statehood and citizenship at the time, the report for the Civil Controller of the Casablanca Region revealed that thirty-four different nationalities were registered for Jews living in Morocco in addition to French and Moroccan.[49] Nevertheless, economic concerns continued to overpower strict implementation of the Statut des Juifs, and by 1942, a report warned that Moroccan Jews formed an integral part of the autochthonous population and their activity proved indispensable for the economy of the Protectorate.[50] While worded in economic terms, this report is representative of the intimate ties Moroccan Jews had in Morocco; it was not only an issue of compassion or human morality but also an economic argument for the leniency with the application of the Statut des Juifs.

Although the impact of Vichy laws on the Jews in Morocco is relatively mild for other communities at the time, a theme that comes across in participants' interviews as presented in Chapter 6, the Protectorate administration did take steps to restrict Jewish rights and livelihood. One such initiative aimed to return Jews back into the medina from the Ville Nouvelle, the European sector.[51] On August 22, 1942, an official decree was issued forcing Jews back into the mellah in Fez and Meknès. French-Moroccan relations deteriorated such that by November 1942 posters around Casablanca advertised a public gathering outside the mellah to begin the process of purifying France.[52] This betrayal of the Protectorate forces created the incentive for Moroccan Jews to take refuge in their dhimmi status as subjects under the sultan or in the rhetoric of Jewish nationalism provided by Political Zionism.

Another consequence of the disenchantment of Moroccan Jews with France is evident in their ecstatic welcome for American troops in Operation Torch, the US-led invasion of North Africa on the morning of November 8, 1942.[53] The Judeo-Arabic song that circulated through the country's mellahs, "Get out O French, Morocco is not yours. America has come to take it, your domination is over!"[54,55] demonstrates this disenchantment. French résident général Charles Noguès attempted to fight back the American troops but was forced to surrender on November 11, 1942.[56] Not only were most Jews pleased to welcome the Americans but in a shock to the Residency, the sultan and many Moroccan nationalists were as well; seeing this as an opportunity to revive their calls for reform which the war had interrupted.[57] In January 1943, the sultan met with Roosevelt at the Anfa Conference much to the displeasure of Protectorate officials. Hoisington suggests that this meeting "fuelled the Sultan's desire to free the country from the French rule."[58]

Moroccan Muslims had remained skeptical of Nazi propaganda and ideology, and as Kenbib points out, "Almost 90% of Muslims were illiterate (so) the masses barely understood Nazi propaganda."[59] Those among the educated elite who were involved in the nationalist movement sensed that Hitler would just as likely target Muslims and "become their deadly foe."[60] European settlers in Morocco at this time echoed the resentment and distrust of the Protectorate administration in their attitudes toward the Americans; "they were receptive to Vichy's ideology and policy... they held the Jews responsible for France's misfortunes" and spread slogans such as "worker, your enemy in the Jew, he exploits you and derives his illgotten gains from your misery."[61] In a surprisingly aware report by the Protectorate administration, the Department of Political Affairs reported that in November 1944, the Jews "consider, first of all, the fact that for the moment, they are deprived of a nationality, as the Muslims consider them not as Moroccans, but as simple protégés of the sultan (dhimmis)."[62]

Though the relationship between the Jewish communities and the Protectorate administration grew strained during the war and the Vichy regime, a new decree designed to regularize the organization of Jewish leadership was introduced in 1945, which challenged the view of the Jews as being the sultan's subjects and under his restricted authority.[63] While it was a way to quiet the Jewish leadership, it was, nevertheless, the structure under which to organize as a branch of the Protectorate. Toward this end, in 1947 the Conseil des Communautés Israélites du Maroc (Jewish Community Council of Morocco—CCIM) was formed.[64] For the first time, Jewish representatives found a place in the Conseil du Gouvernement (Government Council) taking six places in the Moroccan division (as opposed to the European division).[65] With the growing popularity of Political Zionist activity paralleling that of the Moroccan nationalist narrative, the French Protectorate struggled to defend itself against both while building and maintaining its power after the war.

Disillusioned with France, Morocco's Jewish community was pulled toward the two other primary nationalist narratives, Moroccan and Political Zionist, which were both accelerating toward declarations of self-determination. The interwar years and Vichy period had increased "social stratification of the Jewish community"[66] and deepened the divide between Jews and Muslims in the urban centers. Before the Protectorate period the majority of Moroccan Jews lived in "overcrowded mellahs under deteriorating conditions, barely earning a living."[67] The open-door free trade policy introduced in the early years of the Protectorate had led those traditionally working as artisans and peddlers to search for new economic opportunity.[68] For many, this led to the Protectorate and AIU which created a cultural gap not only between themselves and less-educated Jews but also between them and their Muslim peers. This "Francisation" that led to "French culture and Francophile feelings"[69] grew harder to maintain with the defeat of France and coming of the Vichy administration. Meanwhile, Political Zionist organizations began organizing clandestine immigration to Palestine. A recent issue of the Moroccan historical periodical, *Zamane*, accounts for this narrative transition when addressing Moroccan Jewish allegiance to a feeling of religious solidarity in the Jewish nation: "The war has shaken spirits. Moroccan Jews are finally becoming aware of belonging to a 'nation' apart."[70] At the same, the Moroccan Independence Party, Istiqlal,[71] resumed its active anti-colonial calls for independence. Formed in 1943 with the eventual support of the sultan, Istiqlal issued its 1944 Manifest of Independence assuring that equal civil rights would be granted to all by a future independent Morocco. Nevertheless, outbreaks of Muslim-Jewish violence in Morocco during the end of the Second World War continued and amplified with the establishment of the State of Israel in 1948.

The refusal to grant Jews French citizenship, the Vichy period of Nazi-occupied France, and the establishment of the modern State of Israel are all turning points toward the alienation of Moroccan Jewry from France and French Morocco. The post-1942 period, in view of the rise of Moroccan nationalism, the Holocaust, and the outcome of the Arab-Israeli War of 1948, encouraged Jews to consider the Political Zionist idea as an alternative national narrative. Pulled between the contrasting forces of French colonialism, Political Zionism, and Moroccan nationalism, the Moroccan Jews were caught in a reality that blurred and inflated cultural differences, obscured ethnic and national identity, and left Jews the difficult choice between emigration and an uncertain future in the eventual independent state of Morocco. In order to approach the complexities and consequences of the Political Zionist narrative in Morocco, the underlying components of its origins and the nature of orientalism are considered.

Emerging from a colonial discourse of othering imposed upon new and unknown societies by the West, orientalism came to encapsulate a Western representation of the East, most prevalently as stereotyped projections rooted in the colonial narrative. The resulting division was to try and explain indigenous religions as well as indigenous racial types from the analogy of religious systems and racial types that were known to the West. To medieval, Christian Europe the two most obvious forms of the religious other were Jews and Muslims and to some extent this binary construct continued, instructing their initial colonial interactions.[72] One view suggests that because Europeans were so imbued with the Bible, it was the first thing they turned to when in doubt, and thus the ethnography of the Israelites, the Jews, was the most available.[73] By the time that liberalism and humanism became intertwined with Western colonial enterprise, orientalism provided the rhetoric for favoring certain 'superior' cultural behaviors in the colonial setting of divide and rule. This became a way of suggesting that anything fine or noble came from outside the colonial project, either from Europe or from the Middle East. Thus many peoples who appeared to have a more advanced way of doing things or who had "noble physical or social features" were perceived of as coming from elsewhere or from "biblical lands."[74]

While the East could uphold a noble, biblical foundation, the West could bring its superior technology and philosophy to spread the prowess of Europe. This notion of honoring the imagined East while aiming toward a forward-thinking West can be seen in the AIU and Political Zionist narrative alike: the ancient heritage of the East is significant and honorable but its greatest 'return to history' will be in French assimilation, in the case of the AIU, or in realizing a Western respite in the Middle East, in the case of Political Zionism and modern Israel. Western perceptions were therefore locked into an "ideological superstructure with an apparatus of complicated assumptions, beliefs, images, literary productions, and rationalizations (not to mention the underlying foundation of commercial, economic and strategic vital interests)."[75] This cumulative body of theory and practice that arose during the period of colonial expansion beyond its Western origins is known as orientalism.

Said's work on orientalism[76] launched a critique of Western notions of the East and the ways in which orientalist discourse has legitimated colonial aggression and political supremacy of the Western world. According to Said, orientalism refers to three interrelated phenomena. First, "an Orientalist is anyone who teaches, writes about, or researches the Orient." Second, "Orientalism is a style of thought based upon an ontological and epistemological distinction made between the Orient and (most of the time) the Occident." This is a large and fairly amorphous category that would include the thoughts and writings of anyone who effectively divided the world up in this bipolar manner. Third,

> Orientalism can be discussed and analyzed as the corporate institution for dealing with the Orient—dealing with it by making statements about it, authorizing views of it, describing it, by teaching it, settling it, ruling over it: in short, Orientalism is a Western style for dominating, restructuring and having authority over the Orient.[77]

Said's defining features remain the mainstream interpretation or implication when using the word 'orientalism,' though the legacy of the orientalist discourse is varied in its reception and context. Said's work encountered criticism for his lack of anthropological and ethnographical basis. His lack of engagement with the categorizations of culture and ethnocentrism has led anthropologists to defend the use of categorization of peoples along biological or cultural lines with the justification that because all humans share the "biological and social potential to be rational and to cooperate . . . even the most 'exotic' cultures in

Western eyes can be approached as essentially human rather than categorically dismissed as inferior and uncivilized."[78] One of the most outspoken critics of Said, Bernard Lewis, depicts Said's work as political propaganda that is "confused, contradictory, and remarkably inaccurate."[79] While he allows that scholars of any given society will naturally have bias when studying and interpreting the creations of another, he points out that this applies to all humans, Said alike, but that intellectual precision and discipline of academics toward scholarly validity and open discussion diminishes the prevalence of bias. Lewis views orientalism as a product of European humanism but contends this is not inherently connected to colonial expansion.[80]

For the French, the Orient was a special possession that not only provided resources and imperial legitimacy but also enriched cultural validation in this image of the other. That is, in defining the East as other, the definition of the West as its contrasting image was solidified. This discourse became a justifying and supporting ideology for colonial presence. Whereas European Jews adopting an Enlightenment approach led to assimilation and anti-Semitism contributed to Political Zionism, Jews of the Maghreb received these ideas "via the agency of colonialism" rather than organically out of the transformation of society as a whole.[81] Conversely, orientalism has also been embraced as a discourse of the colonized. In the post–Second World War wave of decolonization, the internalization of other provided a rallying point for the colonized to embrace their romanticized past and unify against the colonial power. One example can be drawn from the anti-colonization négritude movement during the decolonization of the French Antillean colonies where the colonized repelled the French ruling other in favor of a return to the qualities that had been internalized as lesser by the colonizing oppressor. In this way, the orientalist discourse can be manipulated to legitimate both colonization and anti-colonization depending on the context and the community.

Because orientalism sometimes entailed a valorization of the Muslim or Arab Other, it could be genuinely celebratory and inspirational. For Jews, such an exercise was often tantamount to a search for roots, for authenticity, and for Oriental role models. Thus, rather than a straightforward means of asserting colonial, corporeal, and cultural authority, "Orientalism could be a profound expression of one's own cultural anxiety and insecurity."[82] This is evident in the fact that for Moroccan Jews, orientalism was present in multiple and contrasting narratives. To the French, Moroccan Jews could be helpful in undermining homogeneous Moroccan (Arab) nationalism while for Political Zionists, Moroccan Jews could be the quintessential victims of diaspora who would benefit from the salvation of Israel. While Jews are distinguished, and distinguish themselves, from Muslims, they do not necessarily do so from Arabs. This religious distinction cannot be assumed to be directly consistent with ethnicity.

The contention that Moroccan Jews emigrated from backward societies to modernity in Israel reflects an orientalist generalization regarding all of North Africa and the Middle East, especially with regard to the role of the Jews in the economies of their countries of origin.[83] For instance, Dahan-Kalev, a Mizrahi-Israeli author, shares her experience upon emigrating to Israel from Morocco in 1949, where,

> according to Eisenstadt (an Israeli sociologist), my father was uneducated, despite his professional experience in banking, and my mother, a cum laude graduate of the Alliance Israélite Universelle, was but another one of the illiterate Mizrakhi immigrants. The fact that both of them had experienced Western culture in the colonial city of Casablanca and through the French education they received in the Alliance was of no value in his eyes.[84]

Having been educated in AIU schools, Dahan-Kalev was torn between "the identity of that imaginative French girl" and books about the Jewish people through the stories of the Shtetl (East European Jewish villages).[85] Neither of these narratives fit her Moroccan Jewish upbringing, a fact that she explains led to alienation from herself and contempt for her parents. Certainly, for some, emigration brought an improvement in the standard of living, but for a substantial stratum, especially those who had been engaged in commerce, administration, and the professions, emigration brought a change for the worse, at least for the first generation that was confined to development camps upon emigrating.

Emerging as a doctrine of Jewish nationalism in nineteenth-century Europe and developed in opposition to anti-Semitism within the European states, the Political Zionist narrative is the framework upon which the State of Israel was founded. It represents the fulfillment of Jewish experience including the recovery of nation-statehood, the restoration to the ancestral homeland, and the resumption of Israel's messianic role in the reconciliation of history. Political Zionism bases its social philosophy on the concept of Jewish regeneration through settlement in Palestine, combining the images of traditional messianic values with foundations in populist idealism of the West. Zionism was the place of the aspired return and the hope for homecoming far before it translated to national activism.[86] In other words, the envisioned return to homeland occupied the place of desire, a return to the land of ancestors, but was not translated into an actual political investment in the possessing of a territory as a fulfillment of such a desire. To acknowledge this distinction, I refer specifically to the self-determination nationalist narrative as Political Zionism.

The colonial period further fueled the environment for the growth in popularity of national movements such as Political Zionism. The form they took was largely a response to the direction of boundary change underway, to growing differentiation or assimilation. Horowitz demonstrates,

> An ethnic group fragmented into subgroups that threatened to overtake the larger group identity might react by reinforcing elements of common culture and common ancestry, suppressing, for example, differences in dialect or stressing descent from a single ancestor (turning to the past to reduce their internal diversity). On the other hand, a group that found itself losing its distinctive identity by absorption in another ethnic group might respond by emphasizing its cultural uniqueness, selectively recalling ancient glories, resuscitating all that distinguishes group members from others, destroying all that links them to others (resort to their history to affirm their distinctiveness from those around them).[87]

Begun by group members who are furthest along in the individual assimilation process, national movements may result in an explosive and violent assertion of group separateness. The cultural revivals that emerged in response reflected an awareness of the danger of a fading group identity. They tended to emphasize the history of separateness and even hostility between the groups. Group identity was thus infused with a new or revived cultural content that served to demarcate the lines between groups more clearly, thereby reducing the ease with which individuals could cross group boundaries.[88] While this understanding is not specific to the Jewish Diaspora or Political Zionism, in particular, it sets the scene of colonial presence and the growth of national self-determination and fits the pattern of fragmented subgroups calling upon a common past or heritage to emphasize uniqueness and unify.

Political Zionism arose in response to the precarious situation of Central and East European Jewry in the second half of the nineteenth century. The experience of pogroms on the territories of the tsarist empire in the late nineteenth and early twentieth centuries, in particular, made a section of Central and East European Jews receptive to the salvation appeal of Political Zionism, which argued that "the solution to the Jewish predicament in much of Europe lay in returning to and reclaiming their ancient homeland in Palestine."[89] Political Zionism aimed to bring the Jewish people back to a position where Jews would live a normal life as a productive and independent nation on its own land. To mainstream Political Zionists, this meant bringing together two seemingly opposing principles: socialism, the most progressive and contemporary of movements, and Jewish spiritual underpinnings reaching back across the millennia to the preexilic Jewish kingdom when the Jews ruled over their own land. Revisionists among the Political Zionist narrative also wanted to follow this general path, or as the Revisionist Zionist leader Jabotinsky[90] claimed, "The Diaspora means that others create and control our history; Zionism means that the Israeli nation begins, as an independent nation, to make its own history."[91]

Although Jews began to emigrate to Palestine beginning in 1882,[92] it was not until 1897 when Theodor Herzl, now known as the father of modern Zionism, convened the First Zionist Congress in Basel, Switzerland, during which 200 participants, representing 17 countries, laid the groundwork for the construction of a highly efficient and sophisticated political narrative and organization.[93] At the Congress, Herzl expanded upon the reasons and ideas he introduced in his 1896 book, *The Jewish State*, such as the need for settlement of Jews in Palestine to escape persecution, a federation of all Jews into local groups throughout their various countries of residence, a strengthening of the Jewish feeling and consciousness, and preparatory steps necessary for the achievement of the Zionist purpose.[94]

In its early years, in order to be realized, Political Zionism could not depend on the existing organizational infrastructure of the European Jewish communities; it had to create an entire state apparatus of its own. Thus the World Zionist Organization, the Jewish National Fund, Political Zionist parties, the Halutz (Pioneer, agricultural labor) movement, the Jewish Agency, and various military organizations came into being. This complex organizational network shares responsibility for the establishment of the Jewish yishuv community in Palestine, and after 1948 it became the foundation of the independent Israeli state institutions. The Political Zionist organizational infrastructure was predominantly Ashkenazi, that is, European, and nearly all of its efforts were oriented originally toward European Jews. It was built to absorb European Jews into the new society, even Jews who were not Political Zionists. Meanwhile, 'Oriental' Jews, sometimes referred to as Mizrahim, did not develop a similar structure, one explanation being because they had not experienced the same crisis of communal existence that the Europeans, especially the East European Jews, had experienced in the latter part of the nineteenth century. On the contrary, the occupation of most of the MENA by European imperialist powers opened new opportunities for the Jews, whether in economic entrepreneurship, imperial administrative positions, or cultural and political activities.[95]

The Balfour Declaration of 1917, drafted by British foreign secretary Balfour as a letter to Baron Rothschild, a leader of the British Jewish community, was crucial in establishing the Political Zionist narrative and garnered legitimacy for the movement. Implicitly recognizing the Jewish need for a national home and setting the foundations for Britain's role to this end, the letter states:

> His Majesty's Government view with favour the establishment in Palestine of a national home for the Jewish people, and will use their best endeavours to facilitate the achievement of this object, it being clearly understood that nothing shall be done which may prejudice the civil and religious rights of existing non-Jewish communities in Palestine, or the rights and political status enjoyed by Jews in any other country.[96]

The Balfour Declaration as well as the growth of nationalism as a political ideology in the period following the First World War and the building up of the Jewish yishuv in Palestine brought a certain attractiveness and prestige to the Political Zionist narrative among Ashkenazim. The period of the British Mandate in Palestine, formalized by the League of Nations in 1922, divided the territory into two administrative areas including Palestine, under direct British rule, and Transjordan under the rule of the Hashemite family. During this time the growth of kibbutzim, collective communities founded on socialist and Political Zionist values, further embodied the persistence of the Political Zionist's pioneering spirit into yishuv life, a trend that continued beyond Israel's declaration of statehood, exemplifying the Political Zionist desire to redeem the land agriculturally, politically, and culturally. The community continued to increase so that by May 1948 it was comprised of approximately 650,000 Jews.[97]

As anti-Semitism grew in Europe during the late nineteenth and early twentieth centuries, Jewish immigration to Palestine began to increase markedly, aggravating and increasing Arab resentment as a result of the land and resources incoming immigrants required. British quotas on immigration, as well as violence between Jewish and Arab communities under the Mandate, seemed to reinforce Herzl's reflection in *The Jewish State*, that the Jewish question persists wherever Jews live in appreciable numbers and gives rise to persecution. This, in turn, reinforced and legitimized the Political Zionist narrative.[98] The Biltmore Program, adopted by a special Zionist conference convened in May 1942, further emphasized the connection of the Jewish people with Palestine, their right to transform it into a Jewish commonwealth, and the ultimate authority of the Jewish Agency with regard to Jewish homelessness and settlement in Palestine.[99]

In effect this established the principle of Western Jewish consensus for Political Zionist aspirations and leadership, and its acceptance in Jewish and international circles between Europe and the West furthered the Political Zionist political agenda. During the following six years, Political Zionist leaders assumed the role of a Jewish government, preparing the foundation of the state and directing the support of the centers of Jewish power in the West. An integral part of this process was the Jewish Agency which, established by the World Zionist Organization in 1929, came to be considered the de facto government of the Jewish homeland before its formal declaration of statehood, and took responsibility for absorption and allocating resources in the resettlement of new immigrants.[100]

With the execution of systemic anti-Semitism under the Hitler Nazi regime, Political Zionists were propelled into urgent organization and action. At the core of the Jewish self-image were feelings of vulnerability and victimhood. Karsh states, "It was hoped that the creation of a Jewish state would strengthen the Jewish psyche in the diaspora. It would not only enable Jews everywhere to stand taller; it would elicit admiration from non-Jews and ensure respect for Jewish rights everywhere."[101] Particularly in the wake of the Holocaust, loyalty to the Jewish faith and commitment to the Jewish people became significant as a stand of solidarity and strength. As a result, pride in one's faith and people became increasingly measured in terms of loyalty to the Political Zionist narrative and the idea of a Jewish state; to support one's religious kin was to support the new project and refuge in Palestine. Through this lens, an internalization of the nation and nationalist sentiments preceded the nation-state itself. By 1948 the Political Zionist narrative and the Jewish Agency were treated as synonymous, and the Jewish Agency was officially recognized as the representative of the Jewish people in all matters concerning the development of the State of Israel. Establishment of formal and recognized statehood constituted a victory for the founders and supporters of Political Zionism and validated the political nationalist narrative. Following the failure of the 1947 United Nations Partition Plan for Palestine (Resolution 181) that proposed an Arab and Jewish state side by side, violence erupted and only increased in ferocity upon Israel's declaration of statehood.

The ensuing war of 1948 (in which Egypt, Iraq, Jordan, Lebanon, and Syria participated) concluded with the 1949 Armistice Agreements from which the Green Line was created; however, despite loss of life, the war did not destroy the Jewish state and therefore solidified the Political Zionist presence in the region resulting in greater confidence and legitimacy among the movement.[102] An internalization of persecution inherent in the desire for a Jewish national home was reinforced by the violent clashes that early citizens encountered; this not only validated the necessity for a Jewish state in the Political Zionist narrative but also gave the narrative greater authority and legitimacy when Israel survived the war victoriously. This highlights the relationship between territory and identity where "securing something requires its differentiation, classification and definition. It has, in short, to be identified in order to secure it."[103]

As a result, Israeli and diaspora Jewry identities and political narratives are shaped, positively or negatively, within and in response to the Political Zionist narrative. Being as it was a movement grown from Western thought and aimed largely at the benefit of the Jews of Western Europe, Political Zionism excluded both orthodox religious Jews and Jews from outside Europe. For instance, the Political Zionist narrative was not successful in reaching all different communities of Jews as seen through the words of an orthodox rabbi in 1900:

> Men who say that the people of Israel should be clothed in secular nationalism, a nation like all other nations, that Judaism rests on three things, national feeling, the land and the language, and that national feeling is the most praiseworthy element in the brew and the most effective in preserving Judaism, while the observance of the Torah and the commandments is a private matter depending on the inclination of each individual. May the Lord rebuke these evil men and He who chooseth Jerusalem seal their mouths.[104]

Soon after the declaration of the State of Israel, the existing community experienced waves of immigrants from various social and cultural areas of the diaspora. The resulting heterogeneous community reflected the appeal of the Political Zionist narrative to an extent but also highlighted its Ashkenazi, Western roots. Sephardim (coming from the Hebrew word for Spain, that is, those expelled from Spain in 1492) and Mizrahim (meaning East or Oriental) Jews, coming from North Africa and the Middle East, arrived in Israel only to be seen by the yishuv as backward and "underdeveloped economically and socially."[105] This created a pluralistic mosaic of ethnic groups that simultaneously fell within the larger collective of the Jewish People. Ben-Gurion, Political Zionist leader and Israel's first prime minister, now viewed aliya (immigration, settlement) and the expansion of industry as the most vital elements in Israel's national security. "The first necessity for ensuring the state's security is mass immigration, at a rapid pace and increasing scope," he stated on the first anniversary of Israel's independence.[106]

The Political Zionist narrative, seeking to provide a national home for the Jewish Diaspora at large, was challenged by subgroups coming from diverse nations suddenly unified as one. Although the exclusion of minority groups is not explicit in the Political Zionist narrative, its ethnic nature naturally excludes those who do not fit within it, therefore defining one's relationship to the state as well as the relationship among its citizens. As a result of the need for national unity that must stand against those who would wish to see the state destroyed, minority communities and rights are often overlooked.[107] Eshkol Nevo's recent novel *Neuland* composes a modern-day microcosm of the utopian ideals that formed the State of Israel. Nevo's characters get a chance to start their lives over in a South American utopia that draws Israelis and other nationals alike to the original Political Zionists' hopes for a secular, ecumenical, and inclusive state. The fact that this theme resonates so powerfully in Israeli culture and beyond is invoked by the title, a play on Herzl's Altneuland and Maurice de Hirsch's efforts to build a Jewish homeland in Argentina.[108] Despite its idealism, Neuland provides a contrast to the actual state of discord and violence in modern Israel, a glaring reflection of the ways in which Herzl's dream has not yet been realized.

The orientalist dimension of the nation has found frequent expression in Political Zionist literature since its formulation, vastly influencing policy. For example, Herzl described in his utopian novel, *Altneuland*, the transformation of the exilic Jew through his emigration to Palestine; a process of regeneration that will lead, ultimately, to the creation of "a Europe in the Middle East" where the Arabs are described as being grateful to the Jews for rescuing them from a state of barbarism.[109] One basic characteristic of the early Political Zionists was the desire to bring the Jewish people back into the general course of world history. This goal would be accomplished by looking simultaneously forward to the West and backward to the East in the form of ancient Israel.

This attraction of the Political Zionist narrative to an Eastern heritage simultaneously reaching 'forward' toward a Western haven in the Middle East continued in the absorption policies of Jews from Middle Eastern states in that they were lauded for their noble heritage but regarded as diseased and backward upon arrival. For instance, a Political Zionist emissary sent to Libya spoke of the people there in the following terms: "They are handsome as far as their physique and outward appearance are concerned, but I found it very difficult to tell them apart from the good quality Arab type."[110] This orientalist attitude internalized within the Political Zionist narrative resulted in Jews from Arab lands being perceived as an abstracted ideal of the primordial Jew, but their present or concrete culture rejected and described as Oriental. The Mizrahim[111] were perceived as upholding the ancient traditions, but incapable of being conscious of its content; Arab-Jewish secularism appeared threatening because it was Arab secularism and was perceived to reflect a different model of secularization and modernization.

The notion of the secular in the Political Zionist discourse was thus a European, cultural identity. Therefore, by extension, the representation and imagining of Jewish collectivity as a national identity took the form of European models. The regeneration of the Jew and the revival of Jewish culture were explicitly their Europeanization, and the binary Political Zionist distinction between Arab and Jew produced an impossible rupture between what had been, until the mass migrations following the establishment of Israel, frequently congruent aspects of identity.[112] A combination of looking back to the East and forward to the West proved to be a contradicting and patronizing narrative to the Jews of Arab lands. 'Negation of exile' (and its complementary 'return to history') demonstrates the theological dimension of Political Zionist national consciousness and the orientalism inherent in secularization. Essentially, 'negation of exile' refers to the consciousness that deems the present Jewish settlement in, and sovereignty over, Palestine as the 'return' of the Jews to the land believed to be their home, and imagined, prior to its 'redemption,' as empty.[113] The negation of exile appeared to be the fulfillment of Jewish history and the realization of Jewish prayers and messianic expectations. According to this perspective, the cultural framework that the Political Zionists wished to actualize and uncover was the authentic Jewish culture, as opposed to the exilic culture, described in orientalist terms as stagnant, unproductive, and irrational. On the other hand, the preference for viewing Oriental Jews as religious was meant to preserve them as carriers of tradition, to which their Arab culture was external and nonessential.[114] Therefore, return was directed toward an imagined East: one that Judeo-Christian Western civilization glorified, constructed in opposition to the Arab-Muslim world. Political Zionism emerged out of this dialectical attitude toward the Orient, a process that ignored and limited the understanding of plural identity.

Political Zionist Revisionist leader Jabotinsky demonstrated the push and pull of East versus West in his criticism of orientalist tendencies within Political Zionism. In a 1927 article, "The Arabesque Fashion," Jabotinsky claimed, "We are going to the Land of Israel in order to advance Europe's moral boundaries to the Euphrates."[115] Jabotinsky challenged the orientalist tendencies that had gained popularity among Political Zionists who saw the East and its inhabitants as morally superior to the West, because the East had not been contaminated by Western civilization and had maintained its original, virtuous characteristics.

According to Jabotinsky, this tendency to romanticize the Orient rested on the false assumption that the East and the West were fundamentally different. The only difference between the two, he claimed, was that while Europe was technologically advanced, the East was not. The East, Jabotinsky claimed, was a primitive expression of Western culture, for example, the historical equivalent of Europe of the Middle Ages.[116] Here he simultaneously criticized and enacted the orientalist dialogue.

Ben-Gurion did not mask his disappointment in the necessity of turning to non-European Jewry. Commenting on the destruction of European Jewry caused by the Holocaust, he remarked in December of 1942, "The destruction of European Jewry is the ruin of Zionism. We will not have with whom to build the Land."[117] Despite this attitude, Political Zionism found a place in the tumult of Moroccan Jewry. A series of factors (including disenchantment with France, the rise of Arab nationalism, the consequences of Vichy France and the Holocaust, and the establishment of the State of Israel) overlapped to set an unstable future for the Jews of Morocco. The onslaught of colonialism and the imposition of Western-style modernity through an orientalist lens transformed all aspects of the Jewish communities of Morocco and much of the Middle East: religious expression, vocational patterns, culture, language, gender conventions, and relations with Muslims. In this sense, the AIU and Political Zionism both functioned as a part of the European colonial presence in Morocco.[118]

The exact date of Political Zionist penetration into the Moroccan communities is not clear; Laskier contends that the earliest organized activity might have commenced after the first Zionist congress of 1897, although the earliest record of organized activity began in 1900 in Tétouan with the Shivat Sion (Return to Zion) association.[119] This association set up a Hebrew-language library to propagate the language and the Political Zionist idea among the Jews. At the same time, a second association was founded in Mogador, known as the Sha'are-Sion (Gates of Zion) and a third association, Ahavat Sion (Love of Zion), was founded in the coastal town of Safi. Laskier uses 1897 as the starting point of Political Zionism in Morocco due to an article found in the Jewish chronicle to Mogador that was written during the first Zionist congress:

> Needless to say, here the Zionist idea finds a loud and sympathetic echo in the hearts of all coreligionists with almost no exceptions. It is quite interesting to note how enthusiastically the rabbis talk over the matter . . . perhaps this feeling of sympathy exists in the hearts of all Jews, only they do not care to expose their sentiments. All Jews may not be in agreement with items of the Congress program, but it seems natural, from some Moroccan-Jewish points of view, that

they should all sympathize with the spirit of the thing, without running the risk of feeling or showing any disloyalty for the native land in which they have been born and bred.[120]

The year 1897 predates many of the complicated years wherein Jewish identity in the Arab world would become more strenuous with the rise of Arab nationalism and growth of European anti-Semitism. However, the spirit that all Jews would sympathize with Political Zionism without showing disloyalty for the native land in which they were born points to the ease with which plural identities can be expressed when allegiances are not in conflict. French Protectorate documents contradict the report of the Zionist congress, claiming that "it is doubtful whether the Zionist exodus will take anyone other than the aged and destitute from Morocco to Jerusalem."[121] Writing in 1918, many years from the first Zionist congress, Colonel Berriau was not entirely wrong; at this point Moroccan Jews were not interested in leaving en masse; however, it overlooks the connection felt by Jews toward Jerusalem without physically leaving their place of birth.

After Herzl's death in 1904, Political Zionist activities in Morocco were temporarily halted, only to be revived in 1907 through the initiative of influential families in the bilad al-Makzhan (in particular Fez, Meknès, and Sefrou) and in 1908 the Hibbat-Sion (Admiration of Zion) society was founded in Fez.[122] Morocco's Jewish community leadership had links through fellow Sephardic exiles throughout Palestine and elsewhere in the Ottoman Empire; however, the organization of Political Zionists strengthened these ties with new fundraising and relief efforts following the First World War. Just as the AIU strived to spread French language and culture through education, so too the first Maghen David school, founded in Casablanca in 1920, taught modern Hebrew, nationalist hymns, and the use of Political Zionist symbols.[123] Others followed into the early 1940s thereby creating a foundation for Jewish cultural nationalism.[124]

From the inception of Political Zionism following the Basel Congress of 1897, a serious conflict had developed between the AIU and the Political Zionists. The latter accused the AIU of sacrificing Jewish goals in favor of national interests (French interests), because in order for the AIU to remain viable, it needed to obtain funds and political support for its educational and political activities. Therefore, the AIU, argued the Political Zionists, had to obtain the consent of the French government for its programs on behalf of the Jews. In encountering early Political Zionist activities, representatives of the AIU were at first concerned with the Political Zionist narrative as a threat to French nationalism, that Political Zionism and Arab nationalism could eventually prove ruinous to

French colonialism. Indeed, among the AIU's critiques was Herzl himself who contended in 1898 that those who refer to the AIU as a Jewish organization might as well describe the "Freemasons as a Judaized association."[125] While the AIU aspired to transform and liberate the Jews in their respective countries through legislative reforms, the Political Zionists, on the other hand, called for the solution to the 'Jewish problem' not through assimilation but rather by physically uprooting the Jews from the diaspora and placing them in a homeland of their own.[126]

Before the Second World War in Morocco, Political Zionist progress was defined by its divisions. No sufficient legislation detaching the Jews completely from the Makhzan jurisdiction was enacted and the Jews, disappointed with the ambiguous social and political status, and seeking political involvement, looked for alternatives for Jewish emancipation. Political events in Palestine, signaling the development of the yishuv, and the increase of Jewish emigration to Palestine from various parts of the diaspora, encouraged segments of Moroccan Jewry to become more involved in the Political Zionist efforts, especially after the French betrayal of the Vichy era. Poverty was still rampant in many communities where the AIU and the Protectorate did not extend their influence or had done so only recently. Despite efforts by various Jewish organizations to help the large number of impoverished Jews in the heavily populated urban centers, poverty remained a major problem[127] and the Political Zionist organizations were there to provide support as an alternative to the Protectorate administration.

It is worth noting that the emigration of Moroccan Jews, particularly to Palestine, began before the First World War. Even during the interwar period, foreign Political Zionist activists made appeals for emigration and tried to cultivate the idea of a return to Israel among the Jewish communities in Morocco. In the southern Moroccan Jewish communities, in particular, Boum stresses that the Political Zionist narrative appealed to "an already existing and deep historical narrative of belonging" that spoke to their feeling of membership in a diasporic community of the Jewish people.[128] Official representatives of Moroccan Judaism as well as French authorities and Moroccan nationalists countered these attempts. During the 1930s, this last group campaigned against Political Zionism, which it considered to be disruptive and incompatible with the Moroccan nationality of the Jews. In 1936, La Nation Arabe acknowledged that the "Jewish people were the object of persecution through the centuries and unfortunately continue to be, especially in civilized countries . . . (but that) until the Balfour Declaration,[129] the harmony between Islam and Judaism was perfect."[130] This did not prevent strong words against Political Zionism; Moroccan nationalists were outraged at what they saw as the Political Zionists' demands for continued immigration to Palestine without limits and with autonomy.[131]

Thus, prior to the Second World War, appeals for emigration garnered little success. As a result, Political Zionist attention before 1939 was largely confined to the spread of the Political Zionist idea in the press and in encouraging Jewish participation in fundraising. Nevertheless, a few aliyah offices in Casablanca and Meknès maintained ties with the emigration section of the Jewish Agency since the early or mid-1930s in an attempt to obtain emigration certificates from the authorities of the Mandate in Palestine. The number of emigrants was limited, partly due to the stiff restrictions imposed by the British over issuance of certificates, and partly due to the lack of regular communications between the Moroccan-based emigration offices and the Jewish Agency.

The period between 1939 and 1945 (arguably until Moroccan independence in 1956) was critical to the growth of Political Zionism and the establishment of ties among world Jewry. This can be understood due to five attributing factors: first, the increasingly separatist demands of an increasingly Arab-Islamic Moroccan nationalist movement after the late 1930s due to heightened French control; second, the landing of the Americans in Morocco in 1942 and the ensuing contacts this established with world, and especially, American Jewry; third, Vichy anti-Semitic laws and the devastation of the Holocaust; fourth, the reorganization of Political Zionist activities such as the rejuvenation of Jewish associations and Hebrew cultural centers in Morocco; and fifth, the penetration of the Jewish Agency representatives in 1944 into Moroccan Jewish communities that undermined the AIU's monopoly of control and influence.[132]

The American arrival did not end French rule in North Africa nor did it immediately revoke the Statut des Juifs but it connected North African Jews to American Jewish organizations which, in turn, pressured Roosevelt to act. More significantly, perhaps, these interactions began a dialogue among the greater Jewish Diaspora that influenced Political Zionist activity throughout the 1940s and beyond. Political Zionist-oriented youth groups, sporting teams, scouting troops, and summer camps were organized in Morocco for Jewish children as was, by the late 1940s, the Revisionist Zionist youth movement, Tel Hai.[133] Once the news of the birth of Israel arrived in these communities, a strong political conception of emigration converged with the mystical-religious attraction the Holy Land had always held. This provided a favorable setting for the Political Zionist narrative, which urged emigration as a means of consolidating the newly created state in the Middle East.

Simultaneously disenchanted with France and, by extension, the AIU, evolués began to express frustration with the notion of emancipation through assimilation and many turned to the Political Zionists for inspiration and opportunity. The radicalization of the Moroccan nationalist stance increasingly identified with Arab political aspirations in Palestine, and these activities greatly enhanced the attractiveness of the Political Zionist narrative. The war had such a profound impact on the diaspora that even the AIU, after 1945, could not remain indifferent to Political Zionism. After the near collapse of the organization in France and the destruction of European Jewry, the AIU took a new position.

As an extension of the Protectorate, the AIU had not been sympathetic to the Political Zionist movement. Worried equally about the spread of pan-Arab nationalist narratives, the Protectorate felt that to allow Political Zionist organizations to act would only cause trouble.[134] Though it never became a Political Zionist-oriented group, the AIU eventually endorsed the need for Jewish emigration to Palestine, particularly the settlement of the victims of Nazi Germany. In 1946, for example, an AIU editorial indicated that the extermination of the Jews in Europe and the practical impossibility for the survivors of emigrating elsewhere made Palestine a natural place for refuge: "The magnificent projects of industrialization in Palestine and the transformation of the country to a modern society, should enable many refugees to settle there, so that both Jews and Arabs could live together."[135]

During the postwar period, Moroccan politics were in transition as well. The Moroccan nationalist movement began concentrating its appeal to Islam and pan-Arab sentiment, references that had considerable impact among the bulk of the Muslim majority. In January 1944, when the Istiqlal (Independence) Party published its Manifesto of Independence engaging it in a power struggle with the French Protectorate powers, the vast majority of Moroccan Jews were caught between allegiances. The Moroccan Jewish communities, while continuing to swear allegiance to the sultan, felt themselves to be more or less outside the struggle for national liberation, and this feeling intensified in 1947 when the primary political forces in Morocco embraced the direction offered by the Arab League. While Muslim political movements were reinforcing their connections to pan-Arabism with the goal of ousting the colonial presence, some Moroccan Jews were turning their backs on these movements and instead heeding the appeals of Political Zionist groups that were organizing aliyah.[136]

The creation in the late nineteenth century of Jewish protégés with special political and legal privileges, the arrival of assimilationist outreach via education in the form of the AIU, and the presence of Political Zionist activity trace the muddled and complex relationship of Moroccan Jews with Europe during the colonial period. Four decades of Protectorate rule reshaped the social, cultural, economic, and political position of the Moroccan Jewish population and challenged the classification of Jews as protégés, dhimmi, subjects, or citizens. Despite efforts to assimilate the Jews, cultural and linguistic identification with France did not guarantee political rights and led to an ultimate betrayal of trust with the arrival of Vichy anti-Semitism. Simultaneously, the presence of Political Zionist organizations in Morocco was also heavily affected by the war. Devastated by the Holocaust and disenchanted with the French, many turned toward Political Zionism in an act of Jewish solidarity toward its own independent nation-state. Though grateful for the efforts of the Moroccan sultan to shield them from these initiatives, Moroccan Jews could not find a clear platform with the Moroccan nationalist parties that often isolated the Jews as other to solidify their own identity.

The creation of the State of Israel in 1948 was an irreversible point of tension between Moroccan Jews and the sultan. While the sultan clearly aligned himself with the Moroccan nationalist movement and the pan-Arab movement led by Nasser in Egypt, Moroccan Jews found themselves a religious minority excluded from both national communities. Nasser's rhetoric appealed to "all countries that speak Arabic" and for the liberation of "Muslims across the world" who are "sibling," "brother," and "neighbor of every African."[137] Nasser spoke of the rights to be self-sufficient, secure, and liberated, though his message was directed at "we the Arabs, we Muslims, we the people of this East—to become one bloc."[138] Though Moroccan nationalists claimed to guarantee equal civil rights and duties to Morocco's Jews, they were marginalized along ethnic and cultural lines as the nationalist movement took on an Arab-Islamic identity.

Many factors cumulated in mass migration of Moroccan Jews, leading many to a new nation-state (Israel) at war with their birth nation. Addressing the first research question, this chapter has demonstrated how the interwoven and overlapping forces of French colonialism and Political Zionism, operating independently but reactively, in the early twentieth century embodied several forms of identity fluidity and a push-pull notion of membership. As demonstrated in the AIU's reach and influence and evidenced in the archived periodicals and colonial documents, the Jews were active and often privileged to the French Protectorate administration. Simultaneously, a new secular nationalist narrative in Political Zionism drew upon the historic internalizations of the nation, Israel and the Jewish people. These concurrent yet contrasting narratives and subsequent demands show the hybrid, overlapping nature of colonialism and Political Zionism and the active role of Moroccan Jews, to varied extents, in both. Having now addressed the first two of three primary nationalist narratives, Chapter 5 turns to examine the transformation of Moroccan Muslim leaders from cooperative calls for reform to demands for independence. The competition of these three predominant narratives enhanced by events in the region ultimately led to an Arab-Islamic conception of Moroccan identity that no longer internalized the Jews as a part of the Moroccan nation.

4

Development and Transformation of Nationalism in Morocco

With this book already having demonstrated the diversity of nationalist narratives that arose during the Protectorate period and examining two, in particular French cultural-linguistic assimilation and Political Zionism, this chapter addresses the development and transformation of an Arab-Islamic Moroccan nationalism, focusing specifically from the beginning of the Protectorate in 1912 to the beginning of the Arab-Israeli War in 1948. This narrative progressed from a reform movement within the Protectorate system to the mobilization of a self-determination autonomous national narrative with calls for independent statehood. Designating two specific events, the 1930 Berber Dahir and the sultan's 1947 Tangier speech, this chapter will follow the same systematic lens of identity and narrative in order to examine both internal and external contexts affecting the evolution of Moroccan nationalism. These two key events were significant catalysts for change and provide in-depth snapshots of the development within the movement's priorities and demands as it transformed from reform to independence. Drawing upon historical literature and periodical and colonial archives, I contend that the development of a specifically Arab-Islamic Moroccan nationalism is consistent with the adaptive ethno-symbolism outlined in Chapter 2 where certain elements are drawn upon purposefully to suit the present needs of the narrative. Finally, from an understanding of the development of the Moroccan nationalist movement, it is possible to address its involvement of, and influence on, Moroccan Jewish identity and narrative. This will address the second research question (in such a case where multiple nationalisms existed simultaneously, why did Moroccan nationalism come to exclude its historic and sizable Jewish brethren?) and will provide the necessary setting for Chapter 6's interview data.

During the course of the Protectorate era, Moroccans and the French administration within Morocco were not isolated from Europe or the rest of the world. Young Moroccans studying in Europe interacted with activists attached to the pan-Arab nationalisms and anti-colonialist movements, and this transfer of ideas, in addition to the impact of the Second World War, had profound influence in the calls for reform and, later, independence in Morocco. Simultaneously, internal changes affected the organization of the Protectorate. Lack of equal access to education and economic hardship before and after the war led to increased migration to the cities and dissatisfaction with the Protectorate administration. While Morocco did not achieve independence until 1956, the groundwork was being laid for significant reforms and separation after only a decade of the Protectorate. This chapter clarifies stages of reform and nationalism as well as the ways in which external and internal influences contributed to the construction of an Arab-Islamic identity as the mainstream Moroccan national identity, thereby excluding a majority of the Jewish population.

The first decade of the twentieth-century partitioning of North Africa among the European powers witnessed agreements between Britain and France over Egypt and Morocco, as well as negotiations with Spain, Germany, and Italy to divide the region. Strategically, Morocco provided France vital access to the Mediterranean passage as well as to French West Africa territories. Moreover, French dominance in Morocco represented a psychological gain: the Protectorate helped France to "maintain its pride and prestige among the great powers of the world,"[1] an image complimented by French colonial rule over neighboring Algeria. The Treaty of Fez on March 30, 1912, differed from France's full colonial control of Algeria and instead enacted an associationist partnership in which France would 'assist' in economic and political development on behalf of the sultan.

The historical divide between blad al-siba and blad al-Makhzan was maintained by uprisings of Berber tribes with one such event in 1911 being used as justification from French assistance. While the Protectorate redistributed traditional veins of power, the power of the sultan, as the center of the blad al-Makzhan, was consolidated and this led to an interesting tension. From the position of figurehead at the center of the blad al-Makzhan, the sultan experienced a centrality to his authority that amounted to "a dominance that had never been achieved before."[2] However, the sultan was simultaneously the figurehead of the Protectorate administration and in this sense his authority altered from its traditional role.

The first French résident général, Hubert Lyautey, remained in his position from 1912 to 1926 and had immense influence in building the Protectorate. His dream that "Morocco would appear one of the most solid bastions of order against the sea of anarchy"³ demonstrates his view of the region at the time as one worthy of the civilizing mission and reveals his motivation to build Morocco into a different colonial entity than Algeria. In Morocco, he consented to "respect Islamic institutions and traditions as well as the Sultan's dignity."⁴ His vision was to "retain an indigenous partner, the Sultan and the Palace administration, in which the trappings of traditional government could be preserved in a reinvented neo-Makhzan to legitimize the French role in the nation-building project."⁵ Thus, the central elements of the traditional system remained but were largely symbolic structures under the actual quotidian rule of the Protectorate administration. Lyautey's desire to see France as aiding in the nation-building project is prophetic, but surely not how he would have envisioned it; in exacerbating societal division while engendering the liberal ideals of the right to self-determination,⁶ it was the existence and actions of the Protectorate that spurred the development of a Moroccan nation-building project that would culminate in independent statehood.

Scholars of Moroccan history vary on how to distinguish between reform and nationalist movements in terms of which reformist goals included a distinct view of nation-state and should therefore be distinguished as nationalist movements; however, the 1930 Berber Dahir is included as a significant turning point in all accounts.⁷ This lack of clarity is an extension of the ambiguity of the arrival of the concept of nationalism to the Moroccan political consciousness. As early as 1846, "Moroccan" and "the people of Morocco" appear as terms used to delineate Moroccans as a "definable entity, different from others, with their own particular cultural, religious, linguistic and political qualities."⁸ Toward the end of the nineteenth century, the use of the word *watan* (homeland) suggests a distinct Moroccan territory;⁹ however, it seems the pervasiveness of the concept of nationalist ideology was not widespread until the ideals of self-determination gained popularity at the close of the First World War.

Three primary networks existed in the early years of the Protectorate, with al-Fassi leading a group of young men from the Qarawiyyin Mosque University, al-Ouezzani leading one from the College Moulay Idriss, and a municipal council of Fez formed of mostly bankers and former protégés.[10][11] As early as 1925, the Qarawiyyin group was formed to study the ways in which the relationship with the Protectorate administration could be reformed.¹² This group was inspired by the Salafiyya movement which "sought to adapt and modernize Islam for a world dominated by European colonialism."¹³ Salafiyyist propaganda cultivated a growing sense of belonging to a single community with a common culture in contrast to that of the "alien French."¹⁴ Interestingly, the Salafiyya current took on an orientalist view in recognizing Muslims' "backwardness in comparison to Western countries" and in having a selective memory when preaching "a return to a past considered as glorious."[15] The desire for a "cultural and religious revival" was "perceived as a precondition for ameliorating the country's standing."[16] This first group was soon thereafter joined by others in Rabat, Tétouan, and Tangier, bringing together individuals from similar social backgrounds, the urban middle class, usually steeped in a predominantly Islamic culture, although some were already participants in the newly introduced French-style educational system. They shared the same aim of Islamic reform as a unifying communal alternative in the face of colonial influence and, meeting together in secret from 1926 onward, these groups shared information about their nationalist sentiment and actions and coordinated events across cities.[17]

This early activity highlights two crucial points: first, the idea of Islam as a unifying alternative to French assimilation and, second, the awareness and influence of external events on Moroccan reformists. These two notions combined for a rhetoric of frustrations with the French and proposed, as an alternative toward prosperity, pan-Arab solidarity. Already before the First World War, Moroccans were inspired by developments of political organization in the MENA region. Joffé cites the example of Kemalist Turkey and later Egypt as well for the rise of pan-Arab authors such as Chakib Arslan who, based in Geneva, served as an intellectual link between nationalist activists from North Africa and the Middle East. In the late 1920s, Arslan had come in contact with Moroccan students studying in Paris, including Mohammed al-Fassi,[18] Ahmed Balafrej, and Mohammed al-Ouezzani who had been instrumental in the formation of the North African Muslim Students Association (AEMNA)[19] and would go on to be key actors in the reform and nationalist movements. This Maghreb presence in Geneva led to the periodical La Nation Arabe, whose writings demonstrate the pan-Maghreb and pan-Islam sentiment that would soon be used to rally support for Moroccan independence. La Nation Arabe defended the autonomy of Morocco while simultaneously threatening the danger of a French-led society:

> It is unnecessary, even foolish, to think that Paris can Frenchify or Christianize the 17 million Muslims who live in Morocco, Algeria, and Tunisia. As long as France, guided by priests, settlers, and its military, nourish the illusion of power, substitute the French language for Arabic, and Christianity for Islam, there will be no difference between the French and the indigenous people.[20]

Though anti-French sentiment was building in educated Muslim circles, reformists in the early Protectorate years struggled to gain support beyond their immediate networks[21] due to low literacy levels of the general public, a state of being that negligible spending on indigenous education by the Franco-Moroccan Makhzan did little to improve, and restrictions on freedom of the press in the form of censoring or forbidding publication.[22] A decree issued on April 27, 1914, created a legal foundation guiding how the press would be regulated under the Protectorate and gave the Residency expansive controls so that the Arabic and French press in Morocco were differentiated, and any Arabic language publications, even if published in Morocco, were considered foreign press that could be prohibited by special decree by the résident général. Later decrees gave the Residency additional powers to forbid any publications necessary to protect order and security.

Unequal access to, and funding of, education was an internal issue that contributed to unrest and frustration with the Protectorate. Education, as a meeting place of the Protectorate administration and its 'protectees,' provides an interesting look at the "reproduction of cultures, the definition of social roles, the categorization of individuals, and the transmission of ideas."[23] Schools can be a space in which colonial collaborators are crafted or divisions are deepened.[24] Chapter 4 has demonstrated how the AIU schools' French curriculum carried with it cultural transformations and created strong ties between the Jewish population and France whereas, for Morocco's Muslim majority, unequal resources led to increased resentment and division.

This motivated students and teachers to work against the curriculum to preserve their culture. Lacking equal resources and equating French colonial education[25] with Gallicization of its young people, reformists founded free schools[26] in 1919 as a Moroccan attempt to create a competitive alternative to the Franco-Muslim schools founded by the Direction of Public Instruction (such as the AIU). By teaching Arabic and Islam as a part of a modern curriculum, these schools played an important role in cultivating a cultural sense of national identity among urban youth based on Islamic ideals. In the mid-1930s, there were 5,000 Moroccan students enrolled, and by the late 1940s this number had increased to 25,000.[27] Reformists noted the tremendous disparity in investment in 'indigenous' education in comparison with the budget allocation for European and Jewish schools in Morocco and continued to criticize the marginalization of instruction in Arabic and Islam. Just before the 1930 Berber Dahir, the Protectorate's education budget allocated 55 million francs for the European and Jewish population, which consisted of 300,000 people with 41,000 students. For the entire Muslim population of over 8 million, there were only 10,000 students in the system and only 17 million francs allocated.[28] By 1935, the situation had not improved markedly; *La Nation Arabe* published a report on the state of education funding in Morocco demonstrating the disparity of resources per capita:

> The sums allocated to the education of Muslim Moroccans are, depending on the year, only 1.3% to 1.8% of the budget of the Moroccan state. For 7 to 8 million Muslim Moroccans, including the school-age population of at least 500,000 people, there are schools for only 11,000 students. By contrast, the European colony, which is 173,000 people, has schools for more than 30,000 students. Moroccan Jews, whose number does not exceed 118,000, have a student population of over 10,500.[29]

In the same manner of motivating French allegiance and membership to Moroccan Jews through AIU funding and resources, the Protectorate administration had the opposite effect on the Muslim population.

The quest to reform Protectorate policy and make it more equitable largely opposed the authoritarian nature of French rule rather than its foreignness. Moroccan proponents of reform criticized the inequalities of a system that provided rights and privileges to French citizens, while denying them to colonial subjects. It is important to note that demands for reform implied a desire for "inclusion and access, not separation. Proponents sought to be treated like Frenchmen were treated; they asked to be regarded as political equals."[30] Toward this end, the realm of education could also provide a meeting place for dissent and rebellion. For instance, in 1923, two years before the reformist group formed at the Qarawiyyin, a student, Abdelqader Tazi, petitioned the administration for reform.[31] In his petition he highlighted the humiliation he experienced at the hands of arrogant and obstinate French who "cannot pass through the streets without unjustly striking or publicly insulting . . . the Muslims whom they encounter. . . . They think of us as their dogs and strike us with their feet."[32] Rather than reject the Protectorate, Tazi called for the French in Morocco to uphold their end of the civilizing mission and act accordingly. However, his petition is interesting in that it shows a proto-nationalist description of the Muslim Moroccan identity that the independence movement would later take on. He warns:

> Be assured that we alone are the people of this country—and that is the reality—and that you are only with us as guests charged with a civilizing mission. . . . Do not forget, where just, that we are Muslims, that this forms a community very attached to its religion, to its country, to its home. . . . The Muslims do not accept injustice; they refuse to perish until the last, by the power of their unity. . . . Three

forces are combined in us. Arab nobility. The Islamic spirit. The sentiment that we are in our own country.[33]

Tazi's letter predates the Istiqlal manifesto by over twenty years but reveals the sentiment of Morocco as possessing an Arab and Islamic spirit. Tazi was removed from Fez and sent to Rabat, though his friends in Fez joined with al-Fassi's Qarawiyyin group and he continued his call for reforms clandestinely in Rabat.[34]

Though reformists were becoming champions of the Moroccan nation and its rights, their agenda to this point was one of reform. In the first issue of Maghreb, an article called for the "modernization of our country . . . but we hold on equally to our past, our traditions, and will never let go of the strong flame of Islam which is so strongly planted in the heart of Barbary."[35] This underscores the distinctive difference from reformist to nationalist: while reformists sought accommodation under French rule, nationalist discourses stressed the right of nations to rule themselves. Nationalist mobilization in favor of independence thus focused on challenging the foreign nature of imperial rule, rather than specific injustices of colonial policy. Whereas reformists sought to democratize rule of the state, nationalists sought to capture it and repel foreign influence. This is not to say that they had nothing in common; indeed, the founding actors of the reform movement would go on to found and play important roles in the nationalist party. However, the student of Moroccan history must not apply these labels to their respective time frame with the outcome already in mind.

A contrasting view sees reformists as 'proto-nationalists' suggesting that these kinds of demands represent an early stage in an evolutionary process toward nationalist resistance aimed at liberating Morocco from colonial rule.[36] Although mobilization during the late 1930s involved a small elite who made no claims about Moroccan independence, this school of thought sees calls for reform as a step on the path toward separatism; before elites try to overthrow colonial rule, they first ask for minor changes. The conditions that promote nationalist mobilization for independence may be quite different from those that facilitate reform movements. For instance, demands for reform came from a small group of European-educated elites, whereas the success of nationalism came from its ability to unify a large majority comprised of different groups. The fate of the reform movement may have prompted nationalist mobilization, as reformists facing failure came to see independence as the only way left to redress the inequalities of colonialism. Moore describes three modes: "Activists seek equality, activists engage in traditional anti-colonialism, and finally modern nationalism, when they achieve full consciousness of their mission."[37] Because this seems clear retrospectively, historians seeking to determine the beginnings of the nationalist movement may consider the reform movement part of the nationalist movement. Further complicating the distinction is the application of language used by the Protectorate and reform actors in their time. For instance, "It was already not uncommon to characterize all opposition to colonial rule as nationalist, regardless of the actual goal of activists."[38] Indeed, the archived periodicals and colonial archives display the term 'nationalist' to describe both the reformists and later those calling for independence.

The very task of seeking the origins of nationalism in the early activities of political leaders tends to homogenize political mobilization and obscure differences in the movements' goals and activities over time. However, those seeking to identify the origins of nationalism in Morocco write with the knowledge that nationalist movements eventually became dominant, not only in Morocco but elsewhere in the colonized world. Even though many of the early reformists shifted their goals over time, it is not possible to say that their demands for reform were purposefully building a nationalist platform at the moment of their conception. Just as identities are dynamic, "One recognizes that goals are not given in advance but are shaped by political context.... Labeling all opposition 'nationalist' inhibits our understanding of how actors come to seek national independence."[39]

This is evident from the writings of one reformer turned nationalist, Allal al-Fassi, the creator of the first reform group in Fez and an eventual Istiqlal leader. Writing in 1954, he stated that the point of the secret societies was to "create a current of reformist thought by propagating the modern Islamic ideologies among the intellectuals in the principal cities of Morocco."[40] He asserts that "nationalist consciousness existed in al-Maghreb before and after the advent of Islam,"[41] though his writings of the reform movement "cannot be separated from the political project of nation-building that he is engaged in at the time he describes those preferences" in 1954.[42]

Nonetheless, al-Fassi's words do emphasize the initial goal of reform within the French system. He also reveals the early attraction of Islam as a unifying platform drawing upon the image of the Moroccan nation founded by the Idrissid dynasty in the late eighth century by Islamization and Arabization. Interestingly, though the reformists rallied for pan-Maghreb and pan-Arab support, they feared becoming like Algeria as it was much more enmeshed with France. Assuaged of this possibility by Lyautey in the first year of the Protectorate, the reformists used his words of respect for Islam, the shari'a, and the habits and customs derived from it against the Protectorate when they felt this promise was not being upheld.

While evaluating the development of Moroccan nationalism, the key distinction between reformists and nationalists can be made from their goals: reformists sought to democratize the state within the Protectorate system, while nationalists sought to control it. The protests that followed the 1930 Berber Dahir can be considered the "seedbed out of which the embryonic nationalist movement emerged,"[43] but the clearest decisive factor in locating a shift in reformists' goals is the 1944 establishment of Istiqlal; in doing so the nationalists demanded autonomous self-rule, a central notion to nationalist ideology.[44] Therefore, herein, the term 'reformists' will be applied to those working for change before 1944, and the term 'nationalists' will be applied to those working for independence from 1944 onward.

While reformists at the beginning of 1930 were still a peripheral, small group, calls for reform did not cease. Forging a new link between the cities of the interior and those of the coast, between the ancient cities of imperial Morocco and the modern urban, commercial centers of the French Protectorate, a sense of Moroccan unity grew to encompass historically divided groups.[45] Increasingly, this caused the French to turn their attention from the conquest of the peripheries of its imperial scope to the reconquest of its center, and in consequence to devise a strategy for urban pacification. Presented on May 16, 1930, the Berber Dahir gave the reformists, "now prepared and ready for political action, a specific target."[46] The decree, signed by the sultan at the request of France's résident général Lucien Saint, gave sanction to Berber tribal (customary) law and placed the Berbers under the French penal code for serious crimes; in doing so, "It officially enshrined customary law, rather than shari'a in the Berber tribal areas."[47] Frustrated by lack of attention to their demands for reform, some Moroccans felt that the decree was designed to destroy the national aspirations of the Moroccan people by dividing the 'indigenous' population, thus isolating the Berber population and bringing them closer to the French tradition and language. The Berber Dahir acted as a spark to ignite an explosion of already lingering frustrations and anti-French feeling throughout Morocco's cities and became one issue on which the reformists built an organized platform. The framing of the French as 'foreign invaders' that would challenge the indigenous sense of belonging only contributed to growing national solidarity.

Claiming that the social and political differences between the blad al-siba and blad al-Makhzan were profound, French Protectorate leaders acted to elevate the distinction by attempting to drive them further apart. The decree itself was a short document which the French claimed merely tidied up some legal points having to do with the system of justice in the Berber lands; they maintained that it continued their traditional respect for Berber common or customary law and was in no way designed to alter or innovate. From the beginning of the Protectorate, Résident Général Lyautey was aware of the "Two Moroccos" the French faced:

> The one we occupy, which is militarily weak and governed by a Makhzen without force or prestige, and the other, much more important, which is comprised of Berber masses who are deeply agitated, fanaticized, and militarily strong, and who, under influences beyond our control, stand united against us.[48]

In order to bring both blad al-Makhzan and blad al-siba under French control, a decree of September 1914 stated that Berber tribes were to be administered according to their own laws and customs and that French authorities would prepare the appropriate legal texts or regulations on behalf of the sultan's Makhzan. The blad al-siba, though aware of the presence of the Makzhan as a "backdrop to the local arena where a new elite based on private ownership of land had developed," was arranged in an increasingly "hierarchical village-based peasantry."[49] The Rif War[50] of the early 1920s put much of the Berber tribal areas between the Rif and France so that their "pacification . . . in the wake of the Rif War was to mark the real beginning of its social and economic integration into Protectorate Morocco"[51] at the end of the 1920s. Following two decades of French attempts to minimize the Arabization and Islamization of the Berber tribes, reformists, who were themselves exclusively from among the urban centers of the blad al-Makzhan, took advantage of the 1930 Berber Dahir labeling it an obstacle to the unification of the Berber lands under Islamic law and, therefore, a threat to Islam.[52]

At the time, France's relations with the Berbers were predicated on two strongly held convictions: that although the Berbers were Muslims, they followed their own religious practices and that their secular resistance to the authority of the sultan's government was based on the "fear, borne out by Arab conquests of the past, of having these customs destroyed."[53] As a result, the French administration concluded that any Berber policy would need to have respect for Berber customs. While an admirable notion, the Berber policy implied a manipulative, Machiavellian hint of divide and rule. Indeed, Résident Général Lucien Saint wrote that French policy aimed at "a state of equilibrium judiciously maintained between two races" and that the Berbers were of "great importance to France's firm establishment in Morocco."[54]

In practice, the new decree created customary tribunals to handle civil, commercial, and personal property cases and removed criminal justice from Berber courts for all cases involving a penalty of more than two years' imprisonment. The transfer of criminal justice to French courts was a startling innovation, depriving the sultan of one of his essential prerogatives in the Berber lands, and the reformists saw this as an intrusion of French authority at the expense of the Makhzan. The discussions before its adoption by those among the French administration illustrate their awareness that the new decree would not be received favorably. Résident Général Charles Noguès, director of the native affairs bureau, and his assistant, Colonel Léopold Bénazet, warned against the possible consequences: the decree "could not pass unnoticed no matter how much care we took to announce it as the simple consecration of an existing state of affairs which is true and as the legitimate, necessary recognition of the aspirations of the Berber people."[55] In altering the scope of Islamic law to accommodate customary law, the decree unsettled religious sensitivities and evoked feelings of religious solidarity. The defense and renewal of Islamic law in the blad al-siba became a central concern and focal point in how the reformists shaped their platform.[56]

The divide and rule nature of the Berber Dahir provided the reformists an opportunity to call for solidarity. Writing in 1932, al-Ouezzani proclaimed that it was an injustice against Islam, the Arabic language, and Moroccan unity because the Berbers are the descendants of Morocco with its grand and glorious history.[57] He continued challenging the Protectorate administration and in 1934 noted, "This is nothing but a Machiavellian colonial project. It symbolized the abominable crusade carried out by the imperialists and priests against Islam and Arab culture."[58] Drawing upon Islamic solidarity and placing themselves as the defenders of the Koran, educated and devout reformists phrased the decree as a new sacrifice imposed on Islam by French pressure and part of a French crusade to Christianize the Berbers. This charge launched a major campaign of protest, using the Latif, the traditional prayer in time of emergency, to alert the populace in mosques throughout the country. Exasperation in the name of religious intolerance exclaimed that Arabs and Berbers could not be isolated in a country where all of its elements intermingled[59] and attacked the decree for trying to introduce French legal code in Morocco defending Islamic law as "neither archaic, nor absurd."[60] Once the religious nature of the protest became apparent, the French resolved not to intervene directly and instructed the sultan to write to the notables of Fez, Meknès, Salé, Rabat, Casablanca, and Marrakech. The sultan described the decree as simply an administrative measure and condemned the young people "devoid of any sort of judgment, heedless of the consequences of their reprehensible actions" who had "misled the crowd and transformed the recitation of the prayers into a political demonstration."[61] The letter forbade the use of mosques as political meeting points[62] yet conceded that any Berber tribe wishing to submit to the jurisdiction of Islamic law would be able to do so.

Protectorate officials hoped that Muslim Moroccans would submit immediately to the sultan's orders. Of the reformists in Fez, the majority agreed to stop the recitation of the Latif, as their sovereign demanded, but determined to send a delegation to discuss the crisis with him. Four days later, however, the Latif was recited in Casablanca, previously untouched by the turbulence, on the guidance of leaders from Rabat and Fez. The leaders and twenty-three of their Casablanca followers were arrested and sentenced to a month in prison. The reformists began organizing delegations in cities throughout the country to transmit their grievances to the Makhzan and presented a memorandum on August 23, 1930, that asserted the Islamization and Arabization of the Berbers of Morocco since the Idrissid dynasty, called for a "unified judiciary administering Islamic law" with the exemption of the country's Jewish minority, demanded the unification of the blad al-Makhzan and blad al-siba with Arabic as the only official language of the country, and an end to missionary activity in all of Morocco. Four days later, the sultan received the Fez delegation. Although he promised to consider their petition, they were sent away without response.

Protests were organized against the decree in multiple towns, and the Latif was recited in mosques throughout the country. As a result, Moroccan reformists were building an image of Moroccan identity in direct opposition to French attempts to preserve a distinct Berber identity. Islamic law and Arabic language became the rallying points on which the nation would be constructed and this led to an attempt at uniform Islamization and Arabization that would exclude groups previously included in the community. The scope of this narrative is consistent with pan-Arab nationalist movements of the same time. Building upon Moroccan discontent with the Protectorate administration, reformists were clear to capitalize on these frustrations. In response to French accusations that the enemies of France were conspiring against them by motivating rebellion in the Maghreb, La Nation Arabe published an article that turned the blame back to France:

> No one is complicit in the agitation which is organized against you in Morocco, Algeria, and Tunisia. The only agitators that move these countries are your own functionaries. This is your tyrannical administration and its absence of any

notion of justice and equality when it comes to the indigenous people, which are at the origin of this hostile movement to France in Muslim countries.⁶³

Interestingly, the early nationalists were aware that "we are all more or less Berbers, some more Arabized than the others; the Arab element in Morocco is tiny. But one fact is certain—that all of Morocco is Muslim."⁶⁴ Whether this statement was made to emphasize Morocco's distinct national character from other Arab nationalist movements in the region or to provide proof of further solidarity against the French administration, the insistence that all of Morocco is Muslim overlooked its sizable Jewish communities. Using Islam within a nation-specific movement highlights the tension between the Islamic notion of the universal community of Muslims, umma, and the territorial sovereignty implied in a nation-specific movement. However, evoking Islam as a common heritage similarly bound together the previously separated blad al-siba and blad al-Makzhan.

French authorities shut down the protests, but the events prompted increased organization in opposition. One such initiative was taken by two reformists, Belafrej and al-Ouezzani, who began the journal *Maghreb* (in Paris due to press restrictions in Morocco) criticizing Protectorate policy.⁶⁵⁶⁶ In the first issue of Maghreb, an article summarized the reformist agenda as it contrasted French assimilation and reaffirmed the significance of Islam to Moroccan culture stating that "if modernization requires sacrificing our own personality, it is natural that we would not want it. In sum, we wish to modernize while remaining ourselves."⁶⁷ In 1933, a second periodical, also in French because the Protectorate denied permission for an Arabic version, was founded in Fez, *L'Action du Peuple*, with Mohammed al-Ouezzani as editor in chief.⁶⁸ Its inaugural issue drew on French leftist ideals applied against itself; al-Ouezzani wrote,

> Our journal will have three categories of readers: Our compatriots who will find here the exposition of their ideas and desires; the local and metropolitan authorities will find the necessary illumination to accomplish their task; and the French living in Morocco will find indispensable information relevant to all that touches the autochthones that form nearly the entire population of the country.⁶⁹

Maghreb was first banned in September 1932 and then permanently banned in 1933 before being discontinued in January 1935. The Fez-based *L'Action du Peuple* was shut down immediately after the controversial reception of the sultan in the medina during his official visit to the city in May 1934. The journals furthered the premise that the Berber Dahir was an attack on the country's historical connection to Islam and argued that the sultan and the Protectorate should officially support Arabization and Islamization policies.

Toward constructing rhetoric of national tradition and commemoration, reformists declared Throne Day as an opportunity to demonstrate their loyalty to the sultan (as opposed to the French) and unite Moroccans in their rich precolonial history and rule. Despite a meager celebration in 1933, Throne Day grew in popularity after 1934 and became one of the major holidays on the Moroccan calendar. Protectorate authorities sought to use the event to symbolically enhance and reinforce the appearance of the Protectorate partnership, but the "reformists continued to be able to use the day's sanctioned banquets and official gatherings to reiterate their own program."[70] After the Second World War when the sultan would affiliate himself with the independence movement, the Throne Day speeches became a strategic opportunity for him to communicate directly to the Moroccan people, reinforcing his symbolic importance in defining the Moroccan national community. In inventing ritual commemorations of anniversaries and taking advantage of opportunities such as an official visit by the sultan, reformists "reached a mass urban audience with a symbolic construction of Moroccan identity"[71] that was beyond the circulation of publications.

The reformist platform was formally articulated in 1934, after the formation of the Moroccan Action Committee (CAM).[72] Initially comprised of a small group of the educated elite, primarily from Rabat and Fez, the group was formed in Paris under the leadership of Allal al-Fassi.[73] With the help of French left-wing sympathizers, they submitted the Plan of Reforms (Plan des Réformes) to the French government in December 1934. The plan did not discuss independence; in fact, it did not question the principle of the Protectorate, but rather it asked for a strict application of the Protectorate as agreed upon in the 1912 Treaty of Fez. This treaty, upon which the Protectorate was founded, provided the reformists with a textual basis for their appeal to the nation, and for a much more specific program of reform. The appeal was concerned with tradition, identity, and culture, though the program was modernist in its demand for political and economic progress.

The plan called for suppression of all direct administration, the administrative organization of Morocco in the sense of administrative and judicial systems, the application of the principle of the separation of powers, the admission of Moroccans on equal terms with Frenchmen to all administrative posts and councils, the formation of a Muslim National Assembly, improvements to the educational system, and the use of Arabic as the official language of the country.[74][75] Achieving no progress on the calls for reform, CAM presented an abbreviated version of reforms in October 1936.[76] This version asked for "democratic freedoms, more primary schools, a unified code of justice, separation of legislative, executive and judicial powers . . . and improved health facilities" as well as several proposals to improve landowner disputes among Moroccans and settlers and farmer credits.[77] It is worth noting the sultan's lack of sympathy, if not hostility, to the CAM's demands for reform. Although he would go on to work with the nationalists' leaders years later, reform to the Protectorate at this time would undermine his role in its government. The democratic government envisioned in the reforms left no clear role for a sultan, and "he realized that a Morocco molded in the image of the Plan of Reforms would be a state wherein his power would be severely curtailed."[78] An alliance with the sultan was not achieved until the platform changed after the Second World War, calling instead for a ruling monarch or a constitutional monarchy.

While the Berber Dahir may not have been the instigator for calls for reform, it was certainly a key catalyst in growth of the reform movement and an opportunistic rallying point to unify Muslim Moroccans outside the educated elite. The inclusion of a later section in the plan calling for the renunciation of the Berber policy and a ban on Christian proselytizing[79] demonstrates the significance of the 1930 decree in the organization of the reformist movement. Another important distinction to make is that by targeting the Berber blad al-siba land, the French policy drove reformists toward unifying the previously divided blad al-siba and blad al-Makzhen. By the mid-1930s, anti-French feeling was strong and pan-Maghreb spirit growing; La Nation Arabe's spring publication invoked the struggling political, economic, and social situation in North Africa as products of the "heavy blows of colonialism" in their country "under the baton and terror" of France.[80] In opposition to the divide and rule perception of the Berber Dahir, the reformists called for the Protectorate to consider all inhabitants of the empire subject of the sultan, excluding foreigners, and "to consider all Moroccans, except the Jews, as Muslims, that is to say that there is not a third religion for Moroccan subjects."[81] This publicly stated awareness of the Moroccan Jews indicates that while reformist rhetoric took on an increasingly Arab-Islamic awareness and unity, they were recognizing and including Jews in the call for equal citizenship as subjects of the sultan.

French language, education, and culture held the attraction of French citizenship and economic advantage and Political Zionism catered to both political nationalism and, for some, religious messianism especially in the wake of the Second World War and the Holocaust. Advantageous educational resources and economic opportunities led Moroccan Jews from the blad al-Makhzan to strengthen their attachment to France and with belief in the unshakeable permanence of French rule in North Africa.[82] Since the inauguration of the AIU in 1862, urban Jews had been exposed to the French language which they adopted as a mother tongue—a language that had paved for them the road to liberal professions, economic progress, administrative capabilities, and new modes of living and thinking. Some had exchanged their Judeo-Arabic names for French ones and adopted French (European) styles of dress and domestic customs. Boum describes this as their "new way of life, a la française, that could not be abandoned."[83] This sentiment is reinforced by the participant interviews presented in the next chapter where some participants express living as in France, as if French.

As for Jewish-Berber relations in the blad al-siba, it should be noted that many Jews lived among, or in proximity to, Berber communities. As merchants, traders, and small artisans in the Atlas mountain villages, Jews often played an intermediary role between Arabs and Berbers, and between different Berber tribal groupings. Moroccan mainstream opinion regarding the war in Europe was resolutely pro-French, and many Moroccan Arab and Berber youth fought in the French army to liberate France in the hope that France would return the favor and grant Morocco its independence after the war.[84] Moroccan Jews, although identifying with France and having expressed their will to join the French army, were absent from this formative experience in the shaping of Moroccan national identity, as had been the case with the Berber Dahir. By the mid-1930s, the reform movement had not contested the rights or participation of Moroccan Jews; however, Jews were omitted from the discussion where Arab and Islamic unity was being evoked to foster solidarity; they were held at the perimeter. Though acknowledging Morocco's Jewish past, the struggle to fit this religious minority into the national rhetoric posed a challenge. This was coupled by the fact that many Moroccan Jews had culturally assimilated and sought French citizenship or, on the other hand, had allied themselves with Political Zionist groups. As the reformist platform transitioned from reform to independence, the urgency to solidify what makes a Moroccan became almost exclusively Arab-Islamic.

The nationalist press of the early 1930s served as a forum for debating these conflicts. One such debate concerned the ambiguities between religious and national identity. According to a 1932 article in Maghreb, the French Civil Controller and local Jewish community in Mogador (Essaouira) were persecuting a Jew who, after practicing Islam for ten years, went to municipal authorities to make his conversion official. The French authorities rejected his request, but after calls from his cousins to divorce his wife and return a dowry, the Adjunct Civil Controller rejected the appeal that as a Muslim he was not under Jewish law and the matter should be decided in the Islamic court. Caught between the French administration, the Makhzan, and Jewish authorities in Mogador, the man was forced to appeal to the sultan.[85] Moroccan reformists were also worried about the prospect of the French naturalizing Morocco's Jews. In *L'Action du Peuple*, al-Ouezzani equated the 1930 Berber Dahir with initiatives to naturalize Morocco's Jews as French citizens and warned that Arabs themselves would end up a persecuted minority. Al-Ouezzani implied that if France granted Jews French naturalization, Arabs would become the minority and be repressed as the inferior population.[86] Evoking fear in this way, the Jews became potential suspects who could undermine Moroccan Muslim authority.

Questions about the status and loyalties of Morocco's religious minority exposed tensions between the ethnic and civic dimensions of the national community that Moroccan reformists were imagining and mobilizing in the 1930s. The 1934 Plan de Réformes outlined the unification of civil, commercial, and penal jurisdictions inspired by Muslim law but included provisions for the continuance of separate rabbinic courts.[87] In proposing equal civil rights, however, it also called for universal suffrage without distinction to religion in the election of Moroccan representative councils at municipal and national levels.

At the same time, Political Zionists started promoting Jewish immigration to Palestine. Nevertheless, some Moroccan Jews joined Arab nationalists calling Political Zionism a "threat to Moroccan Jewry and Judaism as well as the historical Jewish-Muslim symbiosis."[88] Years before, the tension presented by Political Zionism was made clear enough for then résident général Lyautey to write, "The Sultan, the Makhzan and the higher and enlightened Muslim class . . . sees the Zionist activity in the worst possible light. . . . In this, there is an apolitical and governmental factor, unique to Morocco, that cannot be neglected."[89] In response, Lyautey continued to emphasize that the sultan refused "to tolerate any propaganda which would lead to a reduction of the number of his Jewish subjects."[90] Despite these pledges of support, by the late 1930s the Protectorate, pressured by the Arab revolt in Palestine, the rise of Nazi Germany in Europe, and fears that Muslim-Jewish unrest in Morocco would undermine their position in North Africa, limited the freedom of any separatist aspirations of both Political Zionists and Moroccan reformists.[91]

In August 1933, Mohammed el-Kholti wrote a piece entitled "The Jews and Us" in *L'Action du Peuple* focused on the citizenship of Moroccan Jews.[92]

El-Kholti stressed an entente between Muslims and Jews without differentiation "according to race" and criticized the effects of Political Zionism on the maintenance of a positive relationship between Moroccan Jews and Muslims.[93] In response to el-Kholti's writings, the next issue of *L'Action du Peuple* included a response from a Moroccan Jew stating that the Jews "should not forget the hospitality extended" when they were expelled from Spain and Portugal.[94] The word choice of this statement is particularly powerful in two places: first, the "hospitality extended" which implies Jews were historic welcomed guests but second, the reference to the Spanish expulsion of 1492 which simultaneously demonstrates the long Jewish presence in Morocco. Just one week later, a Jewish leader in Fez, Isaac Bendayan, wrote to mention his failed attempt to found the Union of Moroccan Muslim-Jewish Youth in 1928.[95] The fact that the French administration had rejected this attempt demonstrates the extent to which the Protectorate administration upheld a divide and rule policy but also the dialogical engagement of Muslims and Jews through the press.

Not long after his original call for solidarity, a shifting of identity and belonging was under route again with the disruption of Political Zionism in the region. El-Kholti wrote to raise the issue as a factor of disorder in Morocco and that Moroccan Jews should unite in their efforts with Muslims:

> Morocco is for Moroccans, that is for us Muslims and for you Jews. It is our duty to collaborate together to defend our homeland. Say it once for all that you have one homeland (not the Promised Land, but the land where you are now). . . . A Moroccan who loves his country must aspire to work for it. . . . Naturally, our compatriots can be Jews as much as they want. . . . Zionism is a factor of outside domination and disorder in the Moroccan country.[96]

In response, the call of integrationist Jews was launched in the publication of Jewish newspapers that aimed to report on the daily communal issues of the communities. However, a number of local, regional, and international political developments would lead some, including *L'Avenir Illustré*, to change its political position and emphasize "aliyah to Zion."[97] Communicating through the medium of this paper, the Moroccan Jewish community pledged to "walk hand in hand" with their fellow Muslim Moroccans who "had been the strength of our fathers and which needs to continue to be ours."[98] The growing rise and threat of Nazi Germany and anti-Semitism provided another turn toward Muslim-Jewish Moroccan unity with nationalist leader, Ahmed Bouhlal, calling for the Jews to,

> remain in this great family that is the Moroccan nation where . . . they have lived in mutual understanding with the Muslim compatriots. (Preserve) the

indissoluble union between Muslims and Jews, in a strictly Moroccan national framework, for the good of our common patrie, for the general interest of our collectivity.[99]

The nationalist movement looked unfavorably on Jewish emigration to Palestine, seeing it as both treasonous to the mother country and reinforcement of the Political Zionist project. It was in such a spirit that Bouhlal (under the pseudonym Abou Khalil) wrote a scathing article in the Arabic edition of Le Jeune Maghrébin entitled "The Zionist Poison in Morocco." It was a harsh indictment of the Jews, the majority of whom, according to the author, were the "lackeys of Zionism and ingrates toward their country, all because of their love of money."[100] The article provoked a reaction by the Alumni Federation of the AIU of Morocco, whose president, Isaac Dahan, wrote a letter of protest to the French résident général. Dahan accused the editor of Le Jeune Maghrébin of anti-Semitism and alleged that the paper was using the question of Political Zionism in Morocco as "a pretext to call for a campaign of incitement and hatred against Moroccan Judaism."[101]

This back-and-forth was strained further by the outbreak of the Arab revolt in Palestine in 1936 and demonstrations in Meknès in September 1937 that resulted in substantial damage to businesses within the mellah. Meanwhile, increasing anti-Semitic activity by rightist French organizations in Morocco added to the feelings of Jewish insecurity. Amid the confusion of contrasting allegiances and increasing insecurity, Moroccan Jews generally put their hopes in the Protectorate power to repel the Nazi threat only to face the quick reality of Vichy rule that would shake, if not destroy, their confidence in their colonial protector and sully the appeal that cultural assimilation would bring political rights. The Moroccan nationalist movement also increased pressure after the announcement of the United Nation's Palestine partition plan in December 1947. In an anti-Zionist campaign in the spring of 1948, the Independence Party, Istiqlal, distributed tracts attacking partition, affirmed Moroccan identification with the Palestinian Arabs, and criticized the Residency for forbidding Moroccans from volunteering to help fight in Palestine. They also organized a boycott against Jewish businesses and European businesses suspected of pro-Zionist sympathies, despite official proclamations from the sultan and the Residency that warned against provoking anti-Jewish sentiment in Morocco.[102] Writing only five months after his pledge to "walk hand in hand," Sammoun stated,

> We are neither Moroccan, nor French. We have the situation of being Moroccans to whom you freely attribute burdens but not the least privileges. The day

when you tell us exactly what we are, attributing to us our duties as well as our privileges as a citizen, will be the day we will take a position.[103]

Though legally defined as Moroccan, Sammoun raises the second-class status of Jews as subjects of the sultan rather than citizens but Muslim readers who dismissed the Jews for doubting their Moroccan identity did not receive the piece warmly.[104] Following Israel's declaration of independence in May 1948, the sultan addressed his subjects via radio warning them to distinguish between the events in Palestine and the situation of Moroccan Jews:

> They [Muslim subjects] must know that the Moroccan Jews, who have resided in the country under the protection of its rulers for centuries, receiving the best welcome, and who have faithfully testified to their complete loyalty to the throne, are different than the uprooted Jews who have been led from all the corners of the world towards Palestine, which they have unjustly and arbitrarily seized.[105]

The sultan advised his Jewish subjects to avoid supporting any Political Zionist activity or "manifesting solidarity with it" which would threaten their individual rights and Moroccan nationality.[106]

The distinction the sultan attempted to maintain between Moroccan Jews and other Jews became increasingly blurred as Moroccan nationalists used the war in Palestine to mobilize popular support. In one of the newspapers of the Parti Démocratique de l'Indépendance (PDI),[107] the author called for a blanket boycott of all Jewish products in Morocco on the basis of the Koran and a theory of Political Zionist conspiracy. Publications such as this, as well as continued incidents of violence and unrest among communities throughout Morocco's urban areas, eroded Jewish trust in the Protectorate administration as well as the sultan, whom they blamed for provoking the attacks with his May 1948 speech. Despite an official statement issued by Istiqlal clarifying the enemy as Political Zionism, not Moroccan Jewry, the unrest negatively impacted Jews' perceptions of, and involvement with, the independence movement.

With the combined force of what was happening with the Third Reich and within Vichy France, the centrality of the Palestinian issue in pan-Arab ideology, as well as the use of a religious other as a unifying tool in narrative building, the clear line between Political Zionism and Moroccan Jews became blurred and complicated. Henceforth, in the political discourse of L'Avenir Illustré, the messianic side of Zionism was highlighted instead of the secular, nationalist ideology so that Moroccan Jews would be envisaged in a postindependence political and economic Morocco.

With the inception of the Latif protests, Moroccan national identity was defined in direct opposition to French attempts to preserve a distinct Moroccan Berber identity through the preservation of Berber customary law and Berber language. In opposition to this French policy, Islamic law and the Arabic language were used instead as the pillars on which the nation should be constructed. The cry, "death to democratic France. Long live Morocco and Moroccans. Long live noble independence . . . under the vibrant standard of Islam, one and immortal,"[108] demonstrates the steadfastness of Islamization for the national community, keeping the Jews on the periphery of the constructed brotherhood.

More than ten years after the founding of the reformist movement, with Europe on the brink of war, the advent of anti-colonial radicals in Paris, and generally hardening attitudes within the French Protectorate administration, riots and demonstrations were planned and carried out in 1937 throughout Fez, Meknès, Marrakech, and Khemisset.[109] The protests in Khemisset were particularly surprising for the Protectorate regime because their policies were largely based on the assumption that the Berbers would remain loyal, and that "only les Arabes," with their Middle Eastern links, pan-Islamism and pan-Arabism, represented a danger.[110] Indeed, to this point, the reformists had been unable to penetrate the countryside. The young leaders, coming from the commercial and intellectual middle class of the blad al-Makzhan, had the typical distaste and fear of rural Morocco produced by centuries of tension. Their lack of success in the countryside was strengthened by the effectiveness of French control of the rural areas, either direct or indirect, and in the countryside itself, "there was considerable reluctance to engage in activities controlled by urban groups in which there was little local confidence, and which seemed to have little purpose except to complicate an already difficult life."[111] Until this escalation, Protectorate officials reported that the agitation was exclusively an urban phenomenon, "strictly limited to some large Moroccan cities" and had not penetrated the blad al-siba.[112] There was no recognition of the legitimacy of the reformists' demands nor of the French role in the making of the reformists and their discontent. In fact, the organization of reformists and their ideology demonstrated the success of French education: most of the young leaders had attended French schools and were inspired by the French nationalist example.

Despite gaining momentum in unifying the blad al-siba Berbers and blad al-Makhzan Muslim Moroccans, the clashes of 1937 resulted in the exile or imprisonment of its leaders.[113] Due to the deconstruction of the reformist movement, nearly no internal contestation remained active in French

Morocco. Indeed, at the beginning of the Second World War, the French received numerous vows of loyalty and support for the war effort from among the Muslim population.[114] Writing just after the fall of France, Protectorate officials noted that continuation of normal regime administration through the Protectorate's intermediaries was interpreted as "the irrefutable sign of the durability of our Protectorate."[115] Nevertheless, within a year of the allied invasion, the former reformists had founded Istiqlal and had begun to engage in public demonstrations for national independence. Writing in February 1944, Protectorate officials admitted that the ideas of nation and independence were not only acknowledged but truly enacted toward independence.[116] In fact, the French Protectorate officials acknowledged this as early as 1937 in a colonial brief: "We no longer have a choice. The rigorous measures against the leaders of the (nationalist) movement . . . are the only means for assuring the future of French Morocco and to create a new climate that permits us to follow our civilizing action."[117]

The result of 1937 clashes was a first shift from frustrated reformism to anti-colonial nationalism, rejecting the fundamental associationist logic of the Protectorate that Morocco had to share sovereignty with France because it needed its help to develop into a modern country. Reform was no longer the goal of the movement, but the nationalist leadership had to wait until conditions changed after wartime in order to begin to mobilize toward independence. From 1944 onward, their definition of an Arab-Islamic Moroccan national identity was used to justify the nation's right to self-determination and autonomous independence and called for the abrogation of the Treaty of Fez.[118]

Therefore, while the Berber Dahir did not create the reform movement, it did provide the first key catalyst toward what would become calls for independence. The movement then climaxed in the violence of the summer and fall of 1937, struggling to regroup following the exile of its leadership and the unpredictability of the war. The next key catalyst is found in January 1944 with the founding of the Independence Party and the publication of its Manifesto of Independence which brought Moroccan demands for independence into the open thereby separating itself from the previous reform movement. To legitimize their right to independence, the nationalists put forth their own construction of Moroccan identity that emphasized the country's "illustrious Arab-Islamic dynastic history as evidence of its long-standing national unity."[119] The international, external element should not be overlooked: during this period, Morocco's neighbors and much of the Muslim world were mobilizing anti-colonial, nationalist movements which drew beyond their colonial mandates through transnational organizations such as the Arab League and the United Nations.

The outbreak of the Second World War and eventual fall of France resulted in collaborative, indirect German-French colonial rule in Africa. The French defeat, coupled with economic problems that intensified toward the end of the war, fueled the nationalists who "sensed that the colonial empire had collapsed" and that "France would no longer be able to project itself as a colonial power."[120] If there had been any doubt, the fall of France officially sealed the union of the blad al-siba and the blad al-makzhan; the arrival of the German Armistice Commission "coupled with the collapse in the rural economy" led "the indigenous" to the nationalists.[121] The Protectorate administration remained intact as regards to its governing process, though with heavy influence and pressure from the Vichy regime. As a result, the period from June 1940 to November 1942 became an extension of Pétain France. Sultan Mohammed V's behavior during this period remains the subject of debate, though in Moroccan Jewish popular consciousness he is remembered as one who refused to hand over his Jewish subjects to the Nazis. Historians, however, point out that, in his role in Protectorate governance, the sultan signed the decrees that permitted the introduction of all the anti-Semitic laws that had been promulgated by Vichy concerning throughout its colonial reach. The French Law of October 3, 1940, which defined a Jew by race as someone who had three Jewish grandparents, and prohibited Jews from practicing a wide variety of professions, was introduced to Morocco by a royal decree on October 31, 1940. Vichy France repealed the Crémieux decree of 1870 that had given to the Jews of Algeria full citizenship, it removed children from schools, enforced quotas in higher education, confiscated properties, and forced many into forced labor.[122]

Vichy rule ended on November 8, 1942, with Operation Torch, the landing of American troops on the Moroccan and Algerian coasts. Though the Moroccan Jews had experienced the impact of anti-Semitic decrees, the arrival of American troops ensured their physical safety. The majority of the population had been psychologically terrorized, but their daily lives had not been substantially altered. The Jews of the mellahs openly celebrated the American arrival betraying their assumed loyalty to the Protectorate. Violent attacks were propagated by local Muslims against Jews in Casablanca and elsewhere, apparently with the encouragement of French officials.[123] The duration and betrayal of Vichy France undermined Jewish loyalty to the Protectorate and from this point on, Moroccan Jews found themselves in an untenable situation perched between the French authorities and the increasingly Arab-Islamic Moroccan nationalist movement.

Just as European Jews were often faithful to their adopted nation throughout the Holocaust, many North African Jews continued to steadfastly support France. They remained true to "the France of the Revolution, of Clemenceau, of De Gaulle."[124] Precisely those Jews who had fulfilled the French ideas of assimilation were hurt most. Ostracized from the larger French community for their Jewishness, this naturally became a focal point forcing Moroccan Jews inward toward their Jewish community and their Jewish identity. Americans had no policy prepared in respect of Morocco after the war; however, nationalists took the American presence as an opening of political opportunity and nationalists, largely quiescent since the beginning of the war, were prepared to renew their efforts. Capitalizing on the weak image of postwar France, Moroccan Muslims took advantage of the opportunity to call for a shift in orientation with greater emphasis on the need for Arabization of education and respect for native Moroccan traditions.

Like other leaders of nationalist movements in the French empire, the Moroccan nationalist leadership had developed relationships with sympathetic politician friends on the French Left and believed the first socialist coalition to control the French government would finally respond and reform France's illiberal colonial policies. The nationalists again drew up a list of demands, calling it the National Pact, which they presented to the Protectorate authorities and which a delegation presented to representatives of the Popular Front government in Paris. The pact reiterated many of the points in the Plan of Reforms, including demands for democratic, economic, legal, educational, labor, industrial, taxation, and public health reforms. Meanwhile, events in the Middle East escalated, including the outbreak of the Arab revolt in Palestine in the early summer, the signing of the Anglo-Egyptian treaty in August in which the British pledged to withdraw most of its troops, and negotiations between the Syrian National Bloc and the French over independence, and these events contributed to the heightened tensions and expectations in Morocco.[125] The sultan was crucial to both the French and the nationalists. Traditionally, he was the ruler of Morocco and the leader of its Muslim community, with the supreme title of "Commander of the Faithful."[126] The French administration needed to retain his authority to legitimize their authority to govern, but the nationalists also felt the sultan would rally popular support to their cause.

On January 11, 1944, the Independence Party Istiqlal was founded under the leadership of the exiled al-Fassi and al-Ouezzani. This was a turning point for Moroccan nationalists that marked the transition from "a small circle of young intellectuals into a political force that gained momentum throughout the 1940s" calling for a constitutional monarchy with Sultan Sidi Mohammed bin Yusuf, or Mohammed V, as it figurehead.[127] With its aims, action, and naming, the party clearly transformed the notion of reform to independence and sought to construct and nurture an image of the Moroccan nation. Choosing its leader as Ahmed Balafrej, the party's claims for independence were based upon the "failure of the French to fulfill the terms of the Protectorate, the French attempts to split the unity of the Moroccan people, the Moroccan record in both wars, and the principles of the Atlantic Charter."[128] The party's manifesto highlighting the party's Islamic orientation of its Moroccan nation was delivered to the résident général, Gabriel Puaux, the Allies, and the sultan.[129] A 'pyramidal structure' composed of different tiers of leadership was adopted with the "zawiya, made up of a very small group of leaders who knew each other perfectly well" at the summit; below them, a larger group known as the "ta'ifa (whose) purpose was to filter new members" and who did not necessarily know the zawiya;[130] and, as a bottom block which operated openly as opposed to the clandestine nature of the zawiya and ta'ifa, the kutla.[131]

Their choice of party name, Hizb al-Istiqlal, Independence Party, is highly indicative of the transformation from reformists to nationalists and did not go unnoticed by the Protectorate. The French response was rapid. Puaux, while prepared to consider reform, was not prepared to consider independence; on January 13 the Brazzaville Conference made clear that no French colony could consider such an option and on January 16 attempts at mediations between the Protectorate, the sultan, and the nationalists began to try to reach agreement on a reform response. By January 29 the signatories of the independence manifesto were arrested and, following Protectorate instruction, the sultan issued a statement the next day on Moroccan radio reaffirming that "the evolution of Morocco will develop within a framework of French friendship and respect of the treaties."[132]

Though many ties had been strengthened between the urban centers and the countryside, the nationalists still lacked a broad following in the countryside where the economic climate had grown increasingly dire. By 1942, imports from France had ceased, a system of rationing was in place, building, except for military purposes, was forbidden, railroad services were reduced, electric service curtailed, and the cost of living was high and rising rapidly.[133] These extreme conditions were not conducive to nationalist organization in the countryside in the moment though the resulting desperation forced many to the cities where the Independence Party was growing rapidly. Although the Protectorate administration claimed it would not subdue the party, its leaders were arrested by the end of the month of its founding leading to riots and violent clashes which only garnered more popular support for the nationalists.[134] Indeed, following the release of the detained leaders in late 1944 and early 1945, the Istiqlal succeeded in winning the support of the Moroccan Communist Party, including its many Jewish members,[135] despite its initial hostility. The Communist Party felt that their trade union movement, which demanded trade union rights and equal pay for all Moroccan workers, fit well with support for the political demands of the Independence Party. In 1946, the new résident général, Erik Labonne, proposed several reforms such as the release of the remaining detainees, including Allal al-Fassi, and the introduction of a plan of legal, educational, and political reform together with a program of modernization and mechanization for peasant agriculture. Istiqlal rejected them as inadequate, reiterating clearly the transition from reform to national independence.

The development of the Moroccan nationalist movement was certainly accelerated by the Second World War and the windows of political opportunity opened by French vulnerability. Indeed, "The Second World War effectively shook the colonial system and demonstrated its weakness. The defeat of France in 1940 . . . shook the myth of invulnerability and occupation's power."[136] Whereas Morocco was busy enacting the ideals of liberty, equality, and fraternity toward their image of the Moroccan nation, France, under the new leadership of Pétain, turned its rhetoric toward labor, family, and fatherland.[137] The Moroccan nationalist narrative had embraced part of France's civilizing mission and turned its own ideals against the administration.

While the war was certainly a turning point, 1947 was a year of significant change in the nationalists' platform. The return in 1947 of Allal al-Fassi, Mohammed al-Ouezzani, and other leaders after more than a decade of exile generated widespread enthusiasm, including huge banquets and parades in Fez and Rabat. On an organizational level, the nationalist movement worked to build off increasing popular support for the objective of independence and public enthusiasm. In the same year, two years after the creation of the Arab League in 1945, a conference was organized in Cairo to coordinate the activities of the three nationalist movements in North Africa (Morocco, Algeria, and Tunisia), and the Arab Maghreb Office was founded to carry out the recommendations of the conference.[138]

Most significant in the Independent Party's positive momentum was the sultan's Tangier speech in April 1947. French colonial archives demonstrate the Protectorate's vulnerability with the role of the sultan. As early as 1944, French military sources recorded, "If the Sultan were to align with the nationalists, he would take with him the great part of the indigenous chiefs that... have remained indecisive and waiting for the Sultan to declare himself, so they can declare themselves."[139] Fearing the unification of the 'Two Moroccos,'[140] France urged the sultan to discourage and denounce the activist nationalists. Nevertheless, in his April 1947 speech presented for the administration of the International Zone in Tangier, the sultan omitted the customary praise for the French colonial endeavor in Morocco and demanded the unity of the country, an event that was seen both by Moroccans and by the French as a rejection of the symbiotic relationship that had previously existed between Sultanate and Protectorate.[141] Though an implicit omission rather than explicit revolt, the Tangier speech was the first public demonstration of the relationship between Istiqlal and the sultan giving the nationalist movement general respectability and wider scope.[142] It was the developments of 1947, this speech in particular, rather than the Second World War itself that ensured the ultimate success of the Moroccan nationalist movement.

Reasons vary in explaining the sultan's changed stance; one explanation cites growing animosity between Moroccans and Protectorate troops culminating in a bloody confrontation between Senegalese colonial troops and Moroccan demonstrators in Casablanca in which scores of demonstrators had been killed.[143] Another explanation is suspected involvement of the colonial right in their agenda to remove the liberal Labonne.[144] Regardless of motivation, Labonne was removed and the sultan remained on the side of the Independence Party. The sultan's attitude was of immense significance. The nationalists, with his open approval, widened their appeal of the Moroccan nation to the countryside that had suffered greatly during the war and was ready to listen. In addition to the support of the sultan, Moroccan nationalists drew upon similar cases of anti-colonial struggle throughout North African and the Middle East with a pan-Arab solidarity.

However, growing anti-colonial, anti-French sentiment and increased allegiance to pan-Arab organizations resulted in a growing distance between Morocco's Muslims and Jews. The Independence Party's 1944 manifesto included no Jews among its signatories[145] and the sultan's speech in 1947 in Tangier made no mention about the future of the Jews whose status was unclear in the wake of Vichy France. Tsur explains this missed opportunity for inclusiveness by the perception of Moroccan identity at the time:

> It seems the deepest, most fundamental obstacle standing in the nationalist movement's path to pave the way into the Jews' heart was the weak status of

an all Moroccan identity awareness, to be more exact, the lack of established and agreed upon foundations of a uniting political group to get all classes to cooperate harmonically and positively, something along the lines of a common ethnic perception.[146]

To add further complication, on November 29, 1947, the United Nations General Assembly passed Resolution 181 endorsing the partition of Palestine into Jewish and Arab states. From that point onward, Moroccan nationalists, influenced heavily by the Arab League, were vehemently against Political Zionism, and the distinction between Political Zionists and Jews was frequently forgotten. The sultan warned them against disloyalty to Morocco;[147] however, semi-clandestine immigration to Palestine began during this period, as the Political Zionist option was beginning to be seen as a viable one, particularly among poorer Moroccan Jews. Betrayed by the promise and superiority of French assimilation and excluded from the rallying cry of Arab-Islamic unity, Jews were torn between three national narratives all of which drew upon different aspects of their Jewish Moroccan identity. Whereas the majority of Moroccan Jews had seen no contradiction in being Jewish, faithful to the sultan, and beneficiaries of France, the sultan's speech and commitment to the nationalists created a political atmosphere of uncertainty. By achieving the endorsement of the sultan,[148] the independence movement and, by extension, the Moroccan nationalist narrative had the final symbol and actor in place to garner broad support and construct a new Moroccan identity.

From 1930 to the postwar period, the Moroccan nationalist movement developed from an informally networked group of young activist elites into a highly structured mass independence party. The first years of the movement's evolution were hugely significant in laying out the parameters for how nationalists would frame Moroccan national identity and develop a repertoire of contention to carry out their struggle against the French-controlled colonial state in Morocco. Through the reformists' groundwork, it was from the Berber Dahir in 1930 and forward that Muslim and Arab identity became the pillars on which the nationalists built their construction of a Moroccan national community unified for more than a thousand years by Islamization and Arabization under successive ruling dynasties. French Berber policy attempting to preserve Berber cultural identity through the official support of customary law and Berber language was framed as a lethal religious attack on the unity of this community. Subsequent cycles of contention built off this foundational framing, as ritualized protest strategies including the Latif prayer, the commemoration of the Berber

Dahir, and Throne Day became essential sites of contention in the Moroccan repertoire of nationalist contention.[149]

Following the war, the movement shifted from demanding the reform of the Protectorate to demanding its end. French rejection of the reformists' demands and their exile of the movement's leadership closed off possibilities for resuming stable and trusted governance. The Second World War shifted the political opportunity context after France's collapse, and the reformists shifted their demands to independence. Consistent with the rise of pan-Arab nationalist sentiment in the region and much of the Middle East, Moroccan national identity was tied even more closely to the unity of the Arab Maghreb in the postwar period.[150] The sultan's 1947 speech in Tangier implicitly positioned himself at the forefront of the movement toward independence negotiating what the independent Moroccan state would look like and articulating an official state discourse of national identity emphasizing the country's Muslim and Arab heritage. His speech was the key of the movement for Moroccan independence, which after the radicalization of its demands by the Second World War obtained the national following and authority it required for its success.

By drawing from past myths and symbols such as the role of the sultan as 'Protector of the Faithful' and Islam as a unifying bridge between the blad al-siba and blad al-Makzhan, while simultaneously enacting modern political, educational, and social institutional aims and reforms, not to mention Western liberal ideals, the nationalists created a new, pan-Arab and pan-Islamic Moroccan narrative that shifted pre-Protectorate identities. This Moroccan nationalist narrative depicts the adaptive ethno-symbolism laid out in Chapter 2. The construction of new from old fits perfectly well in a country where modernization was essential for the ideas of the national and universal (Moroccan, Arab, Islamic) with an emphasis on community values and tradition. At the same time, and similarly to Moroccan nationalists, Political Zionist leaders made use of Jewish religious myths and symbols such as the memory of delivery from persecution and suffering that spoke to a larger spiritual Jewish consciousness. Moroccan nationalists, in response, attempted to assign the Jews within national Moroccan boundaries while downplaying their spiritual relationships with their kin; however, the combination of Political Zionist symbols that resonated among these rural Jewish communities and social, economic, and political stresses decided the emigration of many when the opportunity to do so arose.[151] The alienation was political and not solely cultural with plural identity traits conflicting in ways they previously had not. For instance, while Jews from European countries could potentially be patriotic and simultaneously identify with Political Zionism, the two were impossible in a Muslim-majority country; to be pro-Moroccan and pro-Zionist was a new contradiction of loyalty.

The Protectorate administration caused rifts among the three narratives that made plural belonging impossible. This meant that the rate of Jewish departure reflected not only the Second World War but later, Arab-Israeli relations, and decolonization in Morocco and its Maghreb neighbors.[152] It is amid these three competing narratives that the interview participants presented in the following chapter were born and continue to live today. From the theoretical and historical background provided thus far, this in-depth look at their Protectorate identities and memories demonstrates the complexity of identity's contextual plurality, the consequences of nation building on individual and collective identity, and the place of Moroccan Jewry among the resulting competing narratives. The secondary literature and periodical and colonial archives presented thus far suggest that the majority of Protectorate-era Moroccan Jews retained their allegiance to France while others embraced the ideas of Political Zionism and a minority of intellectuals chose the option of Moroccan nationalism. This chapter contributes toward answering the second research question which asks why Moroccan nationalism came to exclude its historic and sizable Jewish brethren by examining the rise of pan-Arabism and the solidarity and narrative building capacity of Islam to unite the blad al-siba and the blad al-Makzhan as well as Arab and Amazigh cultures. Second, as a result of the Jews' close relationship with the Protectorate administration or, at the very least, the AIU, the necessarily anti-Protectorate Moroccan nationalist narrative for independence came to exclude those who were so closely aligned with the Protectorate. The next chapter's interview participant data fulfills the method's third point and examines the three primary narratives in depth in order to address the third research question: What does it say of the nation-state and its Jewish minority that there remains a decreased but enduring Jewish community?

Part III

Jewish Moroccan Voices

5

Zohra, Yaakov, and Michel

Preceding chapters have demonstrated the heterogeneity of late nineteenth and early twentieth-century Morocco as a scene for the development and transformation of nationalist narratives. Enticed by the many advantages of aligning oneself with the Protectorate administration and France in general as well as the pull of Political Zionism as a transnational narrative uniting the Jewish diaspora, Moroccan Jews had reason to be drawn toward multiple, and eventually conflicting, nationalist narratives. Tracing the development of Moroccan nationalism from reform movement to nationalist narrative reiterates the significance of historical and political context in that this development cannot be evaluated or explained without its surrounding, complementary, and contrasting narratives. For instance, the followers of parties that would eventually make demands for independent statehood on nationalist grounds could not have flourished without the presence of resentment toward the French Protectorate and, further, the context of the Second World War which shifted political opportunity after the collapse of France. Consistent with the rise of pan-Arab nationalist sentiment in the region and much of the Middle East, Moroccan national identity was tied even more closely to the unity of the Arab Maghreb in the postwar period[1] which, in turn, affected both the status of France and the reception of Political Zionism among the Jewish and Muslim population alike.

Building upon the secondary historical literature as well as the colonial and periodical archives, this chapter will adhere to the three main narratives discussed in Chapters 4 and 5 (French assimilation, Political Zionism, Moroccan nationalism) as broad, primary identity categorizations that arose due to the polarizing context of the Protectorate period. While lacking definitive borders, these categorizations provide broadly demarcated spaces, wherein the oral histories of Moroccan Jews, collected in the form of ethnographic semi-structured interviews in 2013 and 2018, may be shared and analyzed.

Building upon what the existing secondary scholarly literature provides and what archived periodicals and colonial documents capture of the French

Protectorate period and the transition from calls for reform to anti-colonial nationalist narrative, ethnographic semi-structured interviews with Moroccan Jews reveal the complexity of contrasting identity allegiances from those who lived during this time. Having outlined an account of the transition from reform movement to nationalist narrative paralleled by an AIU-led French assimilation movement and growing Political Zionist network in French Protectorate Morocco, I interviewed Moroccan Jews who lived during this time and have remained in the country with the purpose of studying the way they perceived Jewish identity during the Protectorate. I was also fortunate to benefit from the collected data of a few generous colleagues also interested in collecting oral testimonies of Moroccan Jews.[2] I wished to learn about perceptions of Jewish identity amid these potentially contrasting allegiances and how their Jewishness was made significant (or not) in terms of their place in the Moroccan nation and the development of Moroccan nationalism.

Because Morocco's Jewish population is severely decimated with an estimated number of 3,000–4,000 Jews remaining[34] in contrast to well over 200,000 during the Protectorate period, I collected the stories and experiences of a generation of Jews who, though not exposed to the Holocaust in the same ways as Jews on the European continent, carry with them unique and important information of this era. Sadly, from my first visit in 2007 to my most recent in 2018, many have passed away; this only highlights the need to collect such testimonies. Their experiences provide an interesting platform through which to analyze the complexity and plurality of identity, the unique status of Jewishness as ethnicity, and Jewish identity during the development of Moroccan nationalism.

In the following sections, I present three in-depth participant vignettes both supported and complicated by their fellow participants' responses. Multiple narratives can demonstrate varying perceptions of the same event; for instance, the Moroccan nationalist narrative perceived the fall of France as an opening of opportunity upon which to act, whereas the French cultural-linguistic assimilationist narrative perceived this to be a great tragedy and betrayal. This ethnographic approach to semi-structured interviews is deeply contextualized but positioned through the research's presentation of history and theory to situate the context. While highlighting individuals and focusing on the human level may undermine the ability to make group generalizations, the methods are replicable even if the results are not due to this deeply contextualized setting.[5] In such a setting with a small interview pool and an aging population, it allows for a thorough, nonthreatening, guided, but open, meeting. Highlighting the individual prevents the risk of neatly assigning a person into his or her box of identity traits and values the individual's nuances. What follows is three in-depth vignettes that fall into the realm of the three main narratives of French assimilation, Political Zionism, and Moroccan nationalism, respectively, as well as the analysis of all interview responses across four themes: education, religion, language, and politics.

Our Ancestors the Gauls

Born in 1918, Zohra[6] spent her life deeply enmeshed in the AIU. Educated in Tétouan with the AIU and later at the Ecole Normale in Paris to be a teacher, she states, "The Alliance is my life."[7] She began teaching in Marrakech in 1937 before moving to Demnate from 1940 to 1946, returning to Marrakech from 1946 to 1960, before moving to Casablanca from 1960 onward. Being in a privileged position within the AIU, Zohra offers perspective into Jewish life under the French Protectorate. In addressing the special relationship between the Protectorate administration and some Jewish communities, she provides one explanation for a Jewish advantage:

> In the sense that the Jews profited from the Protectorate, because they were already instructed and knew French, I think it is so. With the Alliance schools, Jewish children spoke French, learning French. And when the Protectorate arrived, the French found the most . . . the ones who were closest . . . it was the Jews who already knew French. I think it's like that . . . it was an advantage.[8]

During this time, "everything was French"[9] including the school inspectors and police officers who held all the power. The Department of Public Instruction[10] of France gave government money to help build schools bringing attention to the tension between the AIU as a private or a public school. Zohra insists, "It was for the Jews. It was not public. But we were helped by the government. In principle Muslims could come. But Muslims did not come. It was for the Jews."[11] This issue of funding highlights the complex relations between the French government, the Protectorate administration, and Jewish leadership within the Moroccan communities; on the one hand, it was clear that the AIU came to care specifically for the Jews; however, on the other hand, the application of government funds gave the illusion it could be a public institution. As a result of this connection, Zohra remarks, "One lived [as] in France, practically, as in French, everything was French."[12]

This feeling of belonging with France and with the French language is evident in the AIU curriculum. Zohra recalls, "One had a French culture. France was very grateful to the Alliance for dispensing and teaching French and the history of France. And not the history of Morocco. Our ancestors the Gauls."[13] Also included in the curriculum which was, in her experience, the same throughout the AIU schools in Morocco was French grammar, history, geography, math, science, and eventually Hebrew. This is consistent with existing literature on AIU policy which details the important role of the AIU in teaching and nurturing the communities' children.[14] AIU schools went beyond academic curriculum to include French notions of hygienic care and dress as well with a specific mission to "introduce Jewish children to Western culture."[15] Zohra describes how teachers were instructed to inspect the students' clothing including underwear to make sure they were clean, "When they entered the class, the teacher would check if the pants looked clean. . . . They would pass and look to see if the underwear is clean. It's true, the Alliance took care of everything."[16]

Making a clear, repetitive distinction that politics are not her "department," Zohra's commentary on French anti-Semitism and Vichy France seems to suggest a minor period of misfortune that was soon recovered after the end of the Second World War. This may be the result of a privileged position within the Protectorate where she did not experience too much disruption with the advent of the Vichy-influence administration, or perhaps a desire to move past the troubling times to reconcile her ongoing close affiliation with France. Nevertheless, she admits that the period of Vichy "was not pretty. The Protectorate under Vichy, it was the start of anti-Jewish legislation."[17]

Living and teaching in Demnate during the war, she recalls the tension of life under Vichy as being "very well" in one way but "poorly" in the other: "Very well [because] one lacked nothing. Very bad because one was far away from the city."[18] After the Vichy administration fell, she remarks that order was restored, and if people were upset with the French for what they had allowed, they did not speak of it. "The lack of confidence in France left the moment that Vichy left, there were no more problems. It was a bad moment but it was the war, I think."[19] She is quick to state that she was lucky to be privileged during this time as a teacher of the AIU. Reiterating her lack of interest or involvement in the 'political department,' Zohra was very reluctant to discuss Political Zionism. She recalls calmly that "Zionist organizations had contact with (AIU) teachers. It was personal, but it was not Zionism in the classroom. . . . Officially, we could not."[20] Any other questions about this subject were received more sensitively and guardedly: "It was dangerous. Not prohibited. Dangerous."[21] When asked about the relationship between the AIU and Zionist organizations, she simply said she would tell me if I turned off the recording.

The AIU, and Zohra as an extension of it, demonstrate an intricate combination of Jewish and French affiliations. The AIU was founded and continues today in order to educate Jews against hate and prejudice and ensure that culture replaces ignorance—a mission not so different than that of Political Zionism but with different cultural and geographic aspirations. As a pupil and supporter of the AIU, Zohra displays this commitment to Jewish and French education and the linguistic and cultural threads attached to it. Though quite unwilling to discuss Political Zionism in Protectorate Morocco, her silence indicates she must have had some experience from which to feel so reluctant and sensitive. Nevertheless, she is active in Jewish life in Morocco demonstrating her continued affiliation with her religion and her birthplace.

An interesting point to note that sheds light on the further complexities of Jewish identity in Morocco is a little joke that Zohra recalls when discussing identity. When asked how she self-identified during her youth, she jokes that she left Spain in 1492 alluding to the expulsion of Jews during the Spanish Inquisition. While intending humor, the point is valid: her identity as Tétouanese is a matter of pride and refinement among Moroccan Jewry where there are these little rivalries between Meknès and Fez, Casablanca and Essaouira, etc. Though she has not lived there since she was young, that specific detail is still significant among her plural affinities. Her affinity to her Tétouanese roots contributes to her sense of being European, and this connects her more to Europe (France and Spain) than feeling indigenous to Morocco.

Zohra's education and career devoted to the AIU certainly informs her self-identity as well as narrative affiliation. Her readiness to move past the unfortunate period of Vichy France and reiteration that politics are not her business is consistent with the reputation of France toward the end of the Protectorate and in present-day Morocco. That is, the esteemed place of France in terms of socioeconomic strength and advantage remained high even among the nationalists working to oust the Protectorate administration. For one not politically active, as in the case of Zohra, the contrasting nationalist narratives of France and Moroccan did not need to conflict nor compete; she could remain faithfully French and a contributing member of Moroccan society.

Faith Cannot Deteriorate

Born in 1925 in Safi where his parents had grown up, a commercial port city between Casablanca and Essaouira, Yaakov moved first to Casablanca and, shortly thereafter, to Fez. His mother's parents arrived to Marrakech where her father was a "great rabbi" who ran a yeshivah; therefore, her birth in "1890 or 1900" was into the yeshivah life that honored and valued the Talmud and Jewish study. Completing his primary education in Fez, he moved to Casablanca for his secondary schooling with the AIU. He recalls the different kinds of schools as French (which admitted only French or friends of the French who worked with them), Koranic school (for the Arabs), and Jewish (for they could not go to French nor Koranic schools). He recalls how he studied until the Bac[22] from which Jews were excluded at the time. In his favor, a minister of public instruction in France who was Jewish was able to permit the Jewish students to study in University and Yaakov began in 1946 at the Ecole d'Orsay Judaïque where he stayed until 1950.

Just as with the separation of schools and schoolchildren, Protectorate Casablanca could be conceptualized into established "spaces"—that is, Muslim spaces, Jewish spaces, etc.

> We [can] say that the protectorate had created, it seems, "spaces." Muslim areas. That is to say that Muslims did not fit in the cities. They did not have access. . . . The Arab should remain in the bled.[23] . . . So the Jews had their compartment to them. . . . We lived almost in isolation. There was little assimilation, very little intermarriage. And one lived much more French than with the Arabs. There was exclusion at the time of the war. The Statut des Juifs excluded [Jews] from schools, banks etc. But we cannot say there was pressure as there was in France.[24]

This passage raises several interesting points. First, the general absence of Muslim Moroccans in Casablanca. Second, the mention of very little assimilation and intermarriage followed by the statement that Jews 'lived much more French' than the Arabs. Assimilation here means assimilation to the Muslim Moroccans. Finally, the acknowledgment that the Jewish Moroccan exclusion at the time of the war was not the same pressure on Jewish life of that in France is an oft-repeated one. Yaakov does mention the Liste de Biens in which Jews had to declare their goods and possessions but of the twenty participants in total, every one commented that the Moroccan Jewish experience was far less severe than the European Jewish struggle.

Despite not feeling enormous pressure during the war, Yaakov provides interesting perspectives on the role of the sultan in Vichy France. Saying that the sultan had no power at the time of the French, he questions his political ability to save the Jews as the state rhetoric of this time suggests. Even if the sultan was not against the Jews himself, the limits of his power became clear when the French later expelled him. If the Germans had demanded it, Yaakov says, and if the war had not stopped in 1942, his belief is that the sultan could not have done anything to stop them: "That the king could defend us . . . it is not that he did not want to, it is that he had no power. It is not he who ruled the country, and it is not he who might have had the right to say 'no, it will or it will not happen.' This is not true."[25]

The changes brought on by the landing of American troops in Casablanca provide interesting insight into the Jewish sentiment of France at this time. When asked how the American arrival impacted the Jews, Yaakov recalls that the American landing provided a deliverance from travel, food, and education restrictions to the point that "we felt really equal":

> Because do not forget that we were led by the French. And the French did not like us very much. Do not think that the French were on good terms with the Jews. It was the Jews are a separate race in the Mellahs. . . . And I'll even tell you that there was even a case of racial discrimination between French Jews and Moroccan Jews. And there were French Jews, not French of France: French Algerian (Algerian Jews). You know Algerian Jews who had become French by the Crémieux Decree and who lived here.[26]

This is a particularly poignant statement to highlight his perception of Protectorate-Jewish relations, stating that the "French do not like us. Do not think that the French were on good terms with us" and labeling it racial discrimination is a different frame of reference than that of other interview participants who feel themselves to be French and remember the Vichy period as a regrettable phase.[27] Furthermore, his comments about Algerian Jewish prejudice of Moroccan Jews undermine generalizations that link North African Jews together as one entity.

Arriving in Paris in 1946 to study with the Ecole d'Orsay Judaïque revealed further desolation of French Jewry:

> I arrived in Paris just after the war in 1946 and in 1946 there was a very serious problem. It is that the French Judaism had disappeared, they were no more. First largely by assimilation and the rest by the Holocaust. The few Jews who remained did not know why they were Jews. They did not even know what it is to be Jewish. So there was no longer Judaism in France in 1946. The few survivors who came from Central Europe did not even want to talk that they were Jews. And we ended up in this situation where France was starting without Judaism.[28]

Forming the extent of Jewish life in Paris was the Ecole d'Orsay,[29] where young North African Jews in Paris came together alongside the Ecole des Cadres Juifs, a Jewish scout organization. His experience in Paris in these four years deeply motivated and connected him to a life of devotion toward the regeneration and sustainment of Jewish life. Returning to Protectorate Morocco in 1950 at the age of twenty-five, he became involved with the Jewish education movement linking him to leaders such as Charles Netter and the Israeli scout program.[30] Though he does not speak directly about Political Zionism, he shares how he took the young women of the community to Israel in order to expand and deepen Jewish ties of their community. He speaks sadly of assimilation that leads to non-Jewish youth and compares the process to vinegar disappearing in water:

> So the problem is the proportion. You know . . . and I was saying this the other day. Take a tub. A tub, you put water in it. And a tub where there's vinegar. There are 1,000 liters in one and 1,000 liters in the other. You take half a liter of vinegar, you put it in the [tub of] water. You stir, you call 50 people, and you ask what there is inside. There's water. Where did the half-liter of vinegar go? It disappeared. It's the same thing.[31]

Because young Jews are being absorbed by a non-Jewish majority, the nation is dwindling. He says that at the end of the Second World War, there were eighteen million Jews in the world but that today, while they should be thirty to thirty-two million, they are only sixteen million. He compares it to the Greek assimilation after the fall of the Second Temple and Jews in Morocco today who go to the pool with a cross on their neck for protection.

Yaakov recalls feeling that Moroccans (Jews) must make a gesture for all that Israel has done for them; "All Jewish children being educated, being sent to Israel for free. All we [Zionists] did for emigration." Being Moroccan and being Jewish are central identities wherein faith remains essential to his being today as evidenced by his description of faith as an omnipresent fog:

> It's faith, which is a kind of fog that envelops the spirit or, being in the same fog, merges (with the spirit). And he who has adopted this atmosphere, he lives within it. . . . And that's the power of faith. Why does one say, "Faith saves"? Because everything else can deteriorate, but faith cannot deteriorate.[32]

Though it is not essential for his faith for this fog to be attached physically to the modern State of Israel, he describes a duty and attachment to the state that implicitly combines morality, politics, and religion. Whereas nation-states may come and go from the world map, the Jewish nation bound by its faith cannot be destroyed as it is an omnipresent fog. Recalling the call of Israeli emissaries who came to Morocco shortly after the declaration of statehood in 1948, he makes an interesting point about the idealism of ideology: "And this is not unique to Judaism. There is no longer [today] the patriotism that existed before. Idealism has not prevailed. We fell into the era [of materialism, of wealth]."[33] Consistent with his commitment to Israel and the sustainment of global Jewry, his motives behind his continued attention to this idealism lives on in him: "It's disservice when you know you will be worshiped materially. Or when one gets a lot of money. Doing something that no one will congratulate you for or give you a coin: that is what nobody wants to do today."[34]

Returning to the claims that identity is plural, contextually dynamic and fluid, and arranged hierarchically, it is clear that Yaakov maintains close ties to Morocco while having deep commitment to the Political Zionist project. Being educated in French and, later, in France naturally points to a relationship between language and identity that indicates an affiliation though whether the feeling of belonging is with the language, culture, politics, etc. is not necessarily a one-size-fits-all connection. In the case of Yaakov, his AIU education gave him the preparation and opportunity for a French and Jewish university education in Paris that deepened his connection to Judaism, not specifically spiritually, but rather as a commitment to the Jewish nation worldwide. The fact that despite these resulting deep ties to Israel, Yaakov chose to remain in Morocco demonstrates the negotiation of identity's plurality.

The flux of connection to one's plural affiliations makes identity dynamic, but I want to add a further claim that this movement is not a linear progression from 'I am Moroccan' to 'I am a Zionist' but a fluid mode of reevaluation. Through fluidity it is understandable that a Moroccan-born Jew benefiting from the Protectorate resources is proud to identify with France until Vichy rules pushes her to feel opposed before anti-Zionist tension in the Arab world allows him to return to feelings of being French, etc. In the case of Yaakov, his Jewishness was always present as a result of his mother's background with the yeshiva, though his AIU education instructed him in French language and a more secular French culture. A major turning point in the context of identity affiliations appears to be the confrontation with the desolation of French Jewry that brought forth sympathy and commitment to the Zionist cause of regeneration Jewish life. Nevertheless, lest I oversimplify and apply the label of Political Zionist to Yaakov immutably, his description of faith as an omnipresent and indestructible fog demonstrates his view that one does not have to physically be in Israel to be a good Jew or a good Zionist.

We are Moroccans

Born in Fez in the 1930s, Michel grew up in the Ville Nouvelle,[35] a mixed neighborhood that was also in its infancy in that year. He shares that while many people thought the Ville Nouvelle to be the 'Christian city,' a term he uses interchangeably with the French city, there was, in reality, nothing French about it apart from a street called Avenue de France where there were buildings of up to five levels being built. Eager to register their son in a nearby school, as opposed to the schools within the mellah, Michel's parents registered him in a Christian (French) school, though his brothers continued to go to the AIU school in the mellah.[36] He recalls the options as a very old school predating the Protectorate for mellah residents only, the Alliance school where his father, born around 1889, had studied, or the French schools in the Ville Nouvelle where he was enrolled for his Maternelle[37] studies.

Michel describes vividly the life of the mellah:

> Honestly speaking, I have never seen crowds of people such as in the Mellah anywhere else, even the roofs of houses and basements were full of inhabitants. . . . Do you know what is the meaning of air? It is not only ventilation as you may understand. It is for example, that if you have a roof and you want to build a room on top of it, that roof becomes air that can be sold . . . thus creating massive problems with the registration of ownership of those properties.

This overcrowding, as well as the enticement of French education, was a turning point for his family's move to the Ville Nouvelle. Michel describes his school as predominantly Christian; he was one of only a few Jewish pupils and does not recall any Muslim students there. In fact, he states that while there were surely some Muslim traders and others working in people's homes or businesses, he doubts there were any as inhabitants in the Ville Nouvelle.[38] At the start of his second academic year in 1940, age five years and nine months, he was refused entry into the primary school with the reason that he was not yet six years old. He connects this frustration of being forced to return to the Maternelle school to Christian and, by extension, French anti-Semitism. He believes that from the beginning of the 1930s until the end of the Second World War, the Christians hated the Jews and that it must not be forgotten. While it is unclear if the primary school policies were enforced with anti-Semitic motivation or how much of this sentiment Michel could grasp at such a young age, he certainly connects the event to perceived anti-Semitic tension and fights that plagued him in later years of his schooling. This is evident, for example, in a fight he remembers at age fourteen. He remembers,

> When [the French children] found a Jew, then it was a fight against the Jews, it was a manifestation of their culture. And to defend myself, it was a manifestation of my culture. Of my identity. In addition I was not particularly strong. Well,

that's the child in these circumstances that I hope will not be repeated ever again for any generation.[39]

Living in a mixed neighborhood and being different than the vast majority of his peers in school, Michel recalls his school days with resentment and bitterness that he portrays as the foundation for his later work with the Communist Party and Istiqlal in Morocco. Upon speaking with his sons, they reported similar stories of their father's upbringing. They shared that although their paternal grandparents spoke Arabic at home, they saw that France and Europe was the future and the French education was a powerful link.[40] This adaptability is recalled by a participant of Boum's in his recent publication that recalls Morocco's Jewish past as distinct from their Muslim neighbors: "Local Jews introduced everything new to Akka: the first mill, the first bicycle, and the first truck. Jews understood change; Muslims did not."[41]

Though he grew up in the Ville Nouvelle, Michel's daily life was still in the mellah due to the short distance between the two areas that he recalls as just above 1 kilometer. His family's house was only the third house built in the Ville Nouvelle in the 1920s, and they made this move because the mellah was full to its limit. Indeed, he shares that the Jews, who were tired of living with numbers exceeding 10,000 to 15,000 on 1.5 hectares,[42] built the central core of the city of Fez. With inhabitants occupying buildings, roofs, and basements, space was hard-fought and problems with registration and ownership of properties persisted. Nevertheless, Michel recalls that though the poor were many, the Jewish community had an organized system of solidarity and support with small charities and an Islamic organization called the Hibra.[43] The members of the Hibra were responsible for anything from handling the dead to guaranteeing the safety of the neighborhood with a sheikh, two vice-sheikhs, and seven councilors who were responsible, with his team, for one specific day of the week. Michel states that this organization was able to carry many social works—for example keeping the mellah safe from trespassers and helping to host visitors since the mellah had no hotel facilities at that time. Additionally, the Hibra was responsible for collecting donations to prepare Saturday meals for the poor Jews both in the mellah and in the Ville Nouvelle.

Experiencing firsthand the challenges of being a Jew among Christians at school and witnessing the good will shown by the Hibra in the Jewish communities at home, Michel's exposure to, and respect for, Muslim culture included Arabic language learning or, more specifically, Judeo-Arabic.[44] This instruction happened at the synagogue that, he recalls, was a place to not only pray but also study Hebrew and religion as well as reading and writing Arabic language. This seems to be a point of pride for him both in his childhood and at the time of the interview when he makes conscious transitions from French to Colloquial Moroccan Arabic, darija.

Speaking generally about Jewish life, and without prompting as to the primary narratives addressed herein, Michel categorizes Protectorate-era Jews as being under three groups of pressure and influence[45] that wanted to "win the Jews":[46] French colonizers, Zionism, and those fighting for the sake of independence. With more detail he describes the French as colonizing oppressors though he does note that they (the Protectorate) helped the Jews by stopping Muslims from interfering in the community committees that were responsible for managing the Jewish community. Because part of the law in Morocco was religious (shari'a), these Jewish-led community committees were established before the Protectorate to oversee and manage Jewish neighborhoods and mellahs. When the Protectorate arrived, they stripped the committees of their council duties but left the committees to manage the religious affairs of the Jewish areas. Michel shares that in order for the committees to retain, and maintain, their control, they collaborated with the French and, in this way, the Protectorate administration had complete control over the Jewish communities. Compounding this collaboration was the pre-Protectorate connection between Moroccan Jews and the AIU. Discussing the AIU, Michel says,

> It's a good thing we were taught to read and write . . . but this solidarity rendered the colonization of Moroccan Jews. And that's when we understand why Moroccan Jews, unlike for example the Iranian or Syrian Jews were not taught Arabic. But rather French. . . . Because when Jews became French in France, in the years of the 19th century, that was something for them. It was so huge that they felt a responsibility.[47]

Because the AIU had educated a large portion of the generation of young Jewish Moroccans in French language and culture, the societal links between the Protectorate administration and the Jewish communities already existed when the Protectorate was made official in 1912. This is not to say that the Protectorate administration had direct rule of the AIU but that when the Protectorate officials found a community of French-educated and French-speaking Jews, they were able to use to their knowledge to their advantage and incentivized to continue funding for AIU schools. While Michel is willing to acknowledge the benefits of the work of the AIU for educating the community, he connects their activity to the colonizing oppression of France. His comment about the lack of Arabic language instruction suggests an additional consequence of the AIU-French collaboration; that is, the instruction and use of French and connection with the Protectorate authorities created or exacerbated a divide between the Moroccan Jewish and Muslim communities.

Michel remarks that the French in Morocco before the war had a feeling of hatred toward the other and were always looking for an enemy toward which to express their racist feelings. According to him, when it was convenient to take advantage of the Jews, their hatred was toward the Muslims; however, when Pétain came to power on June 18, 1940, their hatred turned toward the Jews. This was confirmed in his eyes when Noguès applied the Statut des Juifs laws soon thereafter. Being educated in a French school amid this political turmoil, he recalls, "I obviously felt a resentment against Pétain and all that . . . on the first of October 1941 he [Pétain] says, 'the Jews, they go' and touched the flag of France, that also makes you think."[48] Because of his young age at the time of the war, he remembers its effect on his life with a child's scale; for instance, on the Jewish holiday of Purim when children typically receive a gift, he recalls, "I want to play. . . . When you want to play and there are no toys, what are you doing?"[49] Nevertheless, he was fortunate that his parents made arrangements to be able to eat and dress properly. Michel's father resisted making his family's declaration of goods as was required by the Statut des Juifs. According to Michel, his father was aware of the risk of this declaration feeling that if they were to make the declaration of assets, they would be taken or, at least, stripped of their assets.

Continuing unprompted and moving on to his second categorization of pressure and influence to win the Jews, Michel discusses Political Zionism in Morocco. Introducing this subject as the answer of the Jews in Europe to anti-Semitism, he says, "The Zionist movement until the war was not largely important."[50] There was a small start in the 1920s, but he recalls hearing stories from his parents that of this infinitesimal group who left, nearly all of them returned. Beyond this, there were some who made a religious pilgrimage to Jerusalem or went there to die or be buried, but "it's an old thing, that does not change much."[51] Until 1940 when Vichy regime French anti-Semitism came to Morocco and introduced the Statut des Juifs, the Political Zionist movement was not a popular narrative. The war, and a period of uncertainty about the place and security of Jews in postwar Morocco, changed this. Michel describes this as a period as litmus test[52] of sorts that would reveal to the Jews what their country would do to protect or expel them and at this wavering, the Zionist movement seized its opportunity and expanded greatly.[53] At this point, Michel distinguishes himself and his comrades at the time as patriotic Jews—that is,

Jews loyal to Morocco who disassociated themselves from the French and the Political Zionists alike.

Though he reasserts that he had no Muslim friends as a young child, Michel was close with many of the educated Muslim elite calling for independence by the end of the war. He recalls his studies with fellow Fassi students where he shared a room with a Muslim friend to the shock of the school's administration. Though he was now interacting frequently and closely with Muslim students, he says that they never talked about politics. He connects this experience to the stance of the nationalists on Moroccan Jews in general: that they avoided the Jewish people very openly. Nevertheless, this period seems to have been Michel's political awakening due to both his coming of age and the transitional period of postwar, preindependence Morocco. By August 1953 he says the Moroccan public was entering a battle and the Jews, as a part of the Moroccan public, were struck by the inaction of their leading committees. Identifying himself as an elite of the society as a student, he went to Paris to continue his studies and met there other Moroccan Jewish students from areas outside his native Fez who decided to join the Communist Party because the Istiqlal Party was against the student union at the time.[54]

Michel soon discovered that there were many Communist Party cells through the Jewish areas of Morocco. In Fez, in the years 1944–7, he claims that there were seven cells and the same in Meknès, the only Moroccan city where the Jews were the majority. Toward the end of the war, dismayed and, for some, betrayed by the French, Michel states that many Jews gathered under the claim that

> we are Moroccans, we do not want colonialism. . . . Because they saw that it was colonialism. It is never said, but they saw that there were anti-Jewish laws, just for the Jews. It must be said, because they knew it at that time. That we have almost forgotten since. . . . Except it had a consequence: that the Zionist organizations [were more readily accepted]. "If France rejects us, if lalala rejects us. . . . If everyone rejects us, we're going to Israel."[55]

As noted earlier, and consistent with the power of context to shift identity affiliations, the end of the war led some to feel betrayed by France and turn to Morocco or to Israel while, as will be evident in the proceeding sections, it led others to be relieved the war was over and return to their French patriotism.

It seems a significant actor in the loyalty of those Jews who proudly announced themselves Moroccans was the Sultan Mohammed V. Just as Michel outlined the advantageous connection between some Jews and the French Protectorate administration, he is quick to point out that many Jews received similar advantages through a connection with the sultan. Mohammed V continued to claim that Jews had no special status and that they were citizens like everyone else. He urged Moroccan Jews not to help the "Zionist aggression" while he reminded Moroccan Muslims not to forget their Jewish brethren.[56] Many years after the war, upon independence from France in 1956, he formed his government with a Jewish minister and many high administrative roles in the army. Michel thinks that Mohammed V genuinely found Jews to be his people just like any other and acted this way because there were a number of Jews who were academically prepared to handle technical or political positions as appropriate. He recalls Mohammed V's death as a disaster for the Jews with huge crowds of Jewish mourners taking to the streets in their grief.

Though he states that Morocco shares a number of common general features with its neighboring North African countries, Michel specifies that a "deep national identity was created for 1,000 years"[57] in Morocco. Not only were Jews "welcomed when they were expelled from Spain" but there were "already Jews in Morocco. . . . Moroccan Judaism is not Judaism imported from Spain, this is not true."[58] As a result of this historic and ongoing presence, he proudly states that Jews were an important part of the activity in Morocco. Though recent and active literature debates the history of Moroccan Muslims as Arab or as Amazigh (Berber), Michel uses the word Arab to describe his country,

> We are in an Arab country. What does that mean an Arab country? This is a country where 95 to 99% are Muslims, Arabs. So you have this minority in the midst of it. It is true that it requires an understanding of both sides to live together. There are times where that intelligence is not enough.[59]

Despite offering this statistic, he makes the distinction that while Jews are not Muslims, they are Moroccan, an affiliation which eleven of twenty participants share as their primary identity. His fight for his right to be Moroccan further reinforced his commitment to Morocco. He maintains that "it's not a problem of religion, it's a problem of cultural contribution"[60] and takes pride when he claims that today Morocco is the only Arab country where there is still a Jewish community: "The only place where there are still some Jews who play a role, participating in political life, participating in the life of the country, it's Morocco."[61] Investing in this reality of Moroccan pluralism is ultimately the best way to live together.

Michel remains resolutely Moroccan in his self-identity—this is, consistent with the outward identity theory that recognizes the social influence of self-perception. For instance, whereas Jewish Moroccan children attending the schools of the AIU studied French curriculum as Michel did in the French school, their Jewishness was not a differentiating factor and was, in fact, part of the lessons they received in the French language. This key difference resulted in a feeling of belonging to the French culture for many of the Alliance students, whereas Michel makes a clear distinction here between their culture and his culture. The fact that he perceived his difference from his French peers as not only Jewish but also Moroccan demonstrates his simultaneous and plural narrative affiliations. He is able to acknowledge and overcome the Arab-Islamic nature of the independence movement and still locate himself and his fellow Jews within it due to their historical and cultural contributions to Morocco and Moroccan identity. His call for pluralism exemplifies the powerful ability of memory to facilitate plural belonging in an inclusive way that honors heterogeneous groups within the nation.

While the three main narratives provide useful, broad categories of identification, a method reinforced by Michel's classification along the same narrative lines, the plurality and fluidity of identity necessitates the ability for individual diversity and nuance to shine through. For instance, Michel's experience in a French school was unique among his peers due to his family's ability to pursue the best possible education for their son. Similarly, Zohra's pride in her Tétouanese roots is unique among the participant pool and informs her feeling of being European. These individual variations are evident in the participants' remarks in regard to their perceptions of options available at the time. Yaakov says there were no Jews allowed in French schools though Michel was in fact living evidence of this. The discrepancies unearthed here are as significant as the corroboration of participants for their exposure of the complex push-pull of identity affiliations at the time.

Education, Faith, Language, and Politics

The participants in this study present a glimpse into the diversity of the Moroccan Jewish community during the Protectorate and today. The three vignettes selected to demonstrate the primary narratives of French assimilation, Political Zionism, and Moroccan nationalism should not be taken to reduce the diversity of the experience among the participants but rather as three broad categories within which to map the fluid movement of dynamic, plural identities. Narratives, which provide group members with "a shared history, based on common origins, distinct identity and a unique purpose,"[62] take place in religious and national discourses that provide the "temporal framework and cultural schemata" for articulating a collective past.[63] Within these meta-narratives, participants draw from a selection of traits and shared memory in order to provide meaning to the past and purpose for the present and future. Therefore, as contextual needs and circumstances change, affecting identity, the narrative responses adjust and affect the way memories are made, recalled, and shared. Ben-Layashi acknowledges the existence of plural narratives in his theory of the "homey narrative."[64] Examining the unpublished memoir[65] of a seven-year-old Moroccan Jewish child in the 1940s of the mellah of Casablanca, he observes the "contradiction between the official narrative and the homey narrative"[66] where the official narrative concerns the news and rumors about the war in Palestine and the creation of the State of Israel and the transnational political-religious consequences, but the homey narrative is concerned with the mellah's celebration of Purim,[67] the child's parents' stories, and home. Both narratives coincide with, and evoke, the past but from two different perspectives of the same chain of events. The "homey narrative" allows for "debris, layers, elements, meanings, and codes of stories that differ from the local well-known ones that dominate familiar discourse"[68] and, in this way, compliment and supplement the historical reconstruction that assumes or constructs the official state narrative. The method of semi-structured interviews allows for the memories and perspectives of these multiple narratives to come through.

All of the twenty participants identify themselves with multiple characteristics and affiliations wherein context shifts the arrangement of their plural, dynamic, and fluid identity. Furthermore, the primary data reinforces that in addition to context, it is important to acknowledge that no identity is a blank slate but is deeply informed from one's experience and environment. Several key themes occur throughout the participants' interviews and are applied here to provide a systematic lens through which to analyze their stories. Their experiences within the realm of education, their views on religion and language, and political involvement reveal the plurality of Moroccan Jewish identity and are indicative of the Jewish role in the development of Moroccan nationalism.

Perceptions of being a minority versus being among the majority in education seem to be highly influential in the participants' self-identity. Whereas Michel was the sole Jew among French Christians, Zohra and all other AIU and mellah students were among the majority if not a homogeneous peer-group. All those who identify primarily as French[69] received French education and pride themselves on the refined French education they received. In fact, among these five, Zohra and one other participant are still active with the AIU to the present day. Interestingly, while all four who identify primarily as Jewish[70] were educated by the AIU, none of them hold this to be a highly significant factor. In fact, one participant provided a different memory: growing up with Muslim neighbors and very little exposure to the French Protectorate administration, his only experience with French came through his schooling with the AIU, but as his teachers were also Moroccan Jews (as opposed to teachers from France), this did not strike him as living among the French. Even among those who identify primarily as Moroccan, five participants[71] related to me individually that as small children they knew nothing different than the combination of French language instruction and Jewish learning. Given that the majority of participants received a French education, whether through the AIU or schools for French residents, and yet only a minority of this group perceive themselves to be primarily French, it would indicate that education alone did not construct Protectorate identity and narrative affiliation. Certainly, it played a large role, as will be evident in the discussion of political activity; however, what seems to be the most significant factor of education was the experience of being one of a peer-group that comprise the school's majority as in AIU schools where the pupils were all Jews in contrast to being a minority among one's peer-group as in the case of Michel in the French school. Michel, for example, had a childhood full of schoolyard fights with French children and was made to feel lesser than his peers in school for being Jewish; these experiences linger when he speaks of French colonial oppression and anti-Semitic treatment of Moroccan Jews:

> In the thirties, the Christians hated the Jews, it was a time of Christian anti-Semitism, or let's say French anti-Semitism. We should never have forgotten this, but we did. . . . I am generalizing but the majority did, especially in Pétain's time in France, and of course Noguès' time in Morocco. That era was known for its anti-Semitism, and we should not forget it.[72]

The participants' regard of their Jewish faith upholds the theory of fluidity and dynamism as it changes depending on context. When discussing his self-perception of being European, one participant speaks with pride, using the pronoun 'we,' about Jewish history in Morocco and their many cultural contributions. Moreover, he says there is a deep connection between the Jews and Muslims—they are cousins through the religion of Abraham—whereas Christians have historically been the oppressors. The ability of one's Jewishness to take on different significance was highlighted in the report for the Civil Controller of the Casablanca Region which revealed that thirty-four different nationalities were registered for Jews living in Morocco in addition to French and

Moroccan.⁷³ While it did not garner allegiance from the Jewish population as a whole, it is not surprising that the Political Zionist narrative was appealing for its ability to foster unity and solidarity among the Jews. One participant recalls the early stance on Political Zionism, reiterated in the archives,⁷⁴ that only the aged and destitute would immigrate to Israel. Yet, faced with the fear of a dwindling Jewish nation within and beyond Morocco, he was motivated to maintain ties with Israelis of Moroccan origin when aliyah began to increase from the 1950s onward. Both Yaakov and the aforementioned participant identify primarily as Jewish, both are religious leaders within their communities, and are deeply committed to the Political Zionist narrative and works despite remaining in Morocco.

By contrast, Zohra echoes the colonial archive findings that reveal the Protectorate's reluctance to allow Zionist organizations to act, believing that it would only lead to trouble.⁷⁵ Her reluctance to speak about Political Zionism reflects her adherence to Protectorate policy, and she goes only so far as to say that to be involved with Zionist agencies during the Protectorate was something done in private and not in any way related to the AIU. This tension between the Political Zionist narrative and the AIU is interesting as AIU schools educated nearly exclusively Moroccan Jews; however, rather than working together, they remained in competition. All twenty participants identify themselves as Jewish, but the significance of this identity varies and is shaped by the hierarchy of their narrative affiliations. The relationship of Moroccan Jews who remain in Morocco is depicted clearly on a research visit of Andre Levy to Casablanca's Asylum for the Elderly (Asile de Vieillards) where he recalls how an elderly Jewish woman asked him in darija, "Where do you live in France?" After responding that he lived in Israel, she asked if he intended to return there after completing his business in Morocco. He confirmed that he would be returning home to which she replied, "This is no good. One should live in Morocco and die and be buried in Israel."⁷⁶ This regard of return to Israel as a place of burial but not for living highlights the coexisting and important balancing of both Jewish and Moroccan identities.

Though deeply connected to culture, language is a more easily acquired trait that can be chosen by an individual without required the reciprocal acknowledgment of an encompassing group of belonging. That is not to say that to speak the same language as a group necessarily grants membership into that group, but rather that the freedom of choice associated with which language is spoken primarily in the home, for instance, is highly indicative of self-identity perception and preferences. Of the five participants who identify primarily as

French, four[77] speak French as their mother tongue both at home and at school. An interesting exception here is one participant who, born in Tangier, spoke Spanish, his first language, at home, but French at school and in business. Zohra and another participant also speak Spanish, a lingering pride of Tétouanese roots, but name French as their primary language.

Perhaps unsurprisingly due to their roles within the Jewish community, the four participants who identify first and foremost as Jewish speak French as the primary language of communication at home and in their communities, but all raise the importance of the Hebrew language in their work and religious life. The activity of Yaakov and another participant with Political Zionist agencies indicates the need for Hebrew-language proficiency but, more importantly, the practice of prayer and other religious rites and study necessitates it. As keeper of the synagogue keys, P10 enjoyed learning Hebrew from the visiting Jewish families from Israel who came for holidays and pilgrimages. For those who have made their Jewishness a priority on their identity hierarchies, it is not surprising that their immediate circles would bring them into contact with, or necessitate the fluency of, the Hebrew language.

Contrastingly, of those who identify first and foremost as Moroccan, six[78] are explicit about their mastery and use of Moroccan colloquial Arabic, darija. One participant in particular connects the importance of speaking, reading, and writing darija to his success as a businessman in Morocco both during and after the Protectorate period. Though another participant prefers to write in Judeo-Arabic, he speaks darija predominantly; that said, both he and another participant remember Hebrew instruction being a part of their AIU curriculum. Michel was adamant to conduct parts of the interview in darija when discussing the independence movement. The participants' views on language seem consistent with the country as a whole where Arabic and Amazigh language are the official languages but French remains widespread in the urban, commercial, and tourist centers. Nevertheless, the fact that all twenty participants speak French fluently but some make a conscious choice to speak Hebrew or darija is indicative of their self-identity and the community with which they choose to surround themselves.

How the experiences with education, religion, and language lead to allegiance with one or more political narratives is a dynamic path. Of those who identify primarily as French, there are different motives or reasons for adhering to the French narrative of cultural-linguistic assimilation. One participant's telling of the rumors, which circulated in the major cities, that a decree had been negotiated which would naturalize Moroccan Jews as French citizens is consistent with the colonial archive records.[79] The French narrative vignette demonstrates Zohra's affinity for the AIU; her positive exposure to France and French culture allowed her to more quickly excuse the period of Vichy rule as a regrettable but temporary phase. One participant's remembrance of lingering protégé benefits such as being able to travel freely if necessary meant that his family could remain privileged Frenchmen that chose to remain in Morocco rather than being forced to flee. The periodicals reveal the mass support of the Jews for the French in the Second World War;[80] despite the anti-Semitic Vichy laws, the five French participants prove that the support for France remained strong.

The opposite result was also possible; disgraced at their rapid loss of honor, pride, and confidence, some of the Moroccan Jewish population were not able to continue to support France or maintain their sense of French identity. For instance, Yaakov described himself as being a very French-assimilated Jew before he saw the desolation of the French Jewish communities and became devoted to the Political Zionist cause. In other cases, the contextualized change was not a flashbulb instant of change but rather a transformation informed by one's past. The lasting memory and influence of these experiences translated from the classroom to political life where those who had negative exposure to France felt their otherness and those who had positive exposure regarded themselves as French. In fact, of the fifteen participants who identify most closely as Moroccan nationalists or as Jewish, nearly all of them agree about French anti-Semitism and the sultan's lack of ability to protect the Jews despite his best intentions.

It is interesting that for some, these same two claims led to activity with the Moroccan nationalist movement, whereas for others it cemented their Jewishness and led to activity with Political Zionism. Of those who identify as primarily Moroccan, only three participants share Michel's strong feelings about France being a colonizing oppressor. Others among this subgroup of eleven acknowledge France's role as an exacerbating force in the development of Moroccan nationalism but note that they are thankful Morocco did not have the struggle with France like their neighbor Algeria. In fact, one participant points out that it was a good thing Morocco never had its own Crémieux Decree because it kept the Moroccan Jews Moroccan and lauds the sultan for his decision to appoint Jews in political roles in the transition to independence in 1956. Other participants mark the end of the war as a major shift in identity as well. Two in particular describe the Allied landing in Casablanca as a time where they felt proud to be Moroccan and recall celebrations in the streets of Casablanca with Muslim neighbors.

Analyzing the stories of each participant as a sample of Moroccan Jews who lived during the Protectorate and remain in Morocco to this day across the themes of education, religion, language, and politics demonstrate the complexity and diversity of Moroccan identity and nationalist narrative affiliations. Though nearly all participants were educated with French curriculum and language, their experiences in education influenced their identities with dynamic and plural consequences. Similarly, though they all define themselves as Jewish, their Jewishness is embodied in very different ways with some taking part in religious practices and congregation and others finding it less relevant in their identity hierarchy. It is interesting to note that though the secondary literature and archive materials present Moroccan Jews to have played a minor role, if any at all, in the development of Moroccan nationalism, the majority of the interview participants identified first and foremost as Moroccan. This fits within the scope of the participant pool; because I interviewed only those Jews who chose to remain in Morocco when the majority of their coreligionists emigrated, it fits that those who felt most Moroccan would be among those who stayed. And yet, they make up a narrow majority, eleven of twenty, of those who chose to remain. The fact that such contrasting narrative affiliations coexist is a testament to the plurality and fluidity of identity and the power of memory to allow for a common space in which heterogeneous groups can all construct a sense of belonging.

Following Chapter 2's depiction of identity as plural, dynamic, fluid, and socially acquired and constructed through narrative, these theoretical foundations put forth are confirmed by the participant data. Indeed, their stories reveal plural characteristics and affiliations that reflect the social context of the Protectorate and their current lives as their identities and narratives changed, adjusted, or realigned. Though dynamism is evident in the secondary literature and archival sources, it is clearly confirmed in the primary data where identities shift and reconstruct to accommodate new and changing narratives. The fact that the participants included herein have remained in Morocco to the present day demonstrates identity fluidity; for instance, one's change from a supporter of France to an ardent donor to Political Zionist causes demonstrates dynamism, but his continued presence and commitment to Morocco demonstrates fluidity.

Narrative, as the "medium through which we navigate our lives, make sense of our past and project our future,"[81] is ongoing and constant; therefore, one is immersed in narrative whether it is in remembering the past, anticipating present and future actions, or situating oneself on a path for stories to come. Ricoeur agrees that narrative is central and omnipresent when he refers to narrative as the "primary organization tool to give temporal structure, order and meaning to the discordant events of life."[82] Individual and collective memory both relies upon and continually fuels narrative structures often integrating "historical sources, oral traditions and social myths [where] complex historic events . . . help articulate and reinforce particular discourses, ideologies and identities."[83] Narrative, as an extension and transmitter of identity, is similarly plural, fluid, and emotional, and cannot be simplified to a binary understanding. This plurality can be visualized in terms of a shifting hierarchy of traits and narratives; it is when one's affiliations are made to be incompatible that trouble arises. This thought is a recurring one that is present in several interviews herein where a contextual experience influenced, if not demanded, a rearranging of affiliations. Particularly with the signing of the Statut des Juifs under the Vichy government, Jews were simultaneously labeled as distinct by their religion while being partially protected as subjects of the sultan by their birthplace and residency. In this way Moroccan Jews were distinct from French Jews or even Algerian Jews who had received French citizenship decades prior; however, they were still isolated and held apart by a sectarian religious distinction of Jewishness. Being at once identified by their religion, ethnicity, and nationality, Moroccan Jews experienced significant identity strain brought about by the colonial presence and the introduction of Political Zionism. The fact that Jewishness had adapted itself to fit in many different realms of Protectorate Morocco society and was not a unilateral, one-size-fits-all definition is evident in the participant responses.

Furthermore, the adaptive ethno-symbolism theory of the nation as repository from which nationalists can select relevant myths, symbols, and memories in order to link past to future and vice versa is confirmed in the case of the development of Moroccan nationalism. Having described the nationalist in Chapter 2 as one who seeks to provide a suitable and dignified past from which to lend authority to the modern nation, and place it in a certain time and space thereby giving it roots, this holds true, as confirmed by the literature, archival material, and participant comments, of the reformists turned nationalists in Protectorate Morocco. By calling upon Islam and the Arab world's dignified past, and framing France as the enemy and oppressor of Muslims, the nationalists selected useful inspiration from the legitimacy of Islam and the success of growing Arab nationalism, but retained other myths, symbols, and memories such as the use of French language and Berber heritage. Interestingly, the Arab-Muslim narrative that shaped the nationalist narrative at the end of the Protectorate and early decades of independence has, in recent years, transformed to include an Amazigh (Berber) focus. This is significant because the popular dissonance of

Jewish and Arab is not as relevant in a linking of Jewish and Amazigh. That such changes in national narrative are possible is to further assert that context is key; society's dominant majority becomes the one to define oneself within or against.

The role of memory in identity and nation building is paramount; narrative, the bridge that connects the individual to the collective among and between generations, cannot be formed, internalized, nor maintained without memory. Any conceptualization of identity will require reaching to the past to connect or make light of the present being. This putting together of knowledge is sustained, shared, and given significance in and by society; therefore, one's encompassing groups of belonging are constructed through narratives that are formed by the groups' collective memories. Consider the role of memory in the adaptive ethno-symbolism described earlier: the nation is a sum of its memories (its putting back together of knowledge) that undergoes the same selectivity when constructing its identity. This selection, and exclusion, of memories leads to a collection of individuals and a gathering of collectives that necessitate self-awareness of its existence; as a result, the nation can be said to be a product of both remembering and forgetting. Memory collects and preserves the knowledge from which national identity is constructed within its own context. In the case of the three primary nationalist narratives in Protectorate Morocco, memory selectivity and construction is visibly effective. For those taken by the appeal of French assimilation, French curriculum's 'our ancestors, the Gauls' provided the opportunity to reimagine oneself as an encompassing group of belonging that spanned generations and continents. For those inspired or comforted by the Political Zionist narrative, there existed a long history of shared memory (rituals, observance, recitation) from which to draw as a part of the Jewish nation, and a lingering sense of already possessing membership to that encompassing group of belonging by birth rite. Lastly, for those drawn and devoted to the developing Moroccan nationalism, one need only select the memory of birthplace, residence, and fraternity to construct one's identity as Moroccan.[84]

Like identity, memory can be manipulated to reshape past events and can be commissioned for future agendas. Therefore, the ethics of memory is important to human rights and the concept of well-being. This is not to say that memory, in itself, is endowed with an inherent power of agency; "In order to yield any effects, remembering and forgetting have to be tied to human actors within cultural, political, institutional, and social frames."[85] In this sense, memory and forgetting develop the capacity to act "as individuals and to the context of a community . . . memories create identity and memories build community."[86] Indeed, several scholars of memory address the power of memory (and forgetting) to incite fear and legitimize violence as well as its power to heal, warn against and prevent future violence and tragedy, and bring diverse communities together.[87] Drawing from Honneth's theory of recognition that bridges the connection of the personal and collective through self-perception and recognition of self-confidence, self-respect, and self-esteem[88] as well as Durkheim's view of social solidarity wherein people feel connected through similar experiences, education, and kinship,[89] the nation is one such type of interdependent social formation. Because humans exist in social contexts and the modern world is currently divided primarily along nation-state lines, it follows that it is desirable for group and, by extension national, membership to allow for human well-being.

Of course, the challenge here is when well-being of one group conflicts with that of another. "Heterogeneous memories may coexist in the individual as they do in society" with some of these interacting or coexisting neutrally; it is when memories are "in painful states of dissonance, friction and rivalry"[90] that well-being is challenged. Margalit addresses the extent to which humans are ethically or morally bound to others within and beyond their communities of belonging. His terms 'thick' and 'thin' apply to the circles of relations humans hold: thick relations are one's "near and dear" whose binding cement is memory, whereas thin relations are strangers or humanity in general whose relations lack deep roots and are more frequently and easily overturned.[91] Memory is a source of knowledge, of course, but because memories are "subject oriented and perspectival, embedded and intermeshed, isolable and fragmentary" they are dynamic and malleable.[92] The way in which memory is wielded by nations constructs the emotion and trauma that comes with memory, but it can also provide a meeting place in which diverse groups can come together. When tangible documentation of the past does not exist, or is not able to by political or physical restrictions, present identities may be undermined or find they cannot be substantiated by memory alone:

> If memories fall apart and one's own past disappears into the mist, identity becomes brittle; if memories lose their relationship to the present and the past becomes the reference point for orientation, one can no longer establish the continuity of one's own life. A person can be lost in memories unable to find the present.[93]

The necessity for these reference points to retrieve, access, and communicate memory, both internally and socially, is reinforced in Nora's Lieux de memoire in the form of "archives, marked anniversaries, and organized commemorations. ... These tangible reference points enable and validate individuals' and collectives' memories."[94] George Orwell's *Nineteen Eighty-Four* provides a moving example of this crisis of memory. If the past is altered, or reference points destroyed, the assigned memory to the reference point is affected: "For how could you establish even the most obvious fact when there existed no record outside your own memory?"[95] Memory capability, as described through the capability approach, allows for the freedoms to acknowledge and celebrate reference points and can therefore provide a powerful opportunity for bridging diverse communities of belonging and constructing narrative for peace-building.

Developed in a variety of normative theories of social justice and development ethics, the capability approach is applicable across disciplines, particularly across cognitive and social sciences. The theoretical framework of capability approach entails the claims that possessing the freedom to achieve well-being is of primary moral importance and that this freedom can be understood in terms of capability, that is, the opportunity "to do and be what [one has] reason to value."[96] Scholars[97] trace the origins of the capability approach to Aristotle, Adam Smith, and Karl Marx, among others; however, its development is due to the economist and philosopher Amartya Sen.[98] Rather than a precise theory of well-being, Sen's approach[99] is concerned with individuals having the opportunity to achieve well-being as a matter of what they are able to do and be.[100] This conceptual framework allows for "the assessment of individual well-being; the evaluation and assessment of social arrangements; and the design of policies and proposals about social change in society."[101] Rather than focus on subjective states of well-being or 'utility' (the individual is happy) or the material means to well-being, 'commodity,' (the individual has a stable source of income), the capability approach is conceived as a more flexible and multicultural framework where the opportunity to function is more indicative of functioning than the commodities that may be present.[102] Though deeply influenced by the work of Rawls, Sen argues that the Rawlsian social primary goods metric[103] fails to account for the diversity of human beings because an index of primary goods does not acknowledge the reality that "people seem to have very different needs varying with health, longevity, climatic conditions, location, work conditions, temperament, and even body size."[104] For Sen, Rawls's primary goods ignore the scope of human diversity since it focuses on means rather than ends (functionings).[105] By focusing on the capability to be and do what is important to an individual, and the opportunity to realize that being and doing rather than ranking and measuring what that may be for different people, the capability approach is applicable to diverse groups of people and a wide range of study.

The language of the capability approach refers to the desired beings and doings, "various states of human beings and activities that a person can undertake," as human functionings.[106] Functionings may include desired 'beings' such as being well nourished, being educated, being housed or desired 'doings' such as traveling, voting, and caring for one's children. These functionings are not assigned a moral value; rather, their value depends on the context in which they exist. A person's freedom or opportunity to achieve her desired functionings is capability. Capabilities "refer to the presence of valuable options or alternatives, in the sense of opportunities that do not exist only formally or legally but are also effectively available to the agent"[107] so that the person is free to make use of these opportunities or not. A capability "reflects the alternative combinations of functionings from which the person can choose one combination."[108] Sen provides an example in the context of a woman who decides that she would like to go out: there are no particular safety risks and she has "critically reflected on this decision and judged that going out would be the sensible—indeed the ideal—thing to do."[109] The functioning (going out) is achieved when she has the capability (opportunity and freedom) to decide to do so. If, for instance, her freedom is violated by an authoritarian rule that she must go out, the functioning will remain the same, but the capability to decide to do so has been violated.

Sen claims that functionings are constitutive of a person's being, so it follows that any assessment of one's well-being must be based in that person's functionings.[110] This notion echoes the United Nation's Universal Declaration of Human Rights, in that to be human is to have a range of functionings (food, shelter, security, education) and, according to the capability approach, can be conceptualized in terms of human capability to have the desired combination of opportunities to achieve these functionings. Robeyns offers several applications to exemplify: for instance, consider a person's ability to be healthy. The capability approach will ask "whether the means or resources necessary for this capability, such as clean water, adequate sanitation, access to doctors" are present.[111] The functioning in this example, being healthy, is only achieved if people have the capability (opportunity) to reach this outcome.

The capability approach insists on focusing on ends (functionings) in assessing well-being and quality of life rather than the means because people will differ in their ability to convert means, or their desire to do so, into valuable opportunities (capabilities) or outcomes (functionings).[112] Assessing means as a measure of well-being is only useful if people have the same opportunities, capacities, or "powers to convert those means into equal capability sets."[113,114] The means of well-being (such as "the availability of commodities, legal entitlements to them" or social institutions)[115] matter, but they themselves are not the functionings of well-being. Individual differences are significant and by starting from functionings, scholars do not "a priori assume that there is only one overridingly important means to that (functioning) such as income, but rather explicitly ask the question which types of means are important for the fostering and nurturing of a particular capability, or set of capabilities."[116]

In order to evaluate the relationship between types of means and the achievement of functionings, Sen provides three categories of conversion factors that explore the degree in which a person can transform a resource into a functioning.[117] These three categories include personal conversion factors, internal to the person such as physical condition, gender, intelligence; social conversion factors such as public policy, social norms, conceptions of class, gender, or race; and environmental conversion factors such as the geographical location and climate.[118] These three types of conversion factors highlight the complexities between resources (means) and achieving well-being (functioning). For example, Robeyns provides the example of a bicycle as a resource for being mobile; however, "how much a bicycle contributes to a person's mobility depends on that person's physical condition [a personal conversion factor], the social mores including whether women are socially allowed to ride a bicycle (a social conversion factor), and the available of decent roads or bike paths (an environmental conversion factor)."[119] To conceptualize this more broadly, two individuals with the same set of means may have very different opportunities due to personal, social, and environmental factors. Because it is necessary to know much more about the context in which an individual is living in order to assess her well-being, Sen's capability approach provides the lens to evaluate the individual's capability (opportunity made feasible) as it is constrained by various conversion factors. By focusing on both the plurality of functionings and capabilities as well as the acknowledgment of personal, social, and environmental factors, the capability approach takes account of human diversity.

Attempting to move the capability approach from ideal theory to empirical application, Martha Nussbaum, a philosopher who has worked with and contributed to developing the capability approach, endorses a well-defined list of capabilities[120] which should be included in every country's constitution as they are "central human capabilities."[121] These proposed capabilities parallel the Universal Declaration of Human Rights such as "life, bodily health, bodily integrity, senses, imagination and thought, emotions, practical reason, affiliation, other species, play, and political and material control over one's environment."[122] Nussbaum insists that these capabilities are necessary for human dignity and moral entitlements of every human being. Other capability scholars address the need to determine a selection of capabilities as well;[123] for instance, Anderson suggests that humans need to possess "whatever capabilities are necessary to enable them to avoid or escape entanglement in oppressive social relationships" and to be able to function "as an equal citizen in a democratic state."[124] Though not denying the value and benefit of these capabilities for human life, Sen takes issue with the notion of "one pre-determined canonical list of capabilities, chosen by theorists without any general social discussion or public reasoning."[125] The strength of the capability approach is in assessing functionings in terms of the combinations of capabilities people have or use to achieve that functioning; it is not inherently concerned with assigning moral judgments to what constitute oppressive social relationships or what citizenship looks like in a democratic state. The empirical challenge is that while the notion of possessing human dignity is arguably universal, the perception of what possessing human dignity means and the process of public reasoning, on which Sen asserts human rights and capabilities depend,[126] are contextually and temporally sensitive. Indeed, "How can we go about ascertaining the content of human rights and of basic capabilities when our values are supposed to be quite divergent, especially across borders of nationality and community?"[127] Rather than decide which capabilities are to be valued by whom, Sen's capability approach applies universally regardless of birthplace, residence, or economic and governmental systems because it focuses on the opportunity to achieve valuable combinations of human functionings, whatever they may be, for a particular place and time.

Therefore, various capabilities take on a plural, hierarchical existence similar to identity and narrative. Functionings, and the opportunities (capability) to have different combinations of functionings, are assessed and weighted in relation to each other much the same way that national identity affiliation and the opportunities (capability) to have plural different combinations of identity affiliations are. For both, social conditions, and the priorities that the given social conditions suggest, vary but the extent to which they are shaped by narrative is similar. That is, the ways in which individuals come to decide what is important for them to be and do, and the extent to which they know which opportunities exist to achieve these ends, is shaped and informed socially by narrative in the same manner as identity and the nation are constructed. As demonstrated in the preceding discourse, this process is not possible without the presence and use of memory and remembering; however, I extend this claim further by asserting that memory and remembering is a powerful force in healing, mediating human rights, and peacekeeping. In this light, memory, and the ability and freedom to remember, presented as an original notion in this thesis as memory capability, is a capability to achieve well-being.

"The link between human rights and the politics of remembrance is strong and historically specific";[128] indeed, without remembrance the Universal Declaration of Human Rights could not exist. The historical truth, revealed in archives and oral testimony, is directly related to the memory of those who lived it and has "great ethical and transformative power" in its ability to forge "a new powerful link between past atrocities and a peaceful future."[129] Because memory is flexible and transformative, memory can play a key role in transitions toward peace and the maintenance of well-being. The volatility of memory may be seen as unreliable for cognitive psychologists, but the continuous appropriation of knowledge into memory means that it not only is adaptive but also has the capacity to encompass "both obstinate retention and the readiness to fuse old information with new."[130] Of course, it is never the past itself that acts upon a present society, but rather the representations of past events that are "created, circulated and received" within a specific context that gives memory significance.[131]

Just as selecting and rearranging memory constructs nations, so are memories produced through selecting and rearranging knowledge. Remembering always entails some sense of forgetting, so that the "file of memory is never closed; it can always be reopened and reconstructed in new acts of remembering."[132] The history, memory, and identity of individuals and nations alike are interrelated: if society, and what is important to it, changes, then identities and memories will change as well. Assmann and Shortt propose this causal relationship can be inverted: change the memories, or the perception and constructs of memories, and the identity of the collective will change.[133] Therefore, the transition toward peace and well-being that requires reaching new forms of order and legitimacy by changing political and social identity may be achieved, creating new frames of action, through memory capability.

Margalit's exploration of the ethics and morality of memory helps to explain the powerful implications of memory for caring and healing. Looking at the case of an Israeli military officer who could not remember one of the fallen soldiers under his command, Margalit explores the relation between memory and caring wherein to forget is taken to mean that one no longer cares. This same impetus to remember is a common phrase in commemorating tragedy such as the Holocaust or the 2001 World Trade Center destruction. The fear and warning present in the charge to remember not only seeks to protect the innocent in the future[134] but is also thought of as a way to honor the victims and extend caring beyond their suffering. Margalit evaluates the relation between caring and memory by proposing that memory "blends into morality through its internal relation with caring"[135] but the two are not necessarily constitutive; that is, it is possible to care about something or someone without having memory of it (general humanity of thin relations), and it is certainly possible to have memory of something or someone without caring for it. Where this relationship becomes significant is when caring confers importance:[136] "When we care about one another, we find it natural to expect the other to be one with whom we share a common past and common memories."[137] This description fits Margalit's notion of thick relations and can be understood to suggest a way forward toward universal morality; in order to facilitate caring and morality beyond one's immediate encompassing groups of belonging, memory capability needs to be a freedom that nations allow, if not encourage. In this sense, humans can care for even those with whom they do not share memory and, through caring, expect reciprocal morality that can bridge encompassing groups of belonging together.

Of course, this ideal of reconstructing and transitioning memory is not likely to be easily applied in long-reaching, intransitive conflicts. The act of being told to forget is itself an act of remembering as one's attempt at forgetting will naturally recall that which one tries to forget. Furthermore, if forgiveness and healing were to require forgetting, one could not decide to forgive. Rather, forgiveness requires deciding to disregard or move beyond that which needs to be forgiven. Therefore, instead of selective amnesia, the memory capability (opportunity) to 'remember rightly' may validate one's representations of past events and the emotion of how one felt at the time. Emotion provides a "way of grasping the sense and sensibility of past events needed for understanding and assessing the things we care about in the present" thereby affecting behavior.[138] The memory of a past emotion evokes "feelings, sensations, [and] images" but the inability to relive an emotion is an opening for reconstructing memory. For instance, "If I fail to remember vividly someone I hated in the past, I might find it hard to believe that I ever hated him. I might just as well re-evaluate my emotion by downgrading its intensity. I sort of dislike him, but I didn't really hate him."[139] The condition that emotion may be valued differently in the present and future than it was in the past is a modest window toward well-being functionings through memory capability.

Another complication in the notion of universal morality lies at the core foundations of identity construction. Because identity is influenced and formed socially and solidarity is often consolidated through comparison to a distinguished other, can morality hold across national borders and, if so, how will nations maintain their autonomous solidarity? Margalit holds that if such a contrast is necessary, "humanity cannot provide the contrast, since it is the most extensive community imaginable and there is nothing and nobody relevant outside of that community to be contrasted with."[140] Caring, however, does not need to eradicate thick and thin relations. The nation can be an encompassing group of belonging that constructs some myth of common ancestry and common memories as distinct from another without sharing a common hatred for it. Because the solidarity of the nation is constructed on invented or false memory, it is not unreasonable to think of a future where memory can be transitioned for the well-being of each nation's citizens and humanity in general. The ways in which memory is constructed and wielded to justify violence and aggression are evident among nations and perpetrators of such acts;[141] however, the fact that memory is seen to be malleable means that it is equally capable of being wielded as a source of healing and well-being.

The powerful interpretative use of memory is supported by the collection of witness testimonials where the same divide exists between nationalist exceptionalism on the one hand, and universal, transnational memory "toward the global attainment of human rights" on the other.[142] The role of testimony reveals and connects memory across generations as the "witness becomes a bearer of history," an "embodiment of memory" who attests to the past and "to the continuing presence of the past" through transmission to future generations.[143] Witness testimony from survivors of the Holocaust has been appropriated in both ways. In the case of nationalist exceptionalism, Arendt observed that testimonials of Jewish survivors enhanced the legitimacy of the modern State of Israel and collectivized Jewish identity into the Political Zionist narrative.[144] Contrastingly, the same testimonials may "provide the foundations for a new cosmopolitan memory . . . transcending ethnic and national boundaries"[145] thereby facilitating transnational shared memory and universal morality. The freedom of memory capability may very well elicit both types of testimony; however, the idea that individuals have the capability to 'remember rightly' can broaden the field of memory "to include other victims, other perpetrators, and other bystanders" thereby incorporating memories "into an enlarged global arena, making room for additional local, regional, national, and transnational testimonies about slavery, colonialism, genocide, and subordination."[146] Memory capability thus creates a common space amid heterogeneous groups of belonging for transnational remembrance, recognition, and well-being. A freedom to be found in memory capability must include the freedom to retrieve, access, and communicate reference points of memory. Witness testimony can be one such example; monuments, archives, museums, or commemorations are other examples of reference points that acknowledge the opportunity to remember rightly and empower and enable different remembrances of events.

Sen's capability approach claims that possessing the freedom to achieve well-being is of primary moral importance and that this freedom can be understood as the capability (opportunity) to do and be what one has reason to value. Memory capability fits this approach in that the opportunity to remember contributes to the achievement of well-being. The conversion factors that may affect the means or resources necessary for this capability will vary among individuals. For instance, two citizens of the same nation may have the same social conversion factors available to them such as civil liberties or freedom of speech and may share the same environmental conversion factors such as geographical location and climate; however, they may have disparate personal conversion factors relating to their physical or mental condition that allow them the opportunity to 'remember rightly' or not. Not dissimilarly, two individuals of different nation-states with differing social norms and public policy may share the same personal and environmental conversion factors but be limited in their memory capability. In assessing well-being within and among nation-states, functionings of well-being may take on different forms and utility but the freedom to have the opportunity to remember is one capability that can allow humanity to do and be what it has reason to value.

In Morocco, the freedom to have the opportunity to 'remember rightly' can be seen in varying ways. For instance, the inability of the vast majority of Jews to locate or reconcile Jewish identity in the Arab-Islamic myth of common ancestry and memory toward the end of the Protectorate and in the first decade of independence resulted in mass emigration to either France, and other Francophone countries, or Israel. This lack of memory capability prevented Jews from feeling a part of the nation's shared memory and led them to seek encompassing groups of belonging elsewhere. For those who emigrated to France and other Francophone areas, notably Quebec, it should be noted that educational and economic opportunities contributed in drawing French-assimilated Moroccan Jews whereas the same cannot be said for those who made aliyah to Israel. Though a number of Jews may have sought opportunity elsewhere regardless, I contend that the development of an inclusive Moroccan nationalism in which Jews would be central, esteemed colleagues in the narrative would not have seen the massive emigration of Moroccan Jews.

Conversely, the freedom to have the opportunity to 'remember rightly' can be seen to have contributed to the choice to remain in Morocco for others. The fact that Michel acknowledges Morocco's Arabness wherein Jews are a minority does not prevent him from having the opportunity to construct a shared memory based on Arabic language and anti-colonial motivation. The representation of the past for Zohra is able to reconstruct the Vichy period as a temporary blemish that was resolved, and she sees herself as a contributing member of Moroccan society as an educator, wife, mother, and grandmother. Furthermore, Yaakov's freedom to be involved with Political Zionist agencies without persecution from his Moroccan nation provides the memory capability to maintain dual encompassing groups of belonging with which he shares memory. In fact, the existence of the Jewish Museum of Morocco and its Moroccan Foundation of Jewish Cultural Heritage in Casablanca which works to document and educate the value of the Jewish component of Moroccan national culture is itself a fitting example of memory capability; the freedom to have the opportunity to collect and present Jewish shared memory as a part of Moroccan national shared memory and be recognized by the Moroccan government as a Public Utility[147] is a strong reference point that creates and nurtures solidarity and well-being among the nation's various groups.

Why should majority groups among heterogeneous communities desire to ensure the well-being of others? The perceived dichotomy between self-interested utility and altruism implies that if people are inherently selfish and operate for their own self-interest, they cannot also be socially molded by group norms. Paul Anderson's discussion of altruism, "the pursuit of another's utility at the expense of one's own," undermines Thomas Hobbes and, later, Adam Smith's notion of strictly, self-interested economic theory with a discussion of Jean-Jacques Rousseau's assertion that humans are more "inclined to follow group norms than calculate and pursue their own individual utility."[148] Considering altruism in the context of concern for the well-being of fellow citizenships can draw upon both self-interest and socially instructed selflessness: if a ruling majority power allows or even encourages the freedoms associated with memory capability for all its people, diverse coexistence and peace can be sustained. This may be driven by self-interest yet also an act of altruisim.

Like identity, memory is a fluid negotiation of interrelated, potentially conflicting, and "condensed remembrances composed when people experience and participate in intersecting historical legacies, movements and presences."[149] The memories related earlier through participant interviews have been transformed through personal reconstruction in the course of their retelling. Though one's remembering of the past could possibly vary from telling to retelling, the participant interviews are consistent in so much as they shared the same time period of interview with no major contextual shifts in their surrounding sociopolitical arena. I did not encounter participants who found their past difficult to recollect, though several commented that their memories would not be worth sharing or being recorded. As I set out to interview those who had not previously been a part of the public eye or previous scholarly work, the stories of these individuals who feel themselves to be unremarkable were quite the opposite. The methodological criticism that oral sources are unreliable because memory and subjectivity may distort facts is outdated and shortsighted because the memory and subjectivity is itself a presentation of the facts. Oral history is "about the historical significance of personal experience on the one hand, and the personal impact of historical matters on the other."[150] The notion that established documentary sources relay the facts more reliably can also be discounted; however, the method of triangulation serves as a cross-checking tool to avoid falsehoods. Portelli's model of three aspects of oral history brings together the "history of events, history of memory, and history and interpretation of events through memory"[151] that recognizes the role and value of memory and narrative in oral sources.

Discussing the historical validity of memory and, in particular, testimonials, Spence, a psychoanalyst, distinguishes between narrative truth and historical, or factual, truth. For Spence, narrative truth derives from memory and is shaped by circumstances of the present moment in which it is being remembered; "Narrative truth is what we have in mind when we say that . . . a given explanation carries conviction."[152] Historical truth, by contrast, is "time-bound and is dedicated to the strict observance of correspondence rules; our aim is to come as close as possible to what really happened."[153] I agree that memory is shaped by circumstances of the present moment in which it is being remembered; however, in presenting narrative truth as instable and imprecise and applying strict observance of correspondence rules to historical truth, Spence's distinction fails to fully account for meaning. For instance, Hirsch and Spitzer find that when reviewing testimonies of Holocaust survivors, one may come across a factually inaccurate account that tells "them more about the meaning of an event, and about the process of its recall in the present, than about the event itself"; by "expanding the notion of truth and coming to a deeper, more encompassing historical understanding"[154] one can reach a more complete form of truth.

This intersection of history and memory is an area of criticism in Halbwachs's work in which he depicts history as an objective scholarly record of the past with which one no longer has an intimate connection whereas memory is spontaneous and adaptable to the needs and pressures of society. Schwartz argues that collective memory is a "continuous negotiation of historical archive and present concerns" in the same way that historical writing is limited by interpretation and present agenda.[155] For Schwartz, history and memory alike can be selectively exploited. Schudson agrees that memory as a dialectic process includes the present shaping of the past as well as the "legacy of the past enduring in the present."[156] Debating the possibility of making objective claims, Postmodernist scholars undermine the authority of professional historiography challenging that the distinction between knowledge and interpretation is not a clear line just as in the case of history and memory.[157] In fact, history and memory can both be presented as social constructs, "each vying for legitimacy and the power to interpret and represent the past."[158] Certainly, the line of division is more blurred in today's academic disciplines than in Halbwachs's time which goes to support the triangulation method. From a combination of the existing scholarly literature, archived periodicals and colonial documents, and semi-structured interviews with those who lived during the Protectorate period, it is possible to approach the context from various angles, present the viewpoints, and draw analysis from a broad and diversified palate of narratives.

This chapter has addressed all the three research questions, providing answers to be further analyzed and reflected upon in Chapter 7. Using the triangulation of scholarly literature, archived periodicals and colonial documents, and primary data from the participants earlier, the way in which the Jewish minority was present, supported, and active (or not) in the development of various nationalisms has been explored to reveal nuanced complexities and overarching themes. The third research question (what does it say of the nation-state and its Jewish minority that there remains a decreased but enduring Jewish community?) has been addressed primarily through memory capability with further explanation from the solar system diaspora approach. Memory, so vital to identity on individual and collective levels, is a powerful tool in the remembering and forgetting that creates a national unit. Where reference points are forbidden to reflect the full heterogeneity of a community, minorities may struggle to identify with the nation-state. In Morocco, Jews have the freedom and opportunity to remember rightly and the intangible and actual infrastructure to retain their religious and national identities and communities within the state; this memory capability explains the continued Jewish presence in Morocco and has hopeful implications for the well-being and peaceful coexistence of diverse nation-states beyond the place and time of Protectorate Morocco. Building on these assertions, the next chapter will draw a broader analysis from the case of Moroccan Jewry and what it means for Moroccan Jews to possess memory capability. Reflecting upon ways in which its experiences can be related to that of its neighbors and the greater Middle East North Africa region, I will address the ways in which Protectorate Morocco is a unique case study as well as further implications for the theoretical and empirical findings herein.

6

Is Jewish Morocco Exceptional?

The great 'exodus' of Morocco's Jews in the 1950s and 1960s is not unique to the region; population estimates for the number of Jews in the Middle Eastern region[1] illustrate a clear trend. Cohen reports that the number of Jews "may be estimated to have been 400,000 in 1917; 460,000 in 1947; 115,000 in 1968; and 104,000 in 1972."[2] The exact figures are not necessary to see the overall trend of brief population swell (caused by the increased accuracy of census figures due to move toward urban centers and the tumult of Second World War refugees) before its drastic and devastating decline that only continued after the war of 1973 in Israel. Regardless of colonial experience or historical role in their local communities and countries, Jews across the MENA underwent a similar exodus following the establishment of the modern State of Israel. In Morocco, the ensuing tension and conflicting narratives in question amid Muslim-Jewish relations certainly had "critical antecedents"[3] in the foundations that had been laid in the coming of the Protectorate administration; however, the "weight of the war years" and declaration of statehood for the new State of Israel created an irreversible "rupture ... (wherein) an already unstable situation simply got worse."[4]

Expanding upon historical reconstruction with archival material and interview data, it is clear that the lives and stories of Morocco's Jews are shaped by the regional and international context in which these narratives were being constructed; however, the case of Morocco is unique in that its Jewish community, though severely decimated, persists. Morocco's three major waves of Jewish emigration in 1948, 1956, and 1967 correspond to the creation of Israel, Moroccan independence, and the Six-Day War, respectively, and join the regional trend of Jewish emigration that undermined centuries of Muslim-Jewish coexistence. Baïda writes of emigration as an emotional and painful tear where the Jews

> reluctantly (leave) a country that is made for them, that remains a part of them, and that they will never forget. They are torn as they abandon this land, a land

where they have lived, struggled, and prayed, a land where their generations built an earthly residence, a land where their dead lie at rest.⁵

Treated as other by the burgeoning nationalist narrative, struggling economically, humiliated by the period of Vichy anti-Semitism, disappointed and betrayed by the French, and torn over the place of Political Zionism; there are many simultaneous forces that can account for the mass emigration of Morocco's Jews, "ending a millennium of coexistence that had marked Morocco as the most tolerant of Muslim societies."⁶

Though Morocco and Algeria shared a colonial power, the experience as Protectorate as opposed to colony made for significant differences in the extent of assimilation and autonomy in Jewish life. Morocco's lack of Crémieux Decree came to be viewed as a positive when Jews were still thought of as subjects of the sultan rather than French citizens subject to French civil law during the Vichy administration. Furthermore, Morocco's struggle for independence came substantially more peacefully than Algeria's that was much more deeply entrenched as a French colony. Michel points out another factor that highlights his perception of Morocco's uniqueness in relation to its neighbors in the region:

> To what extent is Morocco North Africa? It is not the same thing. . . . We must not forget that Algeria and Tunisia was a part of the Turkish provinces. We have never been a Turkish province. . . . So my deep conviction is that we have a number of common general features with neighboring North African countries, and others further . . . but we have a deep national identity . . . Today when the Arab world rebels, Morocco does not revolt. Why? Because we have already achieved much of what they do not yet have.⁷

This statement is an interesting mix of historical relevance. The reminder that Morocco was not a part of the Ottoman Empire seems to reassert Moroccan's Arab past as opposed to the Turks. However, he then distances Morocco from the Arab world when it comes to the Arab Spring and revolution to assert Morocco's unique national identity. The reference to a deep national identity that is uniquely Moroccan demonstrates the power of memory and narrative to unite and maintain solidarity. Michel clearly furthers the notion of deep national identity to include the Jews and their distinct part in this narrative, and his use of 'we' contrasted against 'they' reinforces his sense of Morocco's unique identity. His final phrase raises another point that is worth mentioning: because these interviews took place in 2013 with follow-up in 2018, following, and partially amid, massive political changes throughout the region, it is possible that interview participants were motivated to present a vision of their past to enhance Morocco's present. That is, taking pride in Morocco's relatively peaceful experience of the Arab Spring and wanting to promote a picture of Morocco as a desirable homeland, were participants keen to present a tolerant, pleasant childhood past? I do not find that this is a significant factor for two principle reasons. First, the participant pool was limited to those who have remained in Morocco as their primary (if not sole) residence continuously since the end of the Protectorate and therefore already represent a group that must take some pride and value in their life in Morocco and Moroccan identity. Second, while every participant spoke affectionately about both the joys and trials of modern Morocco and their life there, this did not prevent diverse stories of the Protectorate past and the different narratives in question in the Protectorate years. Therefore, while it may be claimed that there is an element of pride among participants in the lack of great disruption of Morocco's peace during the revolutions of neighboring countries, it has not significantly affected the variety of memories of experiences during the Protectorate era.

As the interviews herein demonstrate, the inability to find oneself a single component of identity in which to reside is an inevitable and ever-shifting reality that results in individuals being informed from a variety of domestic and external factors and contexts. Torn between various identity affiliations in their birth country, emigrated Moroccan Jews continue to face this tension that is often expressed through a hyphen such as Moroccan-Israeli (or the more vague Mizrahi-Israeli), French-Moroccan, or Moroccan-Canadian. New perspectives on the experience of Morocco's Jews cannot be discovered solely on the colonial archives and periodicals but require oral sources that come from an increasingly small and aging population. Indeed, to write the history of Moroccan Jewry, it is essential to include narrative from Morocco itself in order to avoid the modern binary dichotomy between Arab and Jew. The multidisciplinary mixed methods approach used in this research constructs a big-picture understanding of the complexities of Jewish identity in French Protectorate Morocco while honoring the stories and experiences of individuals who lived through it and still call Morocco home.

Unlike many Arab and/or Muslim states in the MENA region, Morocco's small Jewish population can live comfortably and quite freely as a minority with citizenship rights. The feeling that this relationship with the state is unstable and vulnerable is connected to the Israeli-Arab conflict like many of its neighboring countries. Michel acknowledges this:

> The future of the Jews in Morocco is linked to the future of the Jews in the world, which is linked to the Jewish-Arab problem. . . . The Arab perspective,

in response to a question about the Jews of Morocco (is that) if there is peace, not even peace but an improvement, then there will be a flow of Moroccan Jews returning home to visit or for advantage. I'm not saying that we will have in the future a large Jewish community in Morocco, it is finished, it has passed. But rather that in the world there is a huge community of a million Moroccan Jews.[8]

While nearly all of these mentioned millions reside outside Morocco, this can be seen as another feature of Morocco's uniqueness; that Jews can still return to see the land of their ancestors and it is seen as advantageous for its contribution to tourism. For example, Jewish pilgrimages to tombs of rabbis or sites of holy events continue to draw Moroccan Jews who reside outside Morocco back into the country thereby reaffirming their attachment to the land and its history.[9]

Moroccan Jewish experience is a unique case in regard to its relationship to the State of Israel and the Jewish nation in general. Conceived as the first diaspora community having been forced to maintain distinct Jewish life and practice outside its center since 70 CE, Zionist historiography regards the various diaspora communities around the world as being "part of a model of symbolic relations between the homeland and exile."[10] In this dichotomy, one is either home or in exile therefore implying a negative connotation to diaspora and disregarding the various feelings of homeland within one's country of birth and residence in the nearly 2,000 years since the destruction of the Second Temple. The Political Zionist notion of recapturing the homeland and welcoming its diaspora home is one reason that Political Zionism was not immediately popular in Morocco where Moroccan Jews felt either Morocco or France to have greater socioeconomic appeal and opportunity. Whereas the homeland-diaspora relationship is depicted as requiring diasporic communities to construct and cultivate longing for their symbolic center, the case of Morocco presented herein demonstrates that constructing and cultivating longing is present among Moroccan Jews with Morocco as their center, not only the return to Zion.

Several scholars reject the perception of Jewish exile as negative.[11] If diaspora is considered outside the Political Zionist framework of national autonomy and self-determination, 'exile' can be seen as a success where there remained "exercise and preservation of cultural power separate from the coercive power of the state."[12] That is, if the ultimate goal of territorial control and autonomy is taken away, the diasporic exile is seen to have thrived and flourished in its respective communities. Gilman agrees that the model of exile and homeland "no longer seems adequate for the writing of any aspect of Jewish history, including that of Zionism and of the state of Israel."[13] The obvious response to this is powerful for its exception; the devastation of the Holocaust and Second World War to the

Jewish Diaspora supported the claims for the necessity of territorial autonomy of the Political Zionist narrative; however, this tragic period of Jewish history is not a representative measure of the homeland and exile dichotomy. In fact, Levy rejects this "uni-direction model (as) overly simplistic," evidenced by the "ambivalent attitudes of Moroccan Jews towards both their presumed homeland and their 'exilic' space."[14] Rather, an alternative is proposed to provide a different model to understand Jewish relationships among the diaspora, the solar system model. The model demands visualization of the many diaspora communities working in the context of others rather than all orbiting around the one homeland. In this sense, Moroccan Jews can "see their place in Casablanca not only as part of a global Jewish diaspora, but also as a homeland for a Moroccan Jewish diaspora."[15]

The solar system model allows for multiple homelands as multiple centers, a plurality that fits given the fluid plurality of identity and narrative. Reinforcing the perception of Morocco as one homeland in the diasporic solar system is the "symbolically meaningful (though negligible demographically) stream of Jewish immigration to Morocco."[16] Levy admits this number is very small; in fact, he estimates only fifty to eighty Moroccan-Israelis returning from Israel to Morocco, but the idea of return, whether to live or only as a pilgrimage, reinforces the state of Morocco as a center rather than a place of exile. Cardeira da Silva uses the term 'first-place' instead of 'solar system' to critique this vision of diaspora communities as satellites.[17] Rather, she complicates the linear view of history that sees a diaspora from its origins to its new diaspora in favor of a pluralistic collection of first-places which resonate with members of the diaspora. Further, the notion of first-places allows for the place to resonate with people beyond the diaspora itself. In the case of pilgrimages to saints in Morocco, forty-five Jewish saints and fourteen Muslims saints are noted but thirty-one saints are claimed by both groups.[18]

Much has been said in the preceding chapters about the affect of context on the exertion of an identity trait or affiliation. I claim that a threat to this trait forces a decision or action to be taken that either exerts the trait or leads to abandoning of the trait. In Morocco, because the Jewish demographic is dwindling and so small in number, daily life is shaped by this. The demographic threat to the community reinforces Morocco as a homeland among the solar system while at the same time challenges its continued existence. That is, when faced with their Moroccan diasporas in Israel, France, or Canada, the homeland is Morocco; however, "The demographic inferiority that is far from being concomitant with their self-proclaimed symbolic centrality cannot be overlooked or ignored."[19]

Nevertheless, the solar system model provides a more thorough representation of diasporic homeland because the sense of belonging and exile may shift due to context. Insofar as Moroccan Jews can return freely to visit or live, Morocco is unique among its neighbors in the region.

The idea of Morocco as a window to the region implies the transition of time-bound content into non-time bound, general categories so that the unique case study gives value to other applications. The scholarly consensus among historical studies of the MENA region suggests that the turning of the twentieth century saw a clear trend of Jewish communities taking part in the evolution of modern Arab culture.[20] Alcalay insists that in "Iraq, Syria, Lebanon, and elsewhere in the region, young Jews, whenever the political climate permitted it, became engaged in literary and journalistic pursuits in their respective countries"[21] with Iraqi Jews, in particular, described as "strikingly Arab and specifically Iraqi."[22] By the middle of the century and the two world wars, the situation changed. While the lives of Jews in Arab lands were touched by the Holocaust in very different ways than European Jewry, Syria and Lebanon, for instance, under French mandate control, "faced severe shortages of food and fuel."[23] British mandate and Hashemite clan-controlled Iraq experienced increasingly anti-Jewish treatment with Jewish neighborhoods experiencing extreme violence in which 179 Jews were killed, while "the rioters orphaned 242 Jewish children, looted 586 Jewish owned buildings, and destroyed the homes of more than 12,000 people."[24] Just as proximity to Europe affected the intensity and pervasiveness of persecution during the Second World War, so does proximity to the ongoing Israeli-Arab conflict affect Jewish life in the region today. Whereas Jewish life and pilgrimage can continue in Morocco, Jewish life in Syria, Lebanon, and Iraq would never be the same.

To gain appropriately in-depth perspective of Jews in Arab lands in a more macro sense of the MENA region in general, one must first understand the particular context, actors, and narratives of each of its communities. This research provides one such in-depth look at Protectorate-era Morocco that can inform further-reaching applications of both a theoretical and empirical nature; however, that is not to say that the country-specific complexities should be overlooked. Other scholars have provided similar works on neighboring North African countries Algeria and Egypt that offer interesting accounts with which to compare and contrast. Morocco and Algeria, for instance, shared a colonizing ruler in France, yet the experience of protectorate versus colony amounted to different experiences. With its tradition of emancipation and its self-proclaimed civilizing mission, French policy offered thousands of Jews a cultural and political alternative from dhimmi status. Algeria and Morocco comprise two principal states of the Maghreb in terms of geography and population and also share linguistic, religious, ethnic, and historical elements.[25] Despite the common colonial ruler, the distinction between protectorate and colony as well as their respective battles for independence make the neighboring countries starkly different. As a full colony of France and therefore a piece of France, the use of French language, the presence of French nationals, and the pull of emigration to the metropole were felt much more strongly in Algeria than in French Protectorate Morocco.[26] Colonial law established three personal status regimes in colonial Algeria: one French, one Muslim, and one Jewish. This arrangement gave local religious authorities jurisdiction over Algerian Muslims and Jews for matters pertaining to marriage, family, and inheritance. At the same time, in order to be governed by their faith, colonized subjects sacrificed the rights of citizenship, since only those governed by the French personal status could be candidates for naturalization.[27] In 1870, France's socialist minister of the interior, Adolphe Crémieux, a Sephardic French Jew, issued a decree offering Jews in Algeria the option of full citizenship if they would accept French civil law. This would mean giving up the right to be governed by tribunals of rabbinical judges under Jewish communal law, as had long been local tradition.[28]

At the outbreak of war in 1939, Algerian Jews pledged support to France in calls against "the common enemy," Germany.[29] Upon France's defeat a year later and the decision to seek a collaborationist armistice that resulted in Vichy rule, anti-Semitism was formally adopted as state policy and the Crémieux Decree annulled. More than 105,000 Algerian Jews who had enjoyed French citizenship for up to three generations suddenly found themselves relegated as no longer citizens, but still subject to French civil code.[30] As in Morocco, Vichy's Statut des Juifs was issued in October 1940 and impacted civil, legal, religious, and personal rights of all Jews in Algeria regardless of their citizenship status. Under this law, Jews were barred from almost every public function. They were prohibited from "holding political office or appointments; from any administrative post; from all diplomatic positions; from all teaching posts; and from all governmental or military positions."[31] Shortly thereafter foreign and French Jews alike were sent to transit camps such as Drancy and Pithiviers in France en route to concentration camps throughout Europe.[32]

Further along the Maghreb in British-ruled Egypt, Jews faced similar tensions between long-standing residency and modern pulls of national allegiances. The similarities among these countries in their exposure to Western culture, language, and privileges as well as their conflicted affiliations to birthplace, religion, and ethnic identities unite the Jews of the MENA during this time period in the fluid hierarchy of identity variables and undermine the homeland-exile dichotomy; however, the differences among them, such as the varying types of colonial influence, their experience of, and role in, independence and development of nationalism, and the ability to remain or return reveal striking differences that demonstrate Morocco's uniqueness. While similarities drawn among the region function to increase authenticity of historical accounts and allow the ability to speak generally about Arab-Jewish experiences, the differences among countries in the region highlight country-specific conditions that should not be glazed over through generalizing statements about the experience of Jews from Arab-Islamic lands. In order to avoid such generalizing, I focus on the case of British-occupied Egypt to demonstrate points of similarity and divergence from Protectorate Morocco.

Taking a similar systematic approach from the precolonial to the development of nationalist narratives, the brief comparison presented herein demonstrates the changing role of Jewish status. Like Morocco, Egypt's once-sizable Jewish population boasted a history dating back to ancient times tied to the biblical books of Genesis and Exodus. These deep roots are seen in the distinction between two Jewish communities, Rabbanites, the predominant stream within the Jewish diaspora beginning in the second century CE that places Rabbinic Judaism in the absence of Temple sacrifices, and Karaites, a conservative thread of Judaism which recognizes the Tanakh alone as Halakhic authority without the oral tradition of the Mishnah or Talmud.[33] The latter, estimated at 30 to 40 percent of the total community, was well embedded in Egyptian culture and upheld the Jewish heritage of Egypt linking it to ancient times.[34] The Jewish legacy left behind in Cairo and Alexandria included "splendid synagogues, schools, hospitals, large department stores, and comfortable residences"[35] that demonstrate the duration and affluence of the communities in their prime.

Egyptian Jews enjoyed a similar place to that of Moroccan Jews where the Muslim-majority society afforded equal rights to all Egyptians regardless of race, language, or religion.[36] However, this early notion of nation-state as a territorial and citizenship-based entity[37] was found lacking when many Egyptian Jews were considered stateless since they lacked paperwork to prove citizenship. For instance, in 1948 the Jewish population was estimated to be between 70,000 and 80,000; however, only about 5,000 held Egyptian nationality, 30,000 with foreign nationality, and the remaining approximately 40,000 stateless.[38] Shamir reasons that such high counts of statelessness existed due, in part, to the assumption that Jews aspired to foreign nationalities and had no interest in benefiting from

Egyptian nationality laws but also from the transition from Ottoman to British Empires when Egyptians transformed from Ottoman subjects to Egyptian nationals under British control whose citizenship was determined by the identity and descent of the parents, not by residence.[39] The persisting number of stateless Egyptian Jews can also be linked to high illiteracy and the complications of attaining evidence that would prove residency before 1848, which many autochthonous Jews struggled to produce.[40] Furthermore, religious Jews, such as the aforementioned Rabbanites and Karaites, though among the most ancient-dated Egyptian communities and deeply embedded in Egyptian culture, tended toward exclusiveness and did not engage the Western-educated leaders' calls for nation-state motivated identity. Whereas Jews remained subjects of the sultan throughout the Protectorate years in Morocco, citizenship status, and the benefits that would accompany it, remained far more vague and unclear in Egypt.

Another reason for this lack of clarity regarding state status resulted from increased diversity of Jews in Egypt. By the population census of 1897, the number of Jews counted amounted to 25,000 of whom 12,507 were listed as foreign nationals.[41] This early figure demonstrates that there already existed some measure of distinguishing between the Jews considered to be natives and those considered to be foreign (or who sought foreign nationality for improved economic opportunity). By the 1917 census, the figure jumped to 59,581 with 34,601 listed as foreign nationals.[42][43] In the census classifications, nationalities were separated by race with Egyptians between differentiated into Arab, Armenian, Greek, or Jew whereas British, French, and Italian nationals were divided into categories of Egyptian, Maltesian, or Jew.[44] It is interesting to note this confusing overlap of categories in such an early day of nation-state citizenship categorization where the term 'race' takes on a broad social, anthropological sense that lends itself to overlapping and vague labels. Despite the unclear inconsistencies, Jews are held to be a different category than Egyptian Arab[45] and were often lumped together as a minority group other which gave no attention to the vast difference in "wealth and social position, political commitments, cultural norms, or historical roots,"[46] a reality that would be especially significant when the distinction between Jewish and Zionist became muddled.

The multicultural, multinational sense of diversity[47] brought many perks but also contributed to the sense of an unclear place of Jews in Egyptian society; those who did not learn to read and write Arabic and who attended foreign schools were likely similarly motivated to give their children what they perceived as the best available educational preparation just as Moroccans during this time period; however, these choices led to the Egyptian perception of Jewish superiority and a lack of interest in the country's future struggle for independence. Unlike the expanse of AIU schools in Morocco teaching French language and culture but also religion, Jewish education in Egypt was restricted to a small population despite efforts made in the early 1900s by a handful of Zionist leaders. Though there were several attempts to open religious institutions such as a yeshiva or a community center for Hebrew-language instruction in Cairo and Alexandria, traditional Jewish education was losing potential participants to the expansion of Western, secular education that was taught mainly in French, Italian, or English.[48]

Similar to other Jewish communities in the region, Political Zionism failed at first to appeal to the Western-educated and upper-class Jews who saw "little incentive to risk their comfortable existence . . . to emigrate to Palestine."[49] However, the arrival of more than 11,000 Jews from the yishuv during and after the First World War, the stateless position of the majority of Egyptian Jews, news of Nazi anti-Semitism and the Holocaust, as well as the anti-Zionist Arab Nationalism that often blurred Zionism with Judaism in general all contributed to the growing strength and appeal of Political Zionism in the late 1930s and throughout the 1940s.[50] During this time in Egypt, Political Zionism found support in ha-Ivri ha-Tza'ir (The Young Hebrew), or the Egyptian branch of ha-Shomer ha-Tza'ir (The Young Guard).[51][52] Ha-Shomer ha-Tza'ir embraced Political Zionism and internationalism simultaneously, recapitulating biblical stories in a manner of affirming the ancient bond of Jews with Egypt, hence legitimizing simultaneously their residence in Egypt and their significance in the Jewish world. This history implicitly disputed the positions of Young Egypt and the Society of Muslim Brothers who were, by the late 1930s, antagonistic to the Jewish presence. Five days before the partition of Palestine, on November 24, 1947, the Egyptian representative in the United Nations General Assembly, Haykal Pasha, declared that

> the Arab governments will do all in their power to defend the Jewish citizens in their countries, but we all know that an excited crowd is sometimes stronger than the police. Unintentionally, you are about to spark an anti-Semitic fire in the Middle East, which will be more difficult to extinguish than it was in Germany.[53]

Indeed, a move directed against the Jews had already been made in July of that year, when the Company Law was signed on November 4, 1947. The law was ostensibly directed against foreigners, but among the main victims were the Jews. It stated that most company directors should be Egyptian nationals; while at that time about 20 percent of the Jews were foreign nationals, about two-thirds stateless and only 15 percent Egyptian nationals.⁵⁴ Until November 1947, ha-Shomer ha-Tza'ir opposed establishing a Jewish state and favored a binational Arab-Jewish state. Between 1938 and 1944, five branches of ha-Ivri ha-Tza'ir were established in Egypt, three in Cairo and two in Alexandria, with 700 to 800 members.⁵⁵ This figure is significant in demonstrating the limited popularity of Political Zionism among Jews in Egypt and the limited commitment to aliyah among those who identified with the narrative.

Following the First World War, the trend of aspiring to foreign nationalities among Egypt's Jews shifted toward Egyptian solidarity and patriotism as evidenced by a sudden rise in Jews enrolled in Arabic language lessons.⁵⁶ Indeed, among Egyptian Jewry there were those who spoke, read, and wrote Arabic fluently and even those who aligned themselves with their pro-Nasser, Marxist-Muslim brothers.⁵⁷ By the late 1930s, Jewish intellectuals had formed the Arabic Jewish weekly, al-Shams, which spoke of the "perfect harmony between all the elements constituting the Egyptian nation" and Egypt's chief rabbi, Rabbi Haim Nahum Effendi, called upon the Jews to adopt Egyptian nationality in the 1929 nationality law.⁵⁸ One example urging Jewish-Egyptian solidarity published in al-Shams in September 1944 stated, "It has never yet been heard of an Arab Jew to be opposed to something his government did."⁵⁹ Potentially able to act as loyal intermediaries between Egypt, Europe, and Palestine, Egyptian Jewish leaders failed to take hold among so many Jews left stateless. Despite their long-standing roots in the country, the majority of the Jews were culturally Western-oriented and educated or conservative and held themselves outside the mainstream Egyptian society.

To the Egyptian government, Political Zionism, which, after all, aimed not at overthrowing the political and economic system of Egypt but at creating a national home for the Jews outside the country (though regrettably in neighboring Palestine), seemed much less dangerous than its greatest rival among Jewish youth, communism. The belief grew that "not only were all Jews potential Zionists, but that anyhow all Zionists were communists, and . . . this communist/Zionist combination in connection with the Palestine affair was a danger to all non-communist states."⁶⁰ Indeed, as nationalism and anti-colonial movements grew in popularity throughout the region, Egyptian Jews were forced to respond by attempting to integrate into the Arab-Islamic majority, openly protest and stress ethnic and religious particularism so as to distinguish themselves from the Political Zionist movement, or leave. Shamir recounts the view that Political Zionism opened an "elegant (and inexpensive) way of getting rid of those elements of the community that seemed either unable or unwilling to integrate into Egyptian society and thereby created added job opportunities" for Muslim and Coptic employees and high school graduates looking for employment.[61] It is therefore not surprising that the Egyptian government, its anti-Zionist position notwithstanding, did very little to restrict massive Jewish emigration. By 1949, large-scale emigration was being organized by Zionist emissaries both within Egypt and from Israel and by 1952, 20 to 25 percent of the community, "most of them members of the lower and lower-middle classes," left Egypt for Israel.[62]

Lucette Lagnado's memoir about her family's exodus from Cairo to New York paints a personal, moving story of the flourishing Jewish life in Egypt and the devastation of immigrating from their home.[63] Focusing primarily on her father, a man both fervently religious and equally engrossed in British and French culture and language, the various characteristics of his identity demonstrate the wide range of what it was to be Jewish in wartime and postwar Cairo. Recalling the impact of the Second World War, Lucette writes,

> Cairo was both protected from the Nazis' relentless march across Europe and Africa and profoundly affected by it. Tens of thousands of British troops were now stationed in and around the city. . . . To those who resented the colonial influence and wanted Egypt for the Egyptians, the English were a hated reminder of the foreign domination that had to end, war or no war. But for the Jews and foreigners who lived in terror of the Nazis, les Anglais were their only hope—their protectors and benefactors.[64]

This memory highlights two interesting points. First, in contrast to the anti-Semitic Vichy regime of the French colonial realm, the experience of British colonial Egypt is demonstrated by the reference of crowded movie theaters and cafes. Second, Lucette's point that the war brought the Jews closer to their colonial presence while isolating others for their distaste for foreign domination is similar to Morocco in one regard, that it distanced Moroccans from the colonial power. A distinct difference, however, is that due to the fall of France and the implementation of Vichy rule, Jews and Muslim Moroccans alike grew to feel betrayed or frustrated with the Protectorate regime.

The history of Moroccan and Egyptian Jews is similar for their presence in the region predating the arrival of Islam. This historic longevity does not negate their status as a minority but reveals the centuries of Jewish existence and influence there. Just as with the coming of the AIU and the appeal for European privileges and opportunities in Morocco, the European presence in Egypt presented socioeconomic opportunities for the Jews; however, its Ottoman past and increased diversity of the Jewish communities within Egypt led to unclear citizenship statuses that could both be advantageous and increase vulnerability. Much like the slow rise of popularity for Political Zionism in Morocco, the narrative was not immediately attractive to Egyptian Jews. Two interesting points of contrast here, however, are the geographical proximity to the new State of Israel (seen to be significant both in terms of yishuv refugees and attitudes toward aliyah) and the attitude of the state toward Political Zionism. While Moroccan nationalists expressed disgust at the goals and ideology of Political Zionism and eventually embraced the communist parties into their narrative, Egypt's attitude toward Political Zionism was much more ambivalent or apathetic as a way to dismiss its Jews.

While both countries see the rise of nationalism during the end of the colonial periods, Morocco took on a more distinctive and uniquely Moroccan narrative. Egypt's Nasser and his commitment to pan-Arab nationalism certainly influenced the Moroccan nationalists as discussed in Chapter 5; however, the adherence to its Berber heritage and to Islam distinguishes Morocco. Furthermore, Nasser's nationalist narrative angered Islamists who rejected the nation-state specificity of nationalism and opted rather for the nation as the Muslim *umma*, whereas Morocco, through the endorsement of the sultan, was able to blend Arab and Islam more cohesively for the nation-state. Though Egypt can be seen to fit with the solar system model (Lagnado's 2007 memoir still sees Egypt as a homeland and further, one could claim it as a homeland since Moses led the Exodus from Egypt), Morocco remains unique for its continued Jewish presence in its postindependence era.[65] The dismissal of the Jews from the Middle East and Arab states cannot be disentangled from the politics of colonial rule but neither can their ability and choice to remain. In creating nation-sized units and introducing the resources and ideologies of nationalism to those who would organize against it, colonial influence cannot be divorced from any of the three primary narratives addressed herein.

Concluding Thoughts

The triangulation approach covers various perspectives of the Protectorate period, supplementing and complimenting existing scholarly literature with archives, some of which have only recently been made accessible, and personal accounts of Jewish life and identity during this time. The time frame 1870–1948 is a conscious decision in order to show the pre-Protectorate, "pre-war period, the war, its aftermath, the rise of nationalist narratives, and its by-product, decolonization."[66] Though a multidisciplinary and wide-reaching theoretical and empirical project, this book keeps to the role and experiences of Moroccan Jews during the Protectorate and the development of nationalist narratives and only briefly addresses the arrival of refugees and the existence of internment camps as the sultan's application of the Statut des Juifs protected Jews native to Morocco as subjects of dhimmi status.[67] A further limitation is the focus on the blad al-Makhzan with unequal representation of the blad al-siba. Joffé points out the fact that many Moroccan Jews during the Protectorate lived in the countryside and "the way in which (they) contributed towards independence for Morocco in 1956 is still little examined";[68] however, because the majority of Jews lived in the mellah and under the protection of the sultan, Jewish communities existed in and around the urban centers.

Having detailed the theoretical foundations and approaches for identity, memory, and nations and nationalism in Chapter 2, the triangulated secondary literature, archival materials, and semi-structured interviews provide a lens through which to see these theories in play. Indeed, the approach taken herein that regards identity as contextualized and social, as well as plural, dynamic, and fluid, is personified not only in the archived periodicals but especially in participant interviews. When the sociopolitical context changes, such as the destruction of French Jewry in the Second World War, identity shifts and renegotiates its plural traits and affiliations. In this sense, it is confirmed that identity is not static, but rather dynamic and, to further elaborate, not simply dynamic but fluid in the ability to balance pieces of plural affiliations in different amounts according to context. For instance, this fluidity is apparent in the ability to balance Political Zionist philanthropy with proud Moroccan citizenship and residence while enjoying the economic and cultural privileges of European commerce and culture.

In addition to the insistence on fluidity, the research moves beyond commonly accepted theories of nation and nationalism in applying the adaptive ethno-symbolism theory. The adaptive ethno-symbolist nation is a repository from which the political 'archaeologists' (nationalists) can select relevant myths, symbols, and memories in order to link past to future and vice versa. The meaning and use of the rediscovered, reinterpreted, and regenerated material may be manipulated and applied in ways completely foreign to its original reality and in this sense may be part of inventing the nation but the myths, symbols, and memories do not appear ex nihilo. This is certainly relevant in the postcolonial era where fledgling nations present a mélange of myths, symbols, songs, and so on in order to form the nation. In Protectorate-era Morocco, Moroccan nationalism took inspiration from Arab nationalism in the surrounding regions but the French language and Berber heritage sustained great influence. Just as in individual and collective identity studies, memory is essential in rediscovering, reinterpreting, and regenerating the myths and symbols that are put back together in the modern context to form the nation and its narrative.

I accept that memories are transient, changing, and volatile: "Some undergo changes in the course of time as one grows older and the living conditions are altered; some fade and are lost together."[69] The dynamic volatility of memory and the manipulation of it for different motives may affect the representation of the past due to the circumstances of the present moment; however, "those memories that are tied into narratives and are often rehearsed are best preserved"[70] and carry associations of deep meaning and emotion. The putting together of knowledge is sustained, shared, and given significance in and by society and repeated from generation to generation so that a "group of more or less the same age that has witnessed the same incisive historical events . . . share a common frame of beliefs, values, habits, and attitudes."[71]

In one sense, the memories of an individual "are dissolved with the death of the person who owned and inhabited them."[72] While this may be so insofar as one's death prevents a continued putting together and passing on of knowledge, the participation of that individual in society will have absorbed, enacted, and influenced the memories of the people in her encompassing groups of belonging. If memory can be so dynamic and volatile, why is it significant to remember the past and, more specifically, why is it important to remember the stories of Moroccan Jewry? Further, it is important to acknowledge that remembering rightly, with memory's fluidity implied, is not necessarily a fixed state of memory but rather an analytical framework that interplays with the state's recognition or lack thereof. Several scholars of memory address the power of memory (and forgetting) to incite fear and legitimize violence as well as its power to heal, warn against and prevent future violence and tragedy, and bring diverse communities together.[73] Knowing too much to "bask in complacent innocence" or knowing too little "to have clarity about how one must now come to terms"[74] with a tragic event, the healing power of knowing the truth can be significant in creating common space for memory among heterogeneous nations.

Volf devotes much of his work on the healing power of memory in terms of the role of memory in forgiveness.[75] Using his own past trauma, he connects remembering with struggle, but concludes that salvation and redemption can be found only in memory. Just remembering pleasant experiences can multiply pleasure as the original experience is remembered, so can remembering pain be extremely painful as its pain "breaks into the present and gains a new lease on life."[76] The response then to the question of 'why remember?' is both internal and external: remember internally to heal and find forgiveness (to be able to remain an ethical human), and remember externally to "honor (victims), protect them, render justice to them, (and) keep them in a sense alive."[77] The significance of collecting and preserving the stories of Holocaust survivors, for instance, is considered important in order "to guard against future horrendous acts but it's also used to maintain solidarity and defense against any threat to the nation."[78] Not to remember would be to fail the obligation of justice or to insult the victims of past atrocities[79] and, as a result, to remember past evils and suffering is to prevent against its reoccurrence.

In order to preserve and keep memory alive, stories need to continue to be put together and passed on. With the generation of Holocaust survivors growing older, it is significant to record not only the stories of those who suffered its most devastating consequences in their proximity to Europe but also the generation of Jews who experienced the persecution of European colonial powers and the Holocaust in different ways. The circumstances surrounding the decline of Morocco's Jews in the years following the establishment of the State of Israel witnessed the largest Jewish population in North Africa,[80] in both absolute and proportional terms, dwindling to an estimated 3,000 to 4,000. Of this small number, a smaller minority lived during the Protectorate period; for this reason, the empirical data presented herein is crucial documentation in a piece of Morocco's history. Miller reiterates this: "The period 1939-56 is fast fading from living memory, and the possibility of making use of the personal testimonies that illuminate our understanding of the past is slipping beyond the edge."[81] The vital work of collecting memories of the surviving participants in the dramatic events of the Protectorate and the Second World War is not only preserving a piece of Moroccan history but also preserving a time that demonstrates a chapter of Muslim-Jewish relations that cannot be repeated in the post-1948 world but should be remembered and reflected upon to prevent the ignorant oppositional dichotomy of Arab and Jew.

Furthermore, the original empirical data of this research is significant and should be remembered for the ways in which it highlights the capability of memory to achieve a sense of well-being, even for members of a minority in heterogeneous societies. Building on Sen's capability approach, I insist that memory not only is essential in identity and nation building but also has powerful potential to further human rights and well-being. Indeed, because memory is flexible and transformative, it can play a key role in transitions toward peace and the maintenance of well-being. The ways in which memory is constructed and wielded to justify violence and aggression are evident among nations and perpetrators of such acts; however, the fact that memory is dynamic means that it is equally capable of being wielded as a source of healing and well-being.

When individuals, victims and perpetrators alike, are given common space to remember, heterogeneous groups can construct a sense of belonging along communal memory. For instance, the May 2013 issue of *Zamane* did not merely include a glorification of Morocco's ancient Jewish path or pride in its continued presence; a piece entitled "Souvenirs of Anti-Judaism" addressed events that acknowledged Moroccan Jewish struggle and unfavorable acts committed against them. Writing of the Vichy era, the author states, "Bullying, teasing, pushing, and even massacres. In Morocco, where the coexistence between Jews and Muslims is a cultural and traditional reality, anti-Judaism (had) found its place."[82] By reaffirming Jewish-Muslim culture and tradition but acknowledging the existence of anti-Jewish acts, Moroccan Jews and Muslims alike construct the common space for memory. I claim that memory capability is a key factor in the ability of the participants who lived in the Protectorate period to continue to reside in Morocco today; their capability to construct memories from plural groups of belonging and reconcile them in their individual and national identity demonstrates the potential of memory to achieve well-being. Though the stories of Protectorate-era Moroccan Jewry are deeply contextualized, the theory of memory capability may have implications far beyond this case study.

Notes

Introduction

1. Grosrichard, R. 2013, p. 60.
2. Dans un monde arabe et musulman, marqué par le conflit israélo-palestinian et un antijudaïsme absurde ... le Maroc fait figure d'exception. La Constitution du pays reconnaît l'apport hébraïque à l'identité marocaine. Une communauté juive, réduite certes, continue à vivre au Maroc. Tourabi, A. 2013, pp. 40–1.
3. Miller, S. G. 2014, p. 462.
4. Julien, C. A. 1952, 1978.
5. Miller, S. G. 2014, p. 462.
6. Julien, C. A. 1978, p. 189.
7. Levisse-Touze, C. 1996, 1998.
8. Hoisington, W. A. Jr., 1984, 1995.
9. Baïda, J. 1996, 1999, 2010, 2013, 2014, Boum, A. 2006, 2010, 2013, 2014, Laskier, M. 1983, 1986, 2003.
10. The AIU was a French Jewish education program that aimed to aid Jews and Judaism in the emancipation and moral progress of the Jews, lend support to those who suffered because of their membership in the Jewish faith, and encourage publications to bring an end to Jewish sufferings. Laskier, M. 1983, p. 33.
11. Miller, S. G. 1999, 2001, 2013, 2014.
12. Secondary civil status of Christians and Jews under the rule of Islam as protected people of the Book. Deshen, S. 1989, p. 26.
13. Rivet, D. 2002.
14. Such as the Centre des Archives et Documentation of the French Ministry of Foreign Affairs at Nantes, the Vichy-Maroc series of the French Ministry of Foreign Affairs, now housed at La Courneuve, and the Centres des Archives d'Outre Mer in Aix en-Provence.
15. Kably, M. 2011.
16. Ibid., p. 618. See also Miller, S.G. 2014, p. 465.
17. Satloff, R. 2006, p. 9.
18. Here I drew from the periodicals *L'Action du Peuple, 1933-34, 1937* and *La Nation Arabe, 1930-39*.
19. *Maghreb, 1932-35* and *L'Avenir Illustrée 1926-40*.

20 Ministère des Affaires Etrangères. Archives diplomatiques, Nantes. Service Historique de la Defense- Fond de l'Armée de Terre, Chateau de Vincennes. Also in France, in Aix-en-Provence, rests the Centre des Archives d'Outre Mer.
21 Casablanca, Rabat, Marrakech, Fez, Essaouira.
22 This restriction will be explained in Chapter 7 in terms of the limits of the research implications for urban versus rural Moroccan Jewry. Furthermore, because the majority of Jewish organization resources are available in the urban centers, nearly all elderly Moroccan Jews reside there.
23 Further complicating the precise number is the consideration that many will have family outside of Morocco with whom they reside during parts of the year though they retain a residence in Morocco. Regardless, the general trend is that of a diminishing population from within a smaller portion who will have lived during the Protectorate.
24 The World Religion Database census data from 2008 lists 4,715 or 0.01 percent of the population, whereas Ynet News, the online Israeli news site of *Yedioth Ahronoth*, an Israeli newspaper, estimates around 3,000 Jews in Morocco as of July 2013. http://www.ynetnews.com/articles/0,7340,L-4364864,00.html
25 Lawrence, A. 2012, p. 480.
26 Duara, P. 1995, p. 152.
27 Appadurai, A. 1988, Boum, A. 2010, p. 52, Kenbib, M. 2010, p. 24, Meiland, J. W. 1980, p. 16, Pratt, M. L. 1992, and Trouillot, M. R. 1997, p. 71.
28 Kenbib, M. 2010, p. 26.
29 Boum, A. 2010, p. 73.
30 Ibid., p. 79.
31 Ibid., p. 82.
32 Levy, A. 2001, p. 247.
33 Ibid., p. 18.

Chapter 1

1 Özkirimli, U. 2000, p. 58.
2 Kaufmann, E. 2004, p. 3.
3 The presence of scholarly journals such as *Nations and Nationalism, Nationalism and Ethnic Politics, National Identities, Citizenship Studies, Ethnic and Racial Studies*, and *Journal of Ethnic and Migration Studies*, as well as academic departments and conferences devoted to the topic illustrate this point.
4 Brubaker and Cooper challenge identity as a category of practice versus a category of analysis before suggesting that identity as a concept be abandoned in academia. 2000.

5 Arendt, H. 1958, Honneth, A. 1995a, Horowitz, D. 2000, Lowrance, S. 2006, Maalouf, A. 2003, and Tajfel, H. 1981 to name a few.
6 See Margalit, A. and Joseph Raz, 1990, Brown, D. 1994, and Taylor, C. 1989, 1994.
7 Hobsbawm, E. 1992, Sen, A. 2006, and Somer, M. 1994 in particular.
8 Leading works include Breuilly, J. 1982, Brubaker, R. 1998, 2004, 2012, Gellner, E. 1983, Hobsbawm, E. 1992, Hutchinson, J. and Anthony Smith, 1994, Özkirimli, U. 2000, 2003, and Smith, A. D. 1983, 1986, 1991, 1995, 1998, and 2001.
9 Kenneally, C. 2014.
10 Horowitz, D. 2000, p. 50.
11 Sedmak, C. 2010, p. 515.
12 Human capability here refers to the "potential to realize possibilities; they are means to transform a possibility into an actuality . . . means of changing a situation," ibid., p. 516.
13 Kaufmann, E. 2004, p. 1.
14 Ibid., p. 2.
15 Satloff, R. 2006, p. 2.
16 Schroeter, D. 2002, p. xvi.
17 Lowrance, S. 2006, p. 168.
18 Arendt, H. 1958, p. 41.
19 Lowrance, S. 2006, p. 169.
20 Maalouf, A. 2003, p. 120.
21 Tajfel, H. 1981, p. 255.
22 Honneth, A. 1995b.
23 Explored in depth by Zurn, C. 2005, pp. 89–126.
24 Margalit, A. and Joseph Raz. 1990, pp. 439–48.
25 Ibid., p. 449.
26 Zubaida, S. 2011, p. 9.
27 Taylor, C. 1994.
28 Ibid., p. 34.
29 A connection for Taylor here is the process of finding identity in a space of morality. For instance, questioning what the meaning of life or what it means to find the good life are questions in which one locates her identity. Taylor, C. 1989.
30 Kedourie, E. 1993, p. 141.
31 Hobsbawm, E. 1992, Maalouf, A. 2003, Sen, A. 2006, to name a few.
32 Howbsbawm, E. 1992, p. 123.
33 Ibid., p. 124.
34 Arendt, H. 1958, p. 181. Arendt's work on the social-political behaviors of humankind examines the social nature of human beings and the construction of political life as a venue for individuals to achieve freedom by constructing societies. See Arendt, H. 1951, 1998.

35 Cooper, F. 2005, p. 9.
36 Maalouf, A. 2003, p. 13.
37 Ibid.
38 Sen, A. 2006, p. xiii.
39 Brown, D. 1994, p. 1031.
40 Maalouf, A. 2003, pp. 23–5.
41 Ibid., p. 25.
42 Maalouf, A. 2003, p. 132.
43 Fenton, S. 2010, p. 72.
44 Somer, M. 1994, p. 605.
45 Ibid., p. 621.
46 Ibid., p. 625.
47 Kedourie, E. 1993, p. 2.
48 Margalit, A. 1997, pp. 83–4.
49 Influential to the French Revolution and Enlightenment ideals, Jean-Jacques Rousseau's ideas in *The Social Contract* identify and justify the ideals of classical republicanism with reforms designed to ensure that humans become fully formed members of society through its nurture. In order to do so, the nation must take "men as they are and laws as they might be" (book 1, chapter 1 and 6). See Rousseau, J. J. 1987; 2010, pp. 115–16.
50 Another 'founding father' of the modern nation and nationalism, Johann Gottfried Herder's celebration of national folk cultures formed a foundation for the achievement of national sovereignty and supported the idea of the nation as a natural and unique collective whose cultural heritage is a necessary and powerful force of human creativity. See Herder, J. G. 1966, 2004.
51 Smith, A. 2013, p. 2.
52 Gellner, E. 1983, p. 7.
53 Anderson, B. 2006, p. 848.
54 Smith, A. D. 1995, pp. 3–23.
55 Smith, A. D. 2003, p. 368.
56 Pierre van den Berghe, Joshua Fishman, and Stephen Grosby to name a few.
57 Smith, A. D. 1995, p. 3.
58 Fenton, S. 2010, p. 86.
59 Noteworthy perennialists include Anthony Smith, John Armstrong, Adrian Hastings, and Walker Connor.
60 Smith, A. D. 1995, p. 10.
61 For the *perennial* argument, Smith gives the example of Masada in modern Israel where its historical significance was taken up after generations to be interpreted as a heroic affirmation of national will and dignity in the face of persecution. This shows the 'bedrock of the nation' in a modern application. Ibid., p. 13.
62 Özkirimli U. 2003, p. 341.

63 Ibid., p. 347.
64 Özkirimli U. 2000, p. 48.
65 Smith, A. D. 1995, p. 5.
66 The most oft-cited *modernists* include Ernest Gellner, Benedict Anderson, Eric Hobsbawm, Anthony Giddens, among others. Ibid.
67 Gellner, E. 1983, p. 140.
68 Smith, A. D. 1995, p. 5.
69 Ibid., p. 36.
70 Ibid.
71 Meadwell, H. 2012, p. 565.
72 Ibid.
73 Hastings, A. 1997, p. 9.
74 Hobsbawm, E. and Ranger, T. 1983, p. 13.
75 Taylor, C. 1997, pp. 32–3.
76 Ibid., p. 3.
77 Orwell, G. 1949, p. 284.
78 Taylor, C. 1997, p. 3.
79 Ibid., p. 13.
80 Hastings, A. 1997, pp. 31–2.
81 Ibid.
82 Eriksen, T. H. 1991b, pp. 263–4.
83 Gans, C. 2003, p. 28.
84 Eriksen, T. H. 1991b, p. 269.
85 Where binary understandings exist, national identity and nationalism become a dangerous narrative of 'us versus them' exceptionalism. See Glover, J. 2001 and Nathanson, S. 1997), pp. 176–90.
86 Glover, J. 1997, pp. 22–3.
87 Augustine, 2008.
88 Locke J. 1694, Reprinted in John Perry John, *Personal Identity*. 1975, p. 51.
89 Halbwachs, M. 1925.
90 Taylor, C. 1989.
91 Lichtenberg, J. 1997, pp. 160–2.
92 Assmann, A. 2006a, p. 211.
93 Assmann, J. 1988, p. 129.
94 Margalit, A. 2004, p. 45.
95 Yerushalmi, Y. 1982, p. 62.
96 Deuteronomy is full of appeals and commands to remember. For instance, "Remember the days of old, consider the years of ages past" (Deut. 32:7). "Remember what Amalek did to you" (Deut. 25:7). And with hammering insistence, "Remember that you were a slave in Egypt" (Deut. 5:15, 15:15, 16:12, 24:18). Volf, M. 2006, p. 1051.

97 Margalit, A. 2004, p. 203.
98 Assmann, A. 2006a, pp. 210–24.
99 Assmann, A. 2006a, p. 264.
100 Volf, M. 2006.
101 Arendt, H. 2006.
102 Surely context is significant in remembering; even in shared memories, individuals will have different vantage points from which they remember the event. In this sense, the individuals may "own a set of exclusive memories," but the discrepancies are embedded in the same event. Assman, A. 2006, p. 212.
103 Fragmentary here refers to both the sense that one's memory may not represent the entire scene of a specific episode and the fragmented nature of recollection where memories may "flash up . . . within a network of seemingly random associations without order, sequence, or cohesion." Ibid., p. 213.
104 Winter, J. 2012.
105 Assmann, A. 2006a, p. 212.
106 Ibid., p. 210.
107 Ibid.
108 Margalit, A. 2004, p. 40.
109 Plato's *Phaedrus* (423–348 BCE) explores the connection of memory and external influence in the way that "calling things to remembrance" by relying on "that which is written" can alter or diffuse memory into reminders thereby demonstrating the extent to which memory is socially affected or altered. However, "If a man makes right use of such means of remembrance . . . he and he alone becomes truly perfect." See Plato, 1995 and Nicholson, G. 1999.
110 Augustine, 2008, pp. 185–6.
111 Margalit, A. 2004, p. 40.
112 Ibid., p. 136.
113 Hopkins, L. and McAuliffe, C. 2010, p. 55.
114 Durkheim, E. 2014.
115 Ibid., p. 92.
116 Ibid.
117 Volf, M. 2004, p. 92.
118 Assman, A. 2006a, p. 216.
119 Ricoeur, P. 2004, p. 56.
120 Volf, M. 2006, p. 126.
121 Volf, M. 2006, p. 126.
122 Kedourie, 1993, p. 51.
123 Volf, M. 2006, p. 128.
124 Ibid., p. 60.
125 Plato, *Phaedrus*, Trans. by Paul Woodruff and Alexander Nehamas (Hackett Publishing Company, Inc., [1956], 1995).

126 Volf, M. 2006, p. 64.
127 Wiesel, E. 1990, p. 239.
128 Margalit, A. 2004, p. 54.
129 Ibid., p. 55.
130 Ibid., p. 74.
131 Ibid., p. 81.
132 Assmann, J. 1988, pp. 126–7.
133 Freeman, M. in Radstone, S. and Schwarz, B. (eds.). 2010, p. 263.
134 Assmann, J. 1988, p. 130.
135 Radstone, S. and Schwarz, B. 2010, p. 3.
136 Nora, P. 1989, p. 18.
137 George Orwell's *1984* poses this question, "How could you make appeal to the future when not a trace of you, not even an anonymous word scribbled on a piece of paper, could physically survive?" 2013, [1949], p. 32.
138 Ibid., p. 15.
139 Radstone, S. and Schwarz, B. 2010, p. 554.
140 Halbwachs, M. 1997, p. 132.
141 Zerubavel, Y. 1995, p. 14. By reshaping Jewish memory, Zerubavel is referring to the reinterpretation of the defense of Masada against the Romans in 73 CE or the Bar Kokhba revolt of 133–136 CE where tragedy and death is being envisioned as a symbol of national revival and right to the land.
142 Gurr, T. R. 1994, p. 348.
143 Ibid.
144 Tonnesson, S., and Antlov, H. 1994, pp. 850–1.
145 Gellner, E. 1983, p. 53.
146 Gurr, T. R. 1994, p. 348.
147 Fishman, J. A. 1976, p. 5.
148 Schildkrout, E. 1979, p. 13.
149 Brown, D. 1994, p. 1029.
150 Horowitz, D. 2002, p. 57.
151 Ibid.
152 Fishman, J. A. 1976, pp. 59–60.
153 Eriksen, T. H. 1991b, p. 265.
154 Fenton, S. 2010, p. 187.
155 Eriksen, T. H. 1991b, p. 265.
156 Ibid., p. 22.
157 Hobsbawm, E. 1992, p. 108.
158 Brubaker, R. 2013, pp. 1–20.
159 Conversi, D. 2000, pp. 134–5.
160 Weber, M. 1978, p. 61.
161 Brown, D. 1994, p. 1039.

162 Zubaida, S. 2011, p. 25, 117.
163 Eriksen, T. H. 1991b, p. 263.
164 Fenton, S. 2010, p. 93.
165 Ibid., p. 199.
166 Horowitz, D. 2002, p. 7.
167 Ibid., p. 8.
168 Shamir, S. 1987, p. 74.
169 Horowitz, D. 2000, p. 89.
170 Ibid.
171 Hutchinson, J. 2005, p. 41.
172 Anderson, B., 2006, Barth, F., 1998, Campbell, D., 1992, Gellner, E., 1983, Horowitz, D., 2000, Kedourie, E., 1993, Tonnesson, S., and Antlov, H., 1994.
173 Tonnesson, S. and Antlov, H. 1994, p. 844.
174 Hobsbawm, E. 1992, p. 136.
175 Gans, C. 2003, pp. 12–13.
176 Gellner, E. 1983, p. 6.
177 It is significant to note that though the ideas of nation and nationalism now hold a meaning and resonance in a universal sense, Gellner and Kedourie both remind the reader that this was not always so—an important reminder for the reading of Islamic political contexts when considering the universal applicability of these terms.
178 Eriksen, T. H. 1991b, p. 264.
179 Hastings, A. 1997, p. 4.
180 Eriksen, T. H. 1991b, p. 266.
181 Glover, J. 1997, p. 12.
182 Eriksen, T. H. 1991b, p. 266.
183 Özkirimli, U. 2000, p. 60.
184 Statist nationalism holds that in order for states to realize political values such as democracy, economic welfare, and distributive justice, the citizenries of states must share a homogeneous national culture. Gans, C. 2003, p. 15.
185 Cultural nationalism holds that members of groups sharing a common history and societal culture have fundamental, morally significant interest in adhering to their culture and in sustaining it across generations. Gans, C. 2003, p. 7.
186 Gans, C. 2003, p. 7.
187 Smith, A. 1981, pp. 19–20.

Chapter 2

1 Kalmar, I. D. and D. Penslar. 2005, pp. 85–6.
2 Cohen, M. 1994, p. xviii.
3 Deshen, S. 1989, p. 26.

4   Ye'or, B. 1985, p. 143.
5   Cohen, M. 1994, p. 119.
6   Ye'or, B. 1985, p. 151.
7   Hirschberg, H. Z. 1974, p. 22.
8   Deshen, S. 1989, p. 2.
9   Eickelman, D. 1985, p. 186.
10 Deshen, S. 1989, p. 2.
11 Both words come from Hebrew roots meaning indigenous and expelled, respectively. While this distinction would gradually fade, tension existed between indigenous or native *toshavim* and those who had fled Spain after the fall of Granada in 1492, the *megorashim*. This distinction is significant because by the eve of the Protectorate, the *toshavim* were spread between urban and rural areas while the Sephardic *megorashim* were primarily located in urban areas. Jewish communities of the rural areas were often more integrated in Tamazight (Middle-Central High Atlas) and Tashelhit (High Atlas and Souss) Berber speaking communities, whereas those in urban areas spoke Arabic and Haketiya, a Judeo-Spanish dialect. Gottreich, E. 2007.
12 Deshen, S. 1989, p. 42.
13 Ibid.
14 Brown, K. L. In Morag, S., Ben-Ami, I. and Stillman, N. (eds.). 1981, p. 258.
15 Ibid.
16 The model for the theoretical legal status of non-Muslim *dhimmis*.
17 Kenbib, M. 2010, p. 26.
18 Deshen, S. 1989, p. 91.
19 Thomson, 1889, Sloushchz, 1927, Montagne, 1930.
20 Boum, A. 2013, p. 29.
21 *Mellah*, from the Hebrew word for salt, refers to the walled, Jewish quarter of a Moroccan city.
22 Brown, K. L. In Morag, S., Ben-Ami, I. and Stillman, N. (eds.). 1981, p. 254.
23 Deshen, S. 1989, p. 99.
24 Miller, S. G. 1999, p. 109.
25 Hart, D. M. 1976, p. 280.
26 Ibid.
27 Ibid. p. 63.
28 Holden, S. E. 2010, pp. 150–1.
29 Brown, K. L. In Morag, S., Ben-Ami, I. and Stillman, N. (eds.). 1981, p. 263.
30 Ibid., p. 164.
31 Schroeter, D. 1993, p. 75.
32 This concept of *Gallicization* will be addressed with the arrival of the French. Brown, K. L. In Morag, S., Ben-Ami, I. and Stillman, N. (eds.). 1981, p. 267.
33 Deshen, S. and Zenner, W. 1996, p. 121.

34 Larhmaid, A. 2010, p. 61.
35 Sami Zubaida's recent work, *Beyond Islam: A New Understanding of the Middle East*, details how "it is capitalism that ushers in diverse processes of social transformation. . . . From this perspective, modernity in diverse parts of the world is not the product of cultural influences, imitations and 'invasions' from the West but the consequence of transformation of social relations, powers and authorities brought about by sweeping socio-economic forces." 2011, p. 5.
36 Laskier, M. M., Reguer, S., Simon, R. S., and Stillman, N. 2003, p. 62.
37 Wyrtzen, J. 2009, pp. 41–2.
38 Deshen, S. 1989, p. 41.
39 Ibid., pp. 41–2.
40 Laskier, M. 1983, p. 151.
41 Tangier became an International zone in 1923 and was administered by a legislative assembly that represented the following nations: France, England, Spain, Portugal, the United States, the Soviet Union, Belgium, Italy, and Holland. Laskier, M. 1983, p. 41.
42 Wyrtzen, J. 2009, pp. 13–4.
43 Ibid., p. 43.
44 Schroeter, D. 2002, pp. 3–4.

Chapter 3

1 Miller discusses the widespread availability of radios as a key factor in the spread of national sentiment and awareness. 2014, p. 469.
2 In the precolonial era, the Berber speakers, isolated in the mountains, were outside the scope of the Sultanate in the *blad al-siba* while Arabic speakers were under the control of the Sultanate in the *blad al-Makhzen*. Joffé, E. G. H. 1985, p. 292.
3 Hoisington, W. 1995, p. 433.
4 The implication being that pre-Protectorate Morocco was a primitive disorderly place. SHD-AT. Carton 305. Extrait du rapport du directeur de l'office du Protectorat de la République Française au Maroc. A/S de la participation du Maroc.
5 Bernard, S. 1968, p. 8.
6 Laskier, M. 1983, p. 152.
7 Ibid., p. 151.
8 Wyrtzen, J. 2009, p. 2.
9 إنه واجب على كل واحد (كل الأشخاص) يستطيع ان يقف في وجه فرنسا، عدو الدين الاسلامي، ويعارضها بالدليل والوثائق والأحتجاجات امام الملوك والأمراء والرجال العادلين والدول العادلة: هو واجب عليهم أن يأتون لمساعدة أخوانهم البربر أخيراً وأن يدافعوا عن تراث الدين الأسلامي وعن تقاليد وحقوق الدين.

SHD-AT, Carton 3H 247, Office de Liaison, Rabat. Renseignement, A/S manifestation anti-française en Lybie à l'occasion du dahir du 16 mai 1930 du Sultan du Maroc.

10 SHD-AT, Carton 3H 247. Office de Liaison, Rabat. Renseignement: Protestations d'elements destouriens du Caire a/s de l'indépendence religieuse accordée aux berbères du Maroc (November 27, 1930).

11 SHD-AT, Carton 3H 247, Office de Liaison, Rabat, Renseignement, Sujet: agitation de l'Association Universelle de la Jeunesse Musulmane a l'occasion du Dahir du Sultan du Maroc sur les tribus berbères (November 10, 1930).

12 Boum, A. 2010, p. 63.

13 Schroeter, D. 1994, p. 185.

14 Named for French, Jewish lawyer and statesman, Adolphe Crémieux, the Décret Crémieux allowed for European residents in Algeria and its native Sephardi Jewish community to become French citizens while Muslim Arabs and Berbers were excluded as having indigenous status.

15 Satloff, R. 2006, p. 28.

16 Laskier, M. 1983, p. 154.

17 The first AIU school was established in Tétouan in 1862 immediately after the Spanish occupation of the city (1860–2). Ibid., p. 32.

18 L'Avenir Illustre, January 9, 1930.

19 Ibid., p. 164.

20 MAE-Nantes, Direction de l'Interieur (DI), Questions Juives, Dossier I.

21 Ibid., pp. 164–5.

22 Laskier, M. 1983, p. 168.

23 Kosansky, O. 2010, p. 346.

24 Gottreich, E. B. and Schroeter, D. J. (eds.). 2010, p. 11.

25 Katz, J. G. 2010, p. 296.

26 Ibid., pp. 33–4.

27 Ibid., p. 64.

28 Ibid., p. 87.

29 Katz, J. G. 2010, pp. 283–4.

30 Originally called the International League against Pogroms, it remained LICA in 1929. Boum, A. 2014, p. 557.

31 Wyrtzen, J. 2009, p. 250.

32 Boum, A. 2014, p. 554.

33 Ibid., p. 559.

34 Interestingly, after surviving the camps (Dienien-Bou-Rezg and Djelfa), Lecache returned to Morocco in 1955 where he continued work with LICA. "The pro-entente movement survived into the 1970s, when PLO activist Issam Sartawi and Israeli leftist Uri Avnery launched an Israeli-Palestinian dialogue. In 1976, another

movement known as *Identité et Dialogue* was established in Paris by a Moroccan group." Ibid., p. 567.
35 Laskier, M. 1983, p. 253.
36 Ibid., p. 29.
37 MAE-Nantes, Series Maroc, Cabinet Diplomatique, Carton 670, Dossier General. Note from Director of Sharifian Affairs, State Section (May 28, 1937).
38 MAE-Nantes, Series Maroc, Cabinet Diplomatique, Carton 670, Dossier General. Letter from M. Avonde-Froment, Consul General of France in Tangier to Résident Général Noguès (July 4, 1938).
39 Gottreich, 2020.
40 "It is Israel as a whole rather than each Jew as an individual that must help France and its allies in gaining victory over the common enemy" *L'Avenir Illustre*, December 1939.
41 MAE-Nantes. Series Maroc, Direction de l'Interieur (DI), Carton 111. Letter from Col. Chevroton, Head of the Meknès Region to the Director of Political Affairs (November 15, 1944).
42 An exception was made in Tunisia where Jews could participate in the infantry, but Moroccan Jews, as subjects of the sultan, were still prohibited.
43 Wyrtzen, J. 2009, p. 30.
44 Satloff, R. 2006, p. 254.
45 Ibid.
46 The decree was published in the *Bulletin Officiel*, No. 1463, November 8, 1940, pp. 1054–5.
47 Satloff, R. 2006, p. 110.
48 Wyrtzen, J. 2009, p. 34. The census was not consistent among Moroccan cities with Casablanca being much more thorough than Fez, for example.
49 MAE-Nantes, Series Maroc, Direction de l'interieur (DI), dossier 6, "Statut des Juifs pendant la Second Guerre Mondiale" (August 1940–May 1945).
50 Abu-Lughod, J. L. 1980, p. 259.
51 Interestingly, Jews in the Spanish zone of Morocco lost none of their rights with Spanish government officials even appealing to Sephardic Jews in French Morocco to apply for Spanish nationality; however, this applied only to the *megorashim* Sephardic Moroccan Jews, a distinction that had become strenuous after several centuries.
52 AsZohraf, R. 2005, p. 455.
53 Satloff, R. 2006, p. 38.
54 AsZohraf, R. 2005, p. 466.
55 Anglo-American troops did not immediately liberate the victims of Vichy France but rather deferred to the defeated Vichy officer in all local matters. Free French eventually restored Jewish rights in late 1943. Satloff, R. 2006, p. 38.

56 Baida, J. 2014, p. 518.
57 Ibid., p. 519.
58 Hoisington, W. 1984, p. 241.
59 Kenbib, M. 2014, p. 547.
60 Ibid., p. 548.
61 Kenbib, M. 2014, p. 546.
62 Wyrtzen, J. 2009, p. 267.
63 Tsur, Y. 2001, p. 134.
64 Ibid.
65 Ibid.
66 Kenbib, M. 2014, p. 540.
67 Ibid., p. 541.
68 Ibid.
69 Ibid., p. 542.
70 Mais la guerre vient bousculer les esprits. Les juifs marocains prennent enfin conscience d'appartenir à une "nation" à part. Hatimi, M. 2013, pp. 48–9.
71 Hizb al-Istiqlal or Parti d'Istiqlal. The Arabic word Istiqlal is translated to Independence.
72 Kalmar, I. D. and Penslar, D. 2005, p. 67.
73 Kalmar and Penslar (2005) suggest an additional view that this binary arose also because Western and particularly Protestant missionaries longed for the return of the Christian messiah, before which long-awaited event Jews had to be found in every corner of the globe; thus Jews were 'invented' in the most remote regions to facilitate the Second Coming.
74 Kalmar, I. D. and Penslar, D. 2005, p. 51.
75 Alcalay, A. 1993, p. 196.
76 Widely debated and idealized, Said's 1978 text, *Orientalism*, came at a time of anti-Soviet and anti-American (anti-Western) opposition in the Islamic world. His presentation of orientalism challenged the binary of East and West that contributed to greater understanding of critical theory in postcolonial movements and sparked literary criticism that continues today. Said, E. 1978. See also, Varisco, D. M. 2013, pp. 52–4.
77 Said, E. W. 1978, pp. 82–3.
78 Varisco, D. M. 2004, pp. 93–112.
79 Lewis, B. 1982.
80 Lewis, B. 2004.
81 Schroeter, D. J. and Chetrit, J. 1996, p. 171.
82 Kalmar, I. D. and Penslar, D. 2005, p. 80.
83 Swirski, S. 1989, p. 7.
84 Dahan-Kalev, H. 2007, p. 8.

85 Ibid., p. 3.
86 Hochberg, G. 2004, p. 204.
87 Horowitz, D. 2000, p. 70.
88 Ibid., p. 72.
89 Bose, S. 2007, p. 211.
90 A Russian Jew, Jabotinsky first established the Jewish Self-Defense Organization to help defend against pogroms in Russia before joining the Sixth Zionist Congress in 1903. Though he was originally against expulsion of the Arabs from Mandatory Palestine, his 1923 article "Iron Wall" advocated a separate defensive force (the Haganah) to combat attacks and demonstrate the Jews' resiliency to the Arabs. Jabotinsky, V. 1923; See also, Massad, J. 1996, pp. 53–68.
91 Jabotinsky, Z. 1958, p. 29.
92 In 1882, the Jewish population of Palestine was estimated at 24,000. Karsh, E. 2002, p. 178.
93 Taylor, A. R. 1972, p. 41.
94 Herzl, T. 1896, p. 19.
95 Deshen, S. and Shokeid, M. 1982, p. 46.
96 Ibid., p. 39.
97 Karsh, E. 2002, p. 178.
98 Herzl, T. 1896, p. 53.
99 Taylor, A. R., 1972, p. 42.
100 Ibid., p. 53.
101 Karsh, E. 2002, p. 46.
102 Shenhav, S. R. 2006, p. 253.
103 Campbell, D. 1992, p. 199.
104 Kedourie, E. 1993, pp. 70–71.
105 Laskier, M. 1983, p. 195.
106 Ibid., p. 193.
107 Shenhav, S. R. 2006, p. 256.
108 Baron Maurice de Hirsch, German philanthropist and friend of the AIU, attempted to resettle and regenerate Jews through industrial and agricultural pursuits which led him to create the Jewish Colonization Association and purchase land in Argentina among other places. Though Herzl appealed to him to combine their efforts and provide a political organization in which to rally the Jews, de Hirsch refused and remained dedicated to his philanthropic endeavors. Schwarz, E. and Johan C. Te Velde. 1939, p. 185–203.
109 Herzl, T. 1896, p. 32.
110 Alcalay, A. 1993, p. 222.
111 It is worth noting that the category *Mizrahim* came into use only after the Arab Jews arrived in Palestine, although the attitude toward them had already been defined during the process of their immigration. The collectivity referred to as the Mizrahim

did not exist prior to the establishment of the state, and it is an error to apply this term historically before it gained meaning in Israel. The grouping together of Jews from North Africa and the Middle East is, in itself, an example of the application of Orientalist attitudes. With time, Mizrahim came to denote a reappropriated identity claimed by Arab Jews in response to their shared marginalization within the framework of the Jewish state on the basis of their origin—a hybrid identity produced by both assimilationist policy and the resistance to it. Regardless of their differing experiences in their countries of origin, Arab Jews were described as primitive and incapable of intellectual understanding. Although Jews were exposed to European colonial presence, customs, and languages, they are said to be "savage and primitive." Kalmar, I. D. and Penslar, D. 2005, p. 173.
112 Kalmar, I. D. and Penslar, D. 2005, p. 168.
113 Ibid., p. 167.
114 Ibid., p. 175.
115 Jabotinsky, Z. 1927, p. 213.
116 Ibid., p. 221.
117 Alcalay, A. 1993, p. 223.
118 Laskier, M. 1983, p. 43.
119 Ibid., p. 196.
120 Ibid., p. 197.
121 MAE-Nantes, Cabinet Diplomatique, Carton 668, Dossier 1, Letter from Col. Berriau, head of Intelligence Service, to Adjunct Secretary General of the Protectorate, Cabinet Diplomatique (November 24, 1918). "Il est douteux que l'exode sioniste aura quelqu'un d'autre que les personnes âgées et les démunis du Maroc à Jérusalem."
122 Laskier, M. 1983, p. 199.
123 Wyrtzen, J. 2009, p. 14.
124 MAE-Nantes, Series Maroc, Cabinet Diplomatique, Carton 670, Dossier General, "Etude sur le Sionisme au Maroc" (April 3, 1945).
125 Laskier, M. 1983, p. 199.
126 Ibid., p. 195.
127 Ibid., p. 157.
128 Boum, A. 2010, p. 55.
129 The Arab press came out strongly against what they perceived to be the influence of Jews in England: "Finance and economy, administration and British Parliament, these are the preferred domains of the Jewish demon." "L'influence des Juifs et la crise morale en Angleterre," *La Nation Arabe*, No 8, V Année, Janvier–Avril 1936, p. 475. "Les finances et l'économie, l'administration et le Parlement britannique sont les domains prefers du dèmon israélite."
130 "Les Juifs ont tout calculé sauf la presence des Arabes en Palestine," *La Nation Arabe*, No 9, V Année, Mai–Août 1936, p. 604. "C'est un fait que le peuple juif a été

l'objet de persécutions à travers les siècles et il continue à l'être malheureusement, surtout dans les pays civilisés. Il n'y avait que les Arabes qui lui avaient toujours témoigné un sentiment de sympathie et de pitié, provenant peut-être de la parenté de race . . . Jusqu'à la proclamation de la promesse Balfour, cette harmonie entre l'Islam et le Judaisme etait parfaite."

131 "Pourquoi l'entente est impossible avec les Juifs," *La Nation Arabe,* No 9, V Année, Mai–Août 1936, p. 567.
132 Laskier, M. 1983, pp. 212–13.
133 Ibid., p. 37.
134 MAE-Nantes. Series Maroc, Cabinet Diplomatique, Carton 668, Dossier 2. Letter from Counselor to the Sharifian Government to the head of the Diplomatic Office in Rabat. 'Objet: Propagande sioniste au Maroc.'
135 Laskier, M. 1983, p. 213.
136 Ibid., pp. 322–3.
137 هذا ليس نداء نقوم به, بل هي الحقيقة التي نريد إعلانها. كل الدول التي تتحدث اللغة العربية هي بلادنا, ويجب علينا تحرير بلادنا.
المسلمون حول العالم أخوة، ويجب على الاخوة أن يتعانوا في وقت الشدة.
كل شخص أفريقي هو أخ وجار لباقي الناس في افريقيا، وكل جار له حق المساندة من جاره حتى يصل الجار الى الاكتفاء الذاتي ويصبح آمن وحر.
نحن الشرق، الذي يواجه طمع الغرب، أمة واحدة. هذه هي الاركان الأربعة لسياستنا في هذه المنطقة من العالم. نحن لا نريد القبلية الدينية أو القبلية العرقية أو الأرض، إنما نسعى – ولكن نحن العرب , نحن المسلمون، نحن الشعوب في الشرق - نسعى أن نصبح كتلة واحدة.

Nasser, G. A. 1954.
138 Ibid.

Chapter 4

1 Mitchel, H. 1955, p. 432.
2 Ibid., p. 40.
3 Segalla, S. D. 2009, p. 1.
4 Laskier, M. 1983, p. 151.
5 Wyrtzen, J. 2009, pp. 13–14.
6 Schroeter, D. 1988, p. 150.
7 Even those who dismiss the period 1912–29 as 'the hollow years' of Maghrebi nationalism acknowledge the Berber Dahir as a key catalyst toward mobilization. See Moreau, O. 2003, pp. 58–70, Ait Mous, F. 2013, pp. 737–52.
8 Miller, S. G. 2013, p. 159.
9 Ibid., p. 160.

10 Ait Mous, F. 2013, p. 739.
11 France removed the title of protégé and its benefits in 1930. Berque, J. 1967, p. 297.
12 Joffé, E. G. H. 1985, p. 291.
13 Ibid., p. 292.
14 Ibid., p. 293.
15 Ait Mous, F. 2013, p. 749.
16 Zisenwine, D. 2010, p. 6.
17 Liaisons between groups led to the formation of the Moroccan League (Ligue Marocaine) in 1926 based upon a shared respect for Salafism and distrust of the religious brotherhoods. Halstead, J. P. 1967.
18 Interestingly, Mohammed al-Fassi was the Crown Prince's tutor thereby giving him a link to the sultan, though the scope of his influence is not clear. Joffé, E. G. H. 1985, p. 302.
19 Schroeter, D. 1988, p. 160.
20 "Ce n'est pas par l'assimilation mais par la justice et l'égalité que la France peut réussir dans le Nord de l'Afrique," *La Nation Arabe,* No 4, V Année, Mars–Avril 1935, p. 262. "Il est inutile, et même sot, qu'on pense à Paris à franciser ou à christianiser les 17 millions de musulmans qui habitent le Maroc, l'Algérie et la Tunisie. Tant que la France, guidée par ses prêtres, ses colons, et ses militaires, nourrira l'illusion de pouvoir, avec le temps, substituer la langue française à la langue arabe, et le chretianisme à l'Islam, il n'y aura rien à faire entre Français et indigenes."
21 Because early reformists were from among the education Muslim elite, these local networks "and the actions and spaces around which they developed" were predominantly based in the urban sphere. Ait Mous, F. 2013, p. 738.
22 Schroeter, D. 1988, p. 170.
23 Segalla, S. D. 2009, p. 7.
24 Segalla puts forward the notion of educators as 'salesman of the empire.' See also Cooper, F. 2005.
25 Although the Makhzan retained its authority over traditional Islamic education, the French soon established a separate colonial school system. Segalla, S. D. 2009, p. 7.
26 Free meaning free of government control.
27 Damis, J. 1970, p. 240.
28 "Pour la securite de l'oeuvre franciase faut-il garder les marocains dans l'ignorance?" *Maghreb,* 1932.
29 "Annexes au Plan de Réformes Marocaines," *La Nation Arabe,* No 5, V Année, Mai–Juin 1935, p. 316. "Les sommes affectées à l'instruction des Marocains musulmans représentent, suivant les années, à peine 1,30 à 1,80 % du Budget de l'Etat marocain. Pour 7 à 8 millions de Marocains musulmans, dont la population d'age

scolaire est d'au moins 500,000 ames, il y a des écoles pour à peine 11,000 élèves. Par contre, la colonie européenne, qui est de 173,000 ames, bénéficie d'écoles pour plus de 30,000 élèves. Les israélites marocains, dont le nombre ne dépasse pas 118,000, ont une clientèle scolaire de plus de 10,500."

30 Lawrence, A. 2012, p. 476.
31 Segalla, S. D. 2009, p. 200.
32 Ibid.
33 Ibid., p. 208.
34 Ibid., p. 211.
35 "Al-Maghrebi," "Les aspirations du 'Maghreb,'" *Maghreb*, July 1932, p. 4. "modernisation de notre pays . . . mais nous nous accrochons aussi à notre passé, nos traditions, et nous ne sera jamais lâcher la flamme forte de l'Islam qui est si fortement planté dans le cœur de Barbarie."
36 Lawrence, A. 2012, p. 476.
37 Moore, C. H. 1970, p. 36.
38 Lawrence, A. 2012, p. 482. Further, "In France, student groups and workers had already spoken of independence for North Africa, and Moroccan leaders had contact with these groups during trips to France. Moroccan leaders also met with Arab nationalist Chakib Arslan, who travelled to Tetouan in 1936 to discuss nationalism. . . . Arslan was less interested, however, in encouraging local nationalisms than in promoting the unity of Arab countries. He supported pan-Maghrebism, or the unification of Algeria, Tunisia, and Morocco." See also Julien, C. A. 1952, p. 34.
39 Lawrence, A. 2012, p. 476.
40 Al-Fassi, A. 1954, p. 149.
41 Ibid.
42 Lawrence, A. 2012, p. 480.
43 Miller, S. G. 2013, p. 168.
44 See Gellner's definition of nationalism as the principle that the political and national unit should be congruent. 1983, p. 1.
45 Historically divided groups here refer to the *blad al-siba* and *blad al-Makzhan*.
46 Ait Mous, F. 2013, p. 747.
47 Lawrence, A. 2012, p. 479.
48 Hoisington, W. 1995, p. 47.
49 Joffé, G. 2014, p. 478.
50 Fought between colonial Spain and the Moroccan Berbers of the Rif mountainous region, France later assisted Spain to end the conflict in May 1925. See Pennell, R. 1986.
51 Ibid., p. 482.
52 Lawrence, A. 2012, p. 435.

53 Ibid.
54 Ibid.
55 Ibid.
56 Their inclusive progress is evident by its mention in Allal al-Fasi's reorganization of the Moroccan nationalist movement into twelve urban sections in 1937. Joffé, G. 2014, p. 485. AOM 27H5 Review de la Presse musulmane (Ministère des Colonies), No 1415-9/EMA (April 17, 1937) Paris.
57 "Consequences du dahir berbère," *Maghreb*, October 1932, pp. 6–7.
58 Al-Ouezzani, M. "20eme anniversaire de la politique berbère (1914-1934)," *Maghreb*, May–June 1934, p. 10. "Ce n'est rien mais un projet colonial machiavélique. Il symbolisait la croisade abominable menée par les impérialistes et les prêtres contre l'Islam et la culture arabe."
59 "Consequences du dahir berbère," *Maghreb*, October 1932, pp. 6–7.
60 Letter to the editor submitted to Socialist paper, *Le Cri Marocain*, republished in February 1933 edition of *Maghreb* and titled, "En Marge du dahir berbère," p. 36.
61 Hoisington, W. A. 1978, p. 437.
62 Despite the sultan's order against using mosques as political spaces, activists continued with the justification that "I did not think that anything would be done, because the Security services do not have the right to intervene in the mosques." This awareness demonstrates the strategy behind the Latif protests that attempted to evade the reach of the Protectorate security forces. SHD-AT 250, "Extraits des declarations du nomme Taieb Ben Hassan Janati" (November 1, 1937).
63 "L'oppression française au Maroc," *La Nation Arabe*, No 3, V Année, Janvier–Fevrier 1935, p. 201. Lorsque les nationalistes françqise liront cet article, ils se mettront en colère et commenceront à crier: "Ce sont les ennemis de la France qui répandent ces bruits et qui agitent, à dessein, le monde musulman contre nous! … Messieurs les Français, il ne s'agit ni de Berlin, ni de Londres, ni de New-York. Personne n'est complice dans l'agitation qui s'organise contre vous au Maroc, en Algérie, ou en Tunisie. Les seuls agitateurs qui remuent ces pays, ce sont vos propres fonctionnaires. C'est votre administration tyrannique et l'absence, chez vous, de toute notion de justice et d'égalité, lorsqu'il s'agit des indigènes, qui sont à l'origine de ce mouvement hostile à la France en pays musulmans."
64 Belafrej, A. "Et maintenant?" *Maghreb*, No. 11, May–June 1933, pp. 50–1.
65 Lawrence, A. 2012, p. 477.
66 Contributing to the sense of Islamization and Arabization following the Berber Dahir of 1930 was activity and outrage in other Arab states. Egyptian and Palestinian papers, for example, include among their nationalist propaganda calls for the abrogation of the Berber Policy. SHD-AT, Carton 3H 247, Report from Col. Margot, Service de la Presse Musulman, to Chef du Cabinet Militaire de Monsieur le Résident Général, A/S, Articles d'Al Fateh sur le Maroc (June 16, 1932). SHD-AT,

Carton 3H 247, Office de Liaison, Rabat. Renseignements: A/S Propagande nationaliste (June 23, 1932).

67 "Al-Maghrebi," "Les aspiration du Maghreb," *Maghreb*, July 1932, p. 4. "Si la modernisation exige que nous sacrifions notre propre personnalité, il est naturel que nous ne voulons pas. En somme, nous voulons moderniser tout restant nous-mêmes."

68 Pennell, C. R. 2000, p. 152.

69 "A nos lectures," *L'Action du Peuple*, No. 1, August 4, 1933. "Notre revue aura trois catégories de lecteurs: Nos compatriotes qui trouveront ici l'exposition de leurs idées et désirs; les autorités locales et métropolitaines trouveront l'éclairage nécessaire pour accomplir leur tâche; et les Français vivant au Maroc trouverez des informations indispensables pertinents pour tout ce qui touche les autochtones qui forment presque toute la population du pays."

70 Wyrtzen, J. 2010, p. 186.

71 Ibid., p. 189.

72 Kutlah al-Amal al-Watani or the Comité d'Action Marocaine, referred to herein as CAM.

73 Lawrence, A. 2012, p. 482.

74 Mitchell, H. 1955, p. 428.

75 To this point, the French administration had functioned nearly exclusively in French. Not only did this result in a burgeoning translation industry in the city but also meant that the average Moroccan was issued bank, passport, post office, and other information that he could not understand. This tactic, whether intentional or simply convenient, reinforced the French monopoly of power and required a great effort from Moroccans to puncture past the administrative periphery.

76 Lawrence, A. 2012, p. 486.

77 Ibid.

78 Hoisington, W. A. Jr. 1984, p. 47.

79 Schroeter, D. 1988, p. 179.

80 "Le Nord de l'Afrique," *La Nation Arabe*, No 5, V Année, Mai–Juin 1935, p. 339. "La situation de l'Afrique du Nord, au point de vue politique, économique et social, s'aggrave tous les jours sous les coups violents du colonialisme. En Tunisie, au Maroc, comme en Algérie, les populations musulmanes nord-africaines vivent sous le régime de la matraque et de la terreur."

81 Schroeter, D. 1988, p. 155.

82 Boum, A. 2010, p. 59.

83 Ibid.

84 Ben-Layashi, S. and Maddy-Weitzman, B. 2010, p. 97.

85 "Le scandale Abdellah ben Mohammed," *Maghreb*, December 1932, 17–19.

86 Al-Ouezzani, M. "La Politique berbère," *L'Action du Peuple*, August 18, 1933, 2.

87 Wyrtzen, J. 2009; p. 23.
88 Boum, A. 2010, p. 58.
89 MAE-Nantes, Series Maroc, Cabinet Diplomatique, Carton 668, Dossier 2, letter from Résident Général Lyautey to Minister of Foreign Affairs, "Questions Israelites. Les Juifs Marocains et le Sionisme" (September 17, 1919).
90 MAE-Nantes, Series Maroc, Cabinet Diplomatique, Carton 668, Dossier 2, letter from Résident Général Lyautey to Zionist Organization of London (June 26, 1926).
91 MAE-Nantes, Series Maroc, Cabinet Diplomatique, Carton 668, Dossier 2, letter from Résident Général Noguès to Minister of Foreign Affairs, "A/S Front national juif en Palestine" (November 6, 1936).
92 El-Kholti, M. "Les israelites et nous," *L'Action du Peuple*, August 18, 1933.
93 Al-Ouezzani, M. "La Politique berbère," *L'Action du Peuple*, August 18, 1933, 2.
94 L'amitie Judéo-Musulmane, *L'Action du Peuple*, September 1, 1933, p. 1.
95 Bendayan, I. 'Lettre ouvert a M. Kholti,' *L'Action du Peuple*, September 8, 1933.
96 El-Kholti, M. "Sionisme et patriotisme marocain," *L'Action du Peuple*, March 2, 1934. "Le Maroc est pour les Marocains, c'est pour les musulmans et les juifs. Il est notre devoir à collaborer ensemble pour défendre notre patrie. Dites-le une fois pour toutes que vous avez une patrie (pas 'la terre promise,' mais la terre où vous êtes maintenant) . . . Un marocain qui aime son pays doit aspirer à travailler pour elle . . . Naturellement, nos compatriotes peuvent être Juifs autant qu'ils le veulent . . . le sionisme est un facteur de domination à l'extérieur et le désordre dans le pays marocaine."
97 Yehuda, Z. 1985, p. 31.
98 Sammoun, A. "L'Amitie Judeo-Musulmane," *L'Avenir Illustre,* February 28, 1937, p. 4.
99 Bouhlal, A. "En marge du meeting de la L.I.C.A.," *L'Action du Peuple*, May 6, 1937, 3. "Restez dans cette grande famille qui est la nation marocaine où . . . ils ont vécu la compréhension mutuelle avec les compatriotes musulmans. (Conserver) l'union indissoluble entre les musulmans et les juifs, dans un cadre national strictement marocaine, pour le bien de notre patrie commune, pour l'intérêt général de notre collectivité."
100 Laskier, M. 1983, p. 323.
101 Ibid., p. 324.
102 Ibid., p. 42. After the United States recognized the State of Israel, the boycott was extended to all American products as well.
103 Sammoun, A. "Pour l'entente judeo-arabe au Maroc," *L'Action du Peuple*, July 1, 1937. "nous ne sommes ni marocaine, ni le français. Nous avons la situation d'être des Marocains lesquels vous attribuez librement charges mais non le moindre privilèges. Le jour où vous nous dire exactement ce que nous sommes, nous attribuant nos droits ainsi que nos privilèges en tant que citoyen, sera être le jour où nous prendrons une position."

104 El-Mesquine, "L'entente islamo-judaique ne peut se fair que dans le cadre nationale?" *L'Action du Peuple*, July 15, 1937, p. 3.
105 AsZohraf, R. 2005, p. 521.
106 Ibid.
107 The *Parti Démocratique de l'Indépendance* was a small nationalist faction that eventually broke away from *Istiqlal* in 1946. Joffé, E. G. H. 1985, p. 303.
108 SHD-AT, Carton 3H 250, Analyse d'un tract provenant du "Comite de defense du Maroc" (May 17, 1939).
109 One consequence of the riots and demonstrations was the disbanding of CAM which had renamed itself the National Action Party. The outlawed party later reestablished itself as the National Party for the Realization of the Plan of Reforms under Allal al-Fassi but they too were met with repression, not reform, and many of its leaders were exiled. Lawrence, A. 2012, p. 487; al-Fassi, A. 1954.
110 Joffé, E. G. H. 1985, p. 293
111 Ibid., p. 294.
112 Hoisington, W. 1995, p. 444.
113 Protectorate authorities outlawed key leaders including Allal al-Fassi (initially to Gabon and later to Congo); Mohammed Lyazidi, Omar Ben Abdeljalil, Ahmed Mekouar (all of whom were exiled to remote locations in the Sahara); and Mohammed al-Ouezzani (who was exiled to Itzer in the High Atlas). Schroeter, D. 1988, p. 178.
114 Lawrence, A. 2012, p. 478.
115 Ibid.
116 SHD-AT, Carton 3H 249, Rapport Mensuel sur la Situation Politique en Milieux Indigènes, Commandement Superieur des Troupes du Maroc, Fevrier 1944.
117 SHD-AT, Carton 3H 250, Report by General Noguès to Yvon Delbos, Minister of Freign Affairs, on Moroccan Nationalism (October 9, 1947), 31. "Nous ne avons plus le choix. Les mesures rigoureuses contre les dirigeants de la mouvement (nationaliste) . . . sont les seuls moyens pour assurer l'avenir du français au Maroc et en créer un nouveau climat qui nous permet de suivre notre action civilisatrice."
118 Wyrtzen, J. 2009, p. 138.
119 Ibid.
120 Zisenwine, D., 2010, p. 29.
121 Joffé, G. 2014, p. 485. AOM 27H6 Review de la Presse musulmane (Ministère des Colonies), No 2816-2/EMA, March 27, 1941, Paris.
122 Abitbol, M. 1989, p. 167.
123 Ben-Layashi, S. and Maddy-Weitzman, B. 2010, p. 96.
124 Abitbol, M. 1989, p. 170.
125 Schroeter, D. 1988, p. 192.
126 Joffé, E. G. H. 1985, p. 302.
127 Zisenwine, D. 2010, p. 9.

128 Mitchell, H. 1955, p. 429.
129 Ibid., p. 303.
130 Ait Mous, F. 2013, p. 748.
131 Joffé, E. G. H. 1985, p. 294.
132 Schroeter, D. 1988, p. 206.
133 Ibid., pp. 304–5.
134 Zisenwine, D. 2010, p. 61.
135 The most stable foundation of Jewish supporters for the nationalist movement was the Jewish communists. Leon Sultan, an Algerian Jewish settler in Morocco, established the Moroccan Communist Party in 1943 and had strong ties to the French Communist Party. After his death in 1944, a Muslim leader, Ali Yata, took control before joining forces with Istiqlal. Tsur, Y. 2001, p. 160.
136 Brignon, J. 1968, p. 396.
137 Dompnier, N. 2001, p. 71. "L'Assemblée Nationale donne les pleins pouvoirs au gouvernement de la République, sous l'autorité et la signature du Maréchal Pétain, à l'effet de promulguer par un ou plusieurs actes une nouvelle Constitution de l'État français. Cette Constitution doit garantir les droits du travail, de la famille et de la patrie. Elle sera ratifiée par la nation et appliquée par les Assemblées qu'elle aura créées."
138 Schroeter, D. 1988, p. 212.
139 SHD-AT, Carton 3H 251, Section des Affaires Politique, "L'Agitation Nationaliste" January–February 1944. "si le Sultan devait se aligner avec les nationalistes, il considérera avec lui la grande partie des chefs autochtones qui sont restés indécis et d'attente pour le Sultan de se déclarer, afin qu'ils puissent se declarer."
140 Referring again to the *blad al-siba* and *blad al-Makzhan*.
141 Joffé, E. G. H. 1985, p. 289.
142 By this time the "countryside had recovered from the war and the drought, and was ready to listen. News of the Sultan's speech spread rapidly, assisted by that modern invention, the radio." Ibid., p. 306.
143 Ibid.
144 Julien, C. A. 1978, pp. 199–201.
145 Though the manifesto signing included no Jewish signatures, "American intelligence agents stationed in Morocco reported continuous efforts by nationalist activists to reach out to . . . Moroccan Jews. Some of the new party's leaders sought to impart an all-Moroccan character to the party, and were interest in spreading their message among the country's Jewish population." Zisenwine, D. 2010, p. 50.
146 Tsur, Y. 2001, p. 76.
147 Ben-Layashi, S. and Maddy-Weitzman, B. 2010, pp. 98–9.
148 The sultan's support of the nationalist movement led to his eventual exile to Corsica and later Madagascar in the early 1950s; however, he was allowed back

in November 1955 and concluded an agreement with Paris for Morocco's full independence in February 1956. Satloff, R. 2006, 109.
149 Schroeter, D. 1988, p. 213.
150 Wyrtzen, J. 2009, p. 136.
151 Boum, A. 2010, p. 66.
152 Abitbol, M. and Astro, A. 1994, p. 249.

Chapter 5

1 Wyrtzen, J. 2009, p. 136.
2 Thank you to Vanessa Paloma and Younes Leghrari.
3 Further complicating the precise number is the consideration that many will have family outside of Morocco with whom they reside during parts of the year though they retain a residence in Morocco. Regardless, the general trend is that of a diminishing population from within a smaller portion who will have lived during the Protectorate.
4 The World Religion Database census data from 2008 lists 4,715 or 0.01 percent of the population whereas Ynet News, the online Israeli news site of *Yedioth Ahronoth*, an Israeli newspaper, estimates around 3,000 Jews in Morocco as of July 2013. http://www.ynetnews.com/articles/0,7340,L-4364864,00.html
5 Scott, J. C. 2008, p. 4.
6 Names have been changed per the IRB approval to protect the identity of research participants.
7 "L'Alliance c'est ma vie" (Zohra, 2013, Line 128).
8 "Dans le sens que les juifs les premiers ont profité du protectorat, parce qu'ils étaient déjà instruits et ils connaissaient le français. Je pense que c'est ça. Avec les écoles de l'Alliance, les enfants juifs parlaient français, apprenait le français. Et quand le protectorat est arrivé, les français ont trouvé le personnel le plus ... celui qui était le plus proche ... c'était les juifs qui connaissaient déjà le français. Je pense que c'est comme ça ... ça a été un avantage" (Zohra, 2013, Line 1–9).
9 "Nos écoles étaient inspectées par des inspecteurs français. Ici pendant le protectorat, tout était français. Les agents de police, c'était des français. Dans les administrations c'était des français. C'était eux qui tenaient tout" (Zohra, 2013, Line 71–4).
10 La Direction de l'Instruction Publique.
11 "C'était pour les juifs. C'était pas public. Mais on était aidés par le gouvernement. C'était pas public. En principe les musulmans pouvaient venir. Mais les musulmans ne venaient pas. C'était pour les juifs" (Zohra, 2013, Line 90–4).
12 "On vivait, on vivait comme en France vous savez, à peu près. Comme en France. Tout était français" (Zohra, 2013, Line 150–2).

13 "On avait une culture française. La France était très reconnaissante envers l'Alliance, qui dispensait, qui faisait apprendre le français et l'histoire de France. Et pas l'histoire du Maroc. Nos ancêtres les gaulois" (Zohra, 2013, Line 311–14).

14 Boum, A. 2013, Laskier, M. 1983, and Zafrani, H. 2002.

15 Boum, A. 2013, p. 72.

16 "Et bien quand ils entraient en classe, la maîtresse avant de passer en classe regardait si la culotte était propre . . . Ils passaient et ils soulevaient pour montrer la culotte . . . C'est vrai. L'Alliance, le personnel de l'Alliance, s'occupait de tout. S'occupait de tout" (Zohra, 2013, Line 558–64).

17 "Pendant Vichy, c'était pas beau. Le protectorat, sous Vichy, il y a eu un début de loi anti-juifs" (Zohra, 2013, Line 214–15).

18 "On était très bien dans in sens, et très mal dans l'autre. Très bien: on ne manquait de rien. Très mal: parce qu'on était loin de la ville. Et les médecins n'étaient pas tout ça fait ce qu'il fallait . . . Mais ça, pour les gens notables, mais pas pour tout le monde. Tout le monde avait le sucre ou le thé rationnés, mais pour nous il y avait les rations, plus que les rations. On était avantagés, c'est pour ça, les enfants, on n'a pas souffert du côté nourriture" (Zohra, 2013, Line 237–53).

19 "Le manque de confiance en la France, à partir du moment où Vichy est parti, y'avait plus de problème. Bon, c'était un mauvais moment, c'était la guerre, je pense, et voilà" (Zohra, 2013, Line 288–90).

20 "Les organisations sionistes avaient le contact avec les instituteurs. Ca a été personnel, mais on ne faisait pas de sionisme dans les classes. Vous comprenez ? Officiellement, on ne pouvait pas" (Zohra, 2013, Line 168–71).

21 "C'était dangereux. Pas interdit. Dangereux" (Zohra, 2013, Line 174).

22 The Bac, or baccalauréat, is the end-of-school diploma that students must sit in order to be admitted to university in France.

23 Literally 'the interior.' May refers simply to the city center but has further connotations to the taxable area under the control of the sultan labeled *Blad al-Makzhen* (in contrast to eh Blad al-Siba: the nontax paying areas in rebellion against the sultan's government in the High Atlas Mountains) during the French 'Pacification' period of 1912–25. For more detail refer to Chapter 4.

24 "Disons que le protectorat avait créé, on dirait, des 'espaces.' Des espaces musulmans. C'est à dire que les musulmans ne rentraient pas dans les villes. Ils n'avaient pas accès . . . L'Arabe devait rester dans le bled . . . Alors, les juifs avaient leur compartiment à eux . . . On vivait à peu près en vase clos. Y'avait très peu d'assimilation, très peu de mariages mixtes. Et on vivait beaucoup plus avec les Français qu'avec les Arabes. Il y avait une exclusion, à l'époque de la guerre. Le statut des Juifs: exclus des lycées, exclus des banques etc. Mais on ne peut pas dire qu'il y avait des pressions comme ce qu'il y avait en France" (Yaakov, 2013, Line 239–54).

25 "Que le roi aurait pu nous défendre . . . c'est pas qu'il ne voulait pas, ou c'est pas qu'il n'avait pas envie, c'est qu'il n'avait aucun pouvoir. C'est pas lui qui dirigeait le

pays, et c'est pas lui qui pouvait avoir son droit de dire 'non, ça se fera ou ça ne se fera pas'. C'est pas vrai" (Yaakov, 2013, Line 293–8).

26 "Parce que n'oubliez pas que nous étions dirigé par des français. Et les français ne nous aimaient pas beaucoup. Ne croyez pas que les français étaient en bon terme avec les juifs. C'était . . . les juifs c'est une race à part, dans les Mellahs. . . . Et je vais même vous dire qu'il y avait même une espèce de discrimination raciale entre les juifs français et les juifs marocains. Et qu'il y avaient des juifs français, pas français de France: des français algériens (des juifs algériens). Vous savez des juifs algériens qui étaient devenu français par la loi Crémieux et qui habitaient ici" (Yaakov, 2013, Line 330–9).

27 Zohra, 2013.

28 "Je suis arrivé à Paris tout de suite après la guerre, en 1946. Et en 1946 il y avait un très grave problème: c'est que le judaïsme français avait disparu, il n'y en avait plus. D'abord en grande partie par l'assimilation et le reste par la Shoah. Les quelques juifs qui restaient ne savaient pas pourquoi ils étaient juifs. Ils ne savaient même pas ce que c'est, être juif. Ce qui fait qu'il n'y avait plus de judaïsme en France en 1946. Les quelques rescapés qui revenaient d'Europe centrale ne voulaient même pas parler qu'ils étaient juifs. Et on s'est retrouvés dans cette situation où la France démarrait sans judaïsme" (Yaakov, 2013, Line 147–57).

29 Yaakov describes the Ecole d'Orsay as a kind of Maimonides Judaism as it was more open and less Talmudic than the Ecole Normale Hebrew.

30 Though a founding member of the AIU, Netter went on to be known best as a Zionist leader promoting agricultural labor and Jewish education in the yishuv, and later Israel, communities.

31 "Alors le problème, c'est la proportion. Vous savez . . . et j'ai raconté l'autre jour. Prenez un bac. Un bac, vous mettez de l'eau dedans. Et un bac où y'a du vinaigre. Y'a 1000 litres ici, 1000 litres là. Vous prenez ½ litre de vinaigre, vous le mettez dans le millilitre d'eau. Vous remuez, vous appelez 50 personnes, et vous demandez qu'est ce qu'il y a dedans. Y'a de l'eau. Ou est passé le ½ litre de vinaigre? Il a disparu. C'est la même chose" (Yaakov, 2013, Line 760–6).

32 "C'est la foi, qui est une espèce de brouillard, qui enveloppe, qui enveloppe l'esprit ou l'être dans un même brouillard, et ils se confondent. Et celui qui a adopté cette atmosphère, il vit dedans . . . Et c'est ça la force de la foi. Pourquoi on dit 'La foi sauve ?' Parce que tout le reste peut se détériorer, mais une foi ne peut pas détériorer" (Yaakov, 2013, Line 48–64).

33 "Et c'est pas particulier au judaïsme. Ce n'est plus le patriotisme qui existait avant. Ce n'est plus l'idéalisme qui régnait. On est tombé dans l'ère . . ." (Yaakov, 2013, Line 1284–6).

34 "On rend service quand on sait qu'on va être adoré matériellement. Ou quand on va rapporter beaucoup d'argent. Alors que faire quelque chose que personne ne

viendra vous féliciter ni vous remettre une médaille: ça personne ne veut le faire aujourd'hui" (Yaakov, 2013, Line 1253–8).

35 Meaning the new city, as opposed to the medina; a distinction that still exists today.

36 Michel is the only participant among the subgroup of eleven who was educated in a French colonial school. The other ten participants were educated by either mellah schools or the AIU.

37 'Maternelle' is the French term for nursery school, usually ages three to six.

38 Michel states that the landlords of the properties were either Jews or Spanish or Portuguese, while the French were the minority in the street in which he lived. This reality coupled with the control that the Jews had over Mellah area speaks to a strong Jewish presence in Fez.

39 "Quand ils ont trouvé un juif, alors se battre contre les juifs c'était une manifestation de leur culture . . . Et me défendre, c'était une manifestation de ma culture. De mon identité . . . En plus j'étais pas particulièrement costaud. Voilà, c'est ça l'enfance dans des circonstances qui j'espère ne se répéteront plus jamais pour aucune generation" (Michel, 2013, Line 145–51).

40 P12 and P13, 2013.

41 Boum, A. 2013, p. 65.

42 1.5 hectares is equal to 0.015 square kilometers.

43 The meaning of *Hibra* in this context is an organization responsible for anything to do with funerals; however, if the word organization is explicitly included, *jameiat al-Hibra* can mean any kind of organization. MICHEL recalls that Hibra kept the *mellah* safe from trespassers, hosted visitors, and provided food when needed.

44 Judeo-Arabic refers to writing Arabic in Hebrew characters.

45 اليهود على الأقل ثلاث فئات، هم كانوا تحت ثلاث مجموعات من الضغط في الخارج الذي أثر عليهم. كان عندنا المستعمرين الفرنسيين. ورد اليهود للمعاداة ضد السامية في أوروبا كان الصهيونية. كان عندنا أيضاً المشاكل الداخلية في المغرب، أي محاربة الأستعمار من أجل الأستقلال. الشعب المغربي يدخل معركة ونحن جزء من الشعب المغربي، والجالية اليهودية تقاد من قبل لجان تعاون، وهذه اللجان لا تتصرف. السؤال يبقى: ما هو دورنا في هذا الوضع خصوصاً كيهود

46 "Je t'ai dit qu'il y avait trois . . . trois zones qui voulaient prendre les juifs du Maroc. N'est-ce pas. Enfin qui voulaient prendre l'esprit, qui voulaient gagner, gagner ces juifs" (Michel, 2013, Line 483–4).

47 "C'est une bonne chose, on nous a appris à lire et à écrire . . . Mais dans cette solidarité, on se rend compte de comment les gens de l'Alliance pensaient la colonisation des juifs marocains. Et c'est à ce moment qu'on comprend pourquoi les juifs marocains, à l'opposé par exemple des juifs iraniens ou syriens, on leur a pas appris l'arabe. Que le français . . . Parce que la France . . . quand les juifs sont devenus français en France, dans les années du 19ème siècle, c'était quelque chose de . . . pour eux c'était tellement énorme qu'ils se sentaient une responsabilité" (Michel, 2013, Line 501–18).

48 "Je ressentais un ressentiment évidemment contre Pétain et tous ces trucs-là . . . le 1er octobre 1941, on vous dit : 'Les juifs, ils s'en vont,' et il a touché le drapeau de la France, ça aussi ça fait réfléchir" (Ibid., Line 51–60).
49 "Donc je réfléchissais puis je passais à autre chose, parce que j'avais mon âge aussi, j'avais envie de jouer . . . Quand tu voulais jouer et qu'il n'y a pas de jouets, qu'est-ce que tu fais? Pendant toute la guerre, on n'a pas vu un jouet" (Ibid., Line 61–4).
50 "Le mouvement sioniste jusqu'à la guerre il n'a pas une grande importance" (Ibid., Line 528).
51 "Ca, ça . . . C'est une vieille chose, ça, ça ne changeait pas grand-chose" (Ibid., Line 534–5).
52 "L'épreuve de vérité. L'épreuve de vérité a eu lieu" (Ibid., Line 104).
53 Momentum for the Zionists would sway in their favor again in 1961 with the arrival of Gamal Abdel Nasser, Egypt's and the pan-Arab nationalists' leader. With the horror of the Holocaust and the continuing tension of the Arab-Israeli conflict fresh in the minds of Moroccan Jews, MICHEL states that the Zionist organizations in Morocco used Nasser's visit to rally support for aliya to Israel.
54 According to MICHEL, Istiqlal was opposed to the idea of student unions because they wanted to consolidate their power and claimed that their party was enough for all (Ibid).
55 "Nous sommes marocains, nous ne voulons plus le colonialisme et nous voulons. . . . Parce qu'ils avaient vu ce que c'était le colonialisme. Ca on le dit jamais, mais ils avaient vu qu'il y avait des lois anti-juifs, rien que pour les juifs. Il faut le dire, parce qu'ils l'ont su à ce moment-là. Ca nous l'avons un peu oublié depuis. C'est vrai, parce que c'est pas grave. Ca n'a pas de conséquence grave sur nous. Sauf que ça a une conséquence: c'est que les juifs ont à ce moment-là admis plus facilement le sionisme. 'Si la France nous rejette, si lalala nous rejette . . . si tout le monde nous rejette, on va en Israel'" (Ibid., Line 551–8).
56 Boum, A. 2013, p. 107.
57 "Mais nous avons une profonde identité nationale qui, après 1000 ans . . . qui s'est créée en 1000 ans plus exactement" (Ibid., Line 288–9).
58 "Les juifs ont été accueillis quand ils ont été expulsés d'Espagne, et ça il ne faut jamais l'oublier . . . Bon, mais y'avait déjà des juifs au Maroc . . . Faut pas non plus raconter d'histoires. Le judaïsme marocain, c'est pas un judaïsme importé d'Espagne, c'est pas vrai" (Ibid., Line 416–26).
59 "Nous sommes dans un pays arabe. Ca veut dire quoi un pays arabe? C'est un pays dont 95-99,9% sont musulmans, arabes. Et donc tu as cette minorité au milieu de ça. C'est vrai que ça demande une intelligence de part et d'autre pour vivre ensemble. Y'a des moments où cette intelligence n'est pas suffisante" (Ibid., Line 327–30).

60 "C'est pas un problème de religion, c'est un problème d'apport culturel" (Ibid., Line 618–9).
61 "Le seul endroit où y'a encore quelques juifs qui jouent un rôle, qui participent à leur vie politique, qui participent à la vie du pays etc., c'est le Maroc" (Ibid., Line 671–2).
62 Zerubavel, Y. 1995, p. 8.
63 Larkin, C. 2011, p. 16.
64 Ben-Layashi, S. 2014, pp. 587–601.
65 Atidguie, A. 1989. Unpublished Manuscript cited in Ben-Layashi, S. 2014. Atidguie emigrated to Israel in the early 1960s and in the late 1980s wrote a memoir about being a child in the *mellah* of Casablanca in the 1940s and 1950s.
66 Ben-Layashi, S. 2014, p. 587.
67 Purim is a Jewish holiday that commemorates the deliverance of the Jewish people in the ancient Perisan Empire from destruction, as recorded in the biblical book of Esther. According to this story, an evil plot to destroy Jews by a political figure named Haman was foiled by a Jewish courtier, Mordecai, and his adoptive daughter, who later became Queen Esther. Ibid., p. 599.
68 Ibid., p. 590.
69 P2, P4, ZOHRA, P17, P18.
70 P3, Yaakov, P10, P15.
71 P5, P6, P8, P9, P20.
72 اليهود على الأقل ثلاث فئات، هم كانوا تحت ثلاث مجموعات من الضغط في الخارج الذي أثَّر عليهم. كان عندنا المستعمرين الفرنسيين. ورد اليهود للمعاداة ضد السامية في أوروبا كان الصهيونية. كان عندنا أيضاً المشاكل الداخلية في المغرب، أي محاربة الأستعمار من أجل الأستقلال. الشعب المغربي يدخل معركة ونحن جزء من الشعب المغربي، والجالية اليهودية تقاد من قبل لجان تعاون، وهذه اللجان لا تتصرف. السؤال يبقى: ما هو دورنا في هذا الوضع خصوصاً كيهود
73 MAE-Nantes, Series Maroc, Direction de l'interieur (DI), dossier 6, "Statut des Juifs pendant la Second Guerre Mondiale" (August 1940–May 1945).
74 MAE-Nantes, Cabinet Diplomatique, Carton 668, Dossier 1, Letter from Col. Berriau, head of Intelligence Service, to Adjunct Secretary General of the Protectorate, Cabinet Diplomatique (November 24, 1918).
75 MAE-Nantes. Series Maroc, Cabinet Diplomatique, Carton 668, Dossier 2. Letter from Counselor to the Sharifian Government to the head of the Diplomatic Office in Rabat. 'Objet: Propagande sioniste au Maroc.'
76 Levy, A. 2001, p. 245.
77 P4, ZOHRA, P17, P18.
78 P1, P5, P6, P8, P9, P19.
79 MAE-Nantes, Direction de l'Interieur (DI), Questions Juives, Dossier I.
80 "It is Israel as a whole rather than each Jew as an individual that must help France and its allies in gaining victory over the common enemy" *L'Avenir Illustre*, December 1939.

81 Brooks, P. 1992, p. 3.
82 Ricoeur, P. 1984, p. 15.
83 Larkin, C. 2011, p. 16.
84 The vital distinction that must be raised here, however, is the inclusiveness or exclusiveness of memory that embodies belonging to a community of belonging: because memories are sustained, shared, and given significance by society, belonging necessitates reciprocal acknowledgment so that one's chosen identity construction may not be made available without societal acceptance.
85 Assman, A. and Linda Shortt, 2012, p. 5.
86 Sedmak, C. 2010, p. 519.
87 See Assmann, 1988, giving memory a common space; Volf, 2006, remembering rightly for healing and preventing violence, and Margalit, 2004, when people come together in political life and transform representations of the past into matters of urgent importance in the present.
88 Honneth, A. 1995.
89 Durkheim, E. (1893), 2014. Durkheim's notions of mechanical and organic solidarity are distinguished by having either low division of labor or high, respectively and relate to the level of interdependencies in society. Where society has a high division of labor with specialized tasks, organic solidarity is generated and maintained by interdependence.
90 Assman, A. and Linda Shortt. 2012, p. 4.
91 Margalit, A. 2004, p. 92.
92 Sedmak, C. 2010, p. 521.
93 Ibid., p. 519.
94 Nora, P. 1989, p. 3.
95 Orwell, G. 2013, (1939), p. 41. "Past events, it is argued, have no objective existence, but survive only in written records and in human memories. The past is whatever the records and the memories agree upon. And since the Party is in full control of all records, and in equally full control of the minds of its members, it follows that the past is whatever the Party chooses to make it." Ibid., p. 243.
96 Robeyns, I. 2011, p. 1.
97 Nussbaum, 1988, 1992, Robeyns, 2005, 2011, Sen, 1993, 1999, Walsh, 2000.
98 Awarded the Nobel Prize in Economics in 1998, Sen is an esteemed scholar on the choice of techniques, growth theory, social choice, opportunity, inequality, poverty, and famine. A recurring theme among these various projects is the promotion of well-being and development.
99 Sen's capability approach was introduced in his 1979 Tanner Lecture on Human Values, "Equality of What?," delivered at Stanford University and has been expanded upon in his 1980 publication and the decades since.
100 Sen, A. 1992, p. 48.

101 Robeyns, I. 2011, p. 2.
102 Clark, D. 2005a, p. 3.
103 First described in Rawls's 1971 *A Theory of Justice*, Rawlsian social primary goods focuses on purpose goods (income and wealth, opportunities and liberties, and the social basis of self-respect) and establishing a normative theory of justice before extending it beyond liberal democratic societies or the concept of citizenship. Rawls, J. 1971, 2001, p. 176.
104 Sen, A. 1980, pp. 215–16.
105 Sen also disregards a utilitarian approach where things or actions are valued according to their contribution to individual utilities experienced by people. Gasper, D. 1997, p. 281.
106 Robeyns, I. 2011, p. 2.
107 Robeyns, I. 2011, p. 10.
108 Sen, A. 2005, p. 154.
109 Ibid., p. 152.
110 Sen, A. 1992, p. 39.
111 Robeyns, I. 2011, p. 6.
112 Sen, A. 1992, p. 26.
113 Robeyns, I. 2011, p. 6.
114 Sen offers the example of Gandhi's hunger strike or other instances of fasting: a starving person and a fasting person appear to have the same functioning (hunger) but their capability to be well nourished is not the same as the fasting person is making a choice whereas the starving person has no other opportunity. 1992, p. 52.
115 Robeyns, I. 2011, p. 6.
116 Ibid., p.11.
117 Sen, A. 1992, pp. 19–38.
118 Robeyns, I. 2011, p. 7.
119 Ibid.
120 See Nussbaum, M. 2000, 2003, 2006.
121 Nussbaum, M. 2006, p. 78.
122 Nussbaum, M. 2006, pp. 72–5; 2003, pp. 41–2; 2005, pp. 41–2.
123 See Alkire, 2002, Anderson, 1999, 2010, Robeyns, 2005, 2011, and Crocker, 2008.
124 Anderson, E. 1999, p. 316.
125 Sen, A. 2005, p. 158.
126 Ibid., p. 151.
127 Ibid., p. 152.
128 Winter, J. 2012, p. vii.
129 Assman, A. and Linda Shortt. 2012, p. 1.
130 Schacter, D. L. 2000, p. 120.
131 Assman, A. and Linda Shortt. 2012, p. 4.

132 Ibid., p. 3.
133 Ibid., p. 7.
134 Volf, M. 2002, p. 59.
135 Margalit, A. 2004, p. 32.
136 To elucidate this point Margalit continues, "I do not care about everything that I deem important; and not everything I care about is important to me. Only those that I care for on reflection are important to include." Ibid., p. 31.
137 Ibid., p. 35.
138 Ibid., p. 109.
139 Ibid., p. 140.
140 Ibid., p. 76.
141 Volf offers examples of rebranding memories to fulfill or justify action, for instance, viewing "the arrival of European settlers on the shores of the New World" as "a story of discover and of bringing the light of civilization to dispel the darkness of barbarity" or the Nazi appeal "to the injustice of the Treaty of Versailles to justify their aggression against neighboring countries." Volf, M. 2002, p. 60.
142 Hirsch, M. and Leo Spitzer. 2009, p. 153.
143 Hartman, G. 1996, p. 142.
144 Arendt, H. 2006.
145 Levy, D. and Natan Sznaider. 2006, p. 4.
146 Hirsch, M. and Leo Spitzer. 2009, p. 165.
147 The museum's website boasts of being recognized as a Public Utility by Prime Ministerial decree in February 2001. http://casajewishmuseum.com
148 Anderson, P. 2008, pp. 1–3.
149 Larkin, C. 2011, p. 11.
150 Portelli, A. 1981, p. 4.
151 Ibid., p. 5.
152 Spence, D. 1982, p. 31.
153 Ibid.
154 Hirsch, M. and Leo Spitzer. 2009, p. 401.
155 Schwartz, B. 1982. p. 393.
156 Schudson, M. 1997. p. 15.
157 Larkin, C. 2011 and Veyne, P. 1984.
158 Larkin, C. 2011. p. 13.

Chapter 6

1 Cohen uses this term without precise distinction to which countries he includes; nevertheless, the numbers are indicative of the general trend in the region.

2   Cohen, H. J. 1973, p. 68.
3   Kenbib, M. 2014, p. 540.
4   Levy, S. 2001, p. 121.
5   Baida, J. 2010, p. 321.
6   Miller, S. G. 2013, p. 202.
7   "Le Maroc, dans quelle mesure il est l'Afrique du Nord? Il n'a pas du tout le même tracé . . . Il faut pas oublier que l'Algérie et la Tunisie actuelle, c'était des provinces turques. Nous n'avons jamais été province turque . . . Donc moi ma profonde conviction c'est que nous avons un certain nombre de traits généraux communs avec les pays voisins d'Afrique du Nord, et même de plus loin. Mais nous avons une profonde identité nationale . . . mais y'a que quand aujourd'hui tout le monde arabe est en train de se révolter, le Maroc ne se révolte pas. Pourquoi? Parce qu'il a déjà obtenu une grande partie de ce qu'ils n'ont pas encore" (Michel, 2013, Line 278–96).
8   "L'avenir des juifs au Maroc est lié à l'avenir des juifs dans le monde. Lequel est lié au problème judéo-arabe . . . Du point de vue arabe, en réponse à une question sur les juif du Maroc : parce que s'il y a la paix, s'il y a, même pas la paix, mais une amélioration, il y a un flux de juifs marocains qui reviennent au pays, pour visiter, ou pour d'avantage. Je ne dis pas qu'on va avoir dans l'avenir une grande communauté juive au Maroc, c'est fini ça, c'est dépassé. Mais par contre, dans ce monde entier, il y a une énorme communauté juive d'un million de juifs marocains dans le monde" (Michel, 2013).
9   Larhmaid tells of one story, set "two or three centuries ago" when Rabbi Chaffar Bal led a caravan of followers from the south toward Akka. Because they traveled in severe heat, the people were very thirsty so he "struck the ground with his foot and made gush forth a spring that exists in the place called Talgha'cht, between Akka and Ait Oubelli. . . . By transferring this oral tradition from generation to generation, Jews in this part of the Sous point to the sanctity of the idea that they belong to the region while also highlighting their economic claims to control of the land's resources" (Larhmaid, A. 2010, p. 65). The rabbi's tomb is a site of pilgrimage today.
10 Boyarin, J. and Boyarin, D., 1993, p. 713.
11 Boyarin, J. and Boyarin D. 1993, 2002, Gilman, S. 1999, Levy, A. 2001.
12 Boyarin, J. and Boyarin, D. 2002, p. vii.
13 Gilman, S. 1999, p. 1.
14 Levy, A. 2001, 247.
15 Ibid.
16 Ibid., p. 260.
17 Cardeira da Silva, 2018.
18 Ibid., 171.
19 Levy, A. 2001, p. 260.

20 Alcalay, A. 1993, Al-Rasheed, M. and Vitalis, R. (eds), 2004, Ashford, D. E. 1961, Bernard, S. 1968, Brown, K. 1981, Lagnado, L. 2007, Satloff, R. 2006, Somekh, S. 2007.
21 Alcalay, A. 1993, p. 201.
22 Snir, R. 2002, p. 540.
23 Satloff, R. 2006, p. 24.
24 Ibid., p. 25.
25 Stora, B. 2000, p. 14.
26 McDougall, J. 2003, p. 6.
27 Schreier, J. 2010, p. 153.
28 Satloff, R. 2006, p. 28.
29 Ibid., p. 29.
30 Ibid., p. 30.
31 Ibid., p. 31.
32 Schroeter, D. and Chetrit, J. 2006, p. 197.
33 Shamir, S. 1987, p. 143.
34 Beinin, J. 1998, p. 9.
35 Shamir, S. 1987, p. 33.
36 Ibid.
37 In the 1919 uprising against Britain, the slogan "*al-din li'illah wa'l-watan li'l-jami*" combined the monotheistic religions and the homeland together. Shamir, S. 1987, p. 33.
38 Ibid., p. 34.
39 Ibid., p. 36.
40 Shamir, S. 1987, p. 55.
41 Cohen, H. J. 1973, p. 47.
42 Ibid.
43 Accounting for this rise, Cohen notes that during and after the First World War, the immigration of Jews to Egypt had come largely from the Palestinian *yishuv* against their will. Ibid.
44 Shamir, S. 1987, p. 42.
45 Ibid., p. 44.
46 Ibid., p. 61.
47 Egyptian cosmopolitanism is explored in Zubaida's 2011 work as a product of imperialism. "The presence of particular milieux of social and cultural mixing and hybridity across communal boundaries" offered permeable social boundaries for the "many migrants and entrepreneurs from Europe and the Levant." 2011, p. 132, 148.
48 Cohen, H. J. 1973, p. 109.
49 Shamir, S. 1987, p. 74.

50 Ibid., p. 74.
51 *Ha-Shomer ha-Tza`ir*, the Egyptian branch of the Young Guard, a Marxist-Zionist movement affiliated with the *Kibutz ha-Artzi* federation.
52 Beinin, J. 1994, p. 3.
53 Cohen, H. J. 1973, p. 50.
54 Ibid.
55 Beinin, J. 1994, p. 13.
56 Shamir, S. 1987, p. 52.
57 Matalon, R. 2001, p. 1184.
58 Shamir, S. 1987, p. 54.
59 Ibid., p. 68.
60 Shamir, S. 1987, p. 69.
61 Ibid., p. 76.
62 Ibid., p. 74.
63 I have included Lagnado's memoir for its personal, inside perspective on the situation of Egyptian Jews; this varies from travel narratives that have been purposefully neglected as it is the memoir of one from within rather than a visiting stranger observer with an outsider's perspective.
64 Lagnado, L. 2007, p. 18.
65 Since the 1950s, various institutions have been established to "cope with the demographic dwindling" of Moroccan Jews. The Jewish Community Council "takes care of the living as well as the dead" and runs extracurricular activities such as youth movements and clubs. The AIU, referred to in its Arabic name, Ittihad, runs "day care centers, elementary schools, and high schools" and the community runs an exclusive health-care system and home for the elderly providing social and financial support. Levy, A. 2001, p. 253.
66 Miller, S. G. 2014, p. 465.
67 For deeper accounts of Jewish refugees from Central Europe arriving to Morocco in the period 1933–40, see Boum, A. 2014, Kenbib, M. 2014, Maghraoui, D. 2014.
68 Joffé, G. 2014, p. 476.
69 Assmann, A. 2006a, p. 213.
70 Ibid.
71 Ibid., p. 215.
72 Ibid., p. 213. See also Sontag, S. 2003, p. 85.
73 See Assmann, 1988, giving memory a common space; Volf, 2006, remembering rightly for healing and preventing violence, and Margalit, 2004, when people come together in political life and transform representations of the past into matters of urgent importance in the present.
74 Sedmak, C. 2010, p. 512.
75 Volf, M. 2006.

76 Ibid., p. 21.
77 Ibid., p. 231.
78 Volf, M. 2002, p. 59.
79 This is discussed in detail in Margalit's story of the Israeli commander officer who faced great criticism upon forgetting the name of one of the fallen soldiers under his command.
80 Gottreich, E. and Schroeter, D. 2010, p. 11.
81 Miller, S. G. 2014, p. 461.
82 "Brimades, moqueries, bourrades, heurts et même massacres. Dans un Maroc, où la cohabitation entre juifs et musulmans est une réalité culturelle et traditionnelle, l'antijudaïsme a su trouver sa place." Monjib, M. 2013.

Bibliography

Abdel-Samad, M. "Why Reform Not Revolution: A Political Opportunity Analysis of Morocco 2011 Protests Movements." *Journal of North African Studies* 19(5), 2014: 792–809.

Abitbol, M. *The Jews of North Africa during the Second World War*. Detroit: Wayne State University Press, 1989.

Abitbol, M. and Astro, A. "The Integration of North African Jews in France." *Yale French Studies* (85), 1994: 11. Discourses of Jewish Identity in Twentieth-Century France.

Abu-Lughod, J. L. Rabat. *Urban Apartheid in Morocco*. Princeton, NJ: Princeton University Press, 1980.

Ahmida, Ali Abdullatif (ed.). *Beyond Colonialism and Nationalism in the Maghreb*. New York: Palgrave, 2000.

Ait Mous, F. "The Moroccan Nationalism Movement: From Local to National Networks." *The Journal of North African Studies*, 18(5), 2013: 737–52.

Akhtar, S. "The Immigrant, the Exile, and the Experience of Nostalgia." *Journal of Applied Psychoanalytic Studies*, ½, 1999: 123–30.

Alcalay, A. *After Jews and Arabs: Remaking Levantine Culture*. Minneapolis: University of Minnesota Press, 1993.

al-Fassi, Allal. *Independence Movements in Arab North Africa*. Washington: American Council of Learned Societies, 1954.

Alkire, S. *Valuing Freedoms: Sen's Capability Approach and Poverty Reduction*. New York: Oxford University Press, 2002.

Al-Rasheed, M. and Vitalis, R. (eds.). *Counter-Narratives: History, Contemporary Society, and Politics in Saudi Arabia and Yemen*. London: Palgrave Macmillan, 2004.

Anderson, B. *Imagined Communities: Reflections on the Origin and Spread of Nationalism*. London: Verso, 2006.

Anderson, E. "What Is the Point of Equality?" *Ethics* 109(2), 1999: 287–337.

Anderson, E. "Justifying the Capabilities Approach to Justice." In Brighouse and Robeyns (eds.), pp. 81–100. http://www.san.ed.ac.uk/__data/assets/pdf_file/0005/15269/080519-altruism_article.pdf. 2010.

Anderson, P. "Is Altruism Possible?" *Royal Anthropological Institute Hocart Prize Essay*. http://www.san.ed.ac.uk/__data/assets/pdf_file/0005/15269/080519- altruism_article.pdf. 2008.

Anderson, P. "The Piety of the Gift: Selfhood and Sociality in the Egyptian Mosque Movement." *Anthropological Theory* 11(1), 2011: 3–21.

Anderson, P. "The Politics of Scorn in Syria and the Agency of Narrated Involvement." *Journal of the Royal Anthropological Institute* 19(3), 2013: 463–81.

Appadurai, A. *The Social Life of Things: Commodities in Cultural Perspective*. Cambridge: Cambridge University Press, 1988.
Arendt, H. *The Origins of Totalitarianism*. Cleveland: World, 1951.
Arendt, H. *The Human Condition*. Chicago: University of Chicago Press, 1958.
Arendt, H. *The Human Condition*, 2nd ed. Chicago: University of Chicago Press, 1998.
Arendt, H. *Eichmann in Jerusalem: A Report on the Banality of Evil*. New York: Penguin Classics, 2006.
Armonstrong, J. "Religious Nationalism and Collective Violence." *Nations and Nationalism* 3(4), 1997: 597–606.
Ashford, D. E. *Political Change in Morocco*. Princeton, NJ: Princeton University Press, 1961.
Assmann, A. "Memory, Individual and Collective." In *The Oxford Handbook of Contextual Political Analysis*, edited by Robert E. Goodin and Charles Tilly. Oxford: Oxford University Press, 2006a.
Assmann, A. *The Long Shadow of the Past: Cultures of Memory and the Politics of History*. Auflage, 2006b. Translated in Assman, A. *Shadows of Trauma: Memory and the Politic of Postwar Identity*. Translated by Sarah Clift. New York: Fordham University Press, 2015.
Assman, A. and Shortt, Linda (eds.). *Memory and Political Change*. London: Palgrave Macmillan, 2012.
Assmann, J. *Collective Memory and Cultural Identity in Kultur und Gedachtnis*. Edited by Jan Assmann and Tonio Holscher and translated by John Czaplicka. Frankfurt/Main: Suhrkamp, 1988.
AsZohraf, R. *Une Certaine Histoire des Juifs du Maroc: 1860–1999*. Paris: Gawsewitch, 2005.
Atidguie, A. *Gan Mishulash ha-Mar'ut (The Triangular Garden of Mirrors)*. 2 vols. Tel Aviv., 1989.
Augustine. *Confessions*. Translated by Henry Chadwick. Oxford: Oxford University Press, 2008.
Azagury, Y. "Sol Hachuel in the Collective Memory and Folktales of Moroccan Jews." In *Jewish Culture and Society in North Africa*, edited by E. B. Gottreich and D. J. Schroeter, 193–8. Bloomington: Indiana University Press, 2010.
Baïda, J. *La Presse Marocaine D'expression Francaise: Des Origines a 1956*. Rabat, Morocco: Faculté des Lettres et des Sciences Humaines de Rabat, 1996.
Baïda, J. *La presse juive au maroc entre les deux guerres*. Hesperis-Tamuda, XXXVII, 1999.
Baïda, J. "The Emigration of Moroccan Jews, 1948–1956." In *Jewish Culture and Society in North Africa*, edited by E. B. Gottreich and D. J. Schroeter and translated by A. Macvicar, 321–49. Bloomington: Indiana University Press, 2010.
Baïda, J. "Sidi Mohammed Ben Youssef et les Lois Antijuives." *Zamane* 44(May), 2013: 42–5.
Baïda, J. "The American Landing in November 1942: A Turning Point in Morocco's Contemporary History." *Journal of North African Studies* 19(4), 2014: 518–23.

Barth, F. *Ethnic Groups and Boundaries*. Chicago: Waveland Press, 1998.

Beinin, J. *Egyptian Jewish Identities: Communitarianisms, Nationalisms, Nostalgias*, 1994. https://publishing.cdlib.org/ucpressebooks/view?docId=ft2290045n&chunk.id=fmsec1&toc.depth=1&toc.id=&brand=ucpress. Accessed April 7, 2020.

Beinin, J. "Egyptian Jewish Identities: Communitarianisms, Nationalisms, Nostalgias." https://publishing.cdlib.org/ucpressebooks/view?docId=ft2290045n&chunk.id=fmsec1&toc.depth=1&toc.id=&brand=ucpress. Accessed April 7, 2020

Beinin, J. *The Dispersion of Egyptian Jewry: Culture, Politics, and the Formation of a Modern Diaspora*. Berkeley: University of California Press, 1998.

Benjelloun, A. "Contribution a l'etude du mouvement nationaliste marocain dans l'ancienne Nord du Maroc 1930–1956." PhD dissertation, Universite Hassan II de Casablanca, 1983.

Ben-Layashi, S. "The 1948 Mallah of Casablanca: Viewing Moroccan (Trans)National Sentiment Through Juvenile Trauma." *Journal of North African Studies* 19(4), 2014: 587–601.

Ben-Layashi, S. and Maddy-Weitzman, B. "Myth, History, and Realpolitik: Morocco and its Jewish Community." *Journal of Modern Jewish Studies* 9(1), 2010: 89–106.

Bernard, S. *The Franco-Moroccan Conflict, 1943–1956*. New Haven, CT: Yale University Press, 1968.

Berque, J. *French North Africa: The Maghreb Between Two World Wars*. New York: Praeger, 1967.

Bertagnin, M., Miller, S. G., and Petruccioli, A. "Inscribing Minority Space in the Islamic City: The Jewish Quarter of Fez (1438–1912)." *Journal of the Society of Architectural Historians* 60(3), 2001: 310–27.

Betts, R. *Assimilation and Association in French Colonial Theory, 1890–1914*. New York: Columbia University Press, 1961.

Blumenson, M. *The Patton Papers: 1940-1945*. Boston, MA: Houghton Mifflin, 1974.

Bose, S. *Contested Lands: War and Peace in Israel-Palestine, Kashmir, Bosnia, Cyprus and Sri Lanka*. London: Harvard University Press, 2007.

Boum, A. "Muslims Remember Jews in Southern Morocco: Social Memories, Dialogic Narratives, and the Collective Imagination of Jewishness." PhD thesis, University of Arizona, 2006.

Boum, A. "Southern Moroccan Jewry Between the Colonial Manufacture of Knowledge and the Postcolonial Historiographical Silence." In *Jewish Culture and Society in North Africa*, edited by E. B. Gottreich and D. J. Schroeter, 73–84. Bloomington: Indiana University Press, 2010.

Boum, A. *Memories of Absence: How Muslims Remember Jews in Morocco*. Stanford, California: Stanford University Press, 2013.

Boum, A. "Partners Against Anti-Semitism: Muslims and Jews Respond to Nazism in French North African Colonies, 1936–1940." *Journal of North African Studies* 19(4), 2014: 554–70.

Bowie, L. "An Aspect of Muslim-Jewish Relations in Late Nineteenth-Century Morocco: A European Diplomatic View." *International Journal of Middle East Studies* 7(1), 1976: 17–19.

Boyarin, D. and Boyarin, J. *Powers of Diaspora: Two Essays on the Relevance of Jewish Culture*. Minneapolis, MN: University of Minnesota Press, 2002.

Boyarin, J. and Boyarin, D. "Diaspora: Generation and the Ground of Jewish Identity." *Critical Inquiry* 19, 1993: 693–725.

Brass, P. R. *Ethnicity and Nationalism: Theory and Comparison*. Newbury Park, CA: Sage, 1991.

Breuilly, J. *Nationalism and the State*. Manchester: Manchester University Press, 1982.

Brignon, J. *Histoire du Maroc*. Hatier; Casablanca: Librairie nationale, 1967.

Brooks, P. *Reading for the Plot: Design and Intention in Narrative*. Cambridge: Harvard University Press, 1992.

Brown, D. "Ethnic Revival: Perspectives on State and Society." In *Nationalism*, edited by J. Hutchinson and A. D. Smith. Oxford: Oxford University Press, 1994.

Brown, K. "Mellah and Madina: A Moroccan City and Its Jewish Quarter (Sale ca. 1880–1930)." In *Studies in Judaism and Islam*, edited by S. D. Goitein, S. Morag, I. Ben-Ami and N. Stilmman. Jerusalem: Magnes Press, 1981.

Brubaker, R. "In the Name of the Nation: Reflections on Nationalism and Patriotism." *Citizenship Studies* 8(2), 2004: 115–27.

Brubaker, R. "Religion and Nationalism: Four Approaches." *Nations and Nationalism*, 18(1), 2012: 2–20.

Brubaker, R. "Language, Religion and the Politics of Difference." *Nations and Nationalism* 19(1), 2013: 1–20.

Brubaker, R. and Cooper, Frederick, "Beyond Identity." *Theory and Society* 29(1), 2000: 1–47.

Brubaker, R. and Laitin, D. "Ethnic and Nationalist Violence." *Annual Review of Sociology* 24, 1998: 423–52.

Buchanan, A. and Moore, M. (eds.). *States, Nations, and Borders: The Ethics of Making Boundaries*. Cambridge: Cambridge University Press, 2003.

Burke, E. *Prelude to Protectorate in Morocco: Precolonial Protest and Resistance, 1860–1912*. Chicago: University of Chicago Press, 1976.

Burke, P. "History as Social Memory." In *Memory: Culture, History and Mind*, edited by T. Butler, 97–113. New York: Blackwell, 1989.

Calhoun, C. *Nations Matter: Culture, History, and the Cosmopolitan Dream*. London: Routledge, 2007.

Campbell, D. *Writing Security: United States Foreign Policy and the Politics of Identity*. Minneapolis: University of Minnesota, 1992.

Canetti, E. *The Voices of Marrakesh*. London: Marion Boyars, 2003.

Cardeira da Silva, M. "Moroccan Jewish First-Places: Contraction, Fabrication, Dissipation." *International Journal of Heritage Studies* 24(2), 2018: 167–80.

Chatterjee, P. *The Nation and Its Fragments: Colonial and Postcolonial Histories.* Princeton: Princeton University Press, 1993.

Chetrit, S. S. *Intra-Jewish Ethnic Conflict in Israel: White Jews, Black Jews.* New York: Routledge, 2010.

Clark, D. A. "The Capability Approach: Its Development, Critiques and Recent Advances." Global Poverty Research Group, Economic and Social Research Council. GPRG-WPS-032, 2005a.

Clark, D. A. "Sen's Capability Approach and the Many Spaces of Human Well-Being." *Journal of Development Studies*, 41(8), 2005b: 1339–68.

Cohen, H. J. *The Jews of the Middle East 1860–1972.* Jerusalem: Israel Universities Press, 1973.

Cohen, M. *Under Crescent and Cross: The Jews in the Middle Ages.* Princeton: Princeton University Press, 1994.

Cohen, Y. "The Migrations of Moroccan Jews to Montreal: Memory, (Oral) History and Historical Narrative." *Journal of Modern Jewish Studies* 10(2), 2011: 245–62.

Conversi, D. "Autonomous Communities and the Ethnic Settlement in Spain." In *Autonomy and Ethnicity: Negotiating Competing Claims in Multi-ethnic States*, edited by Y. Ghai, 122–46. Cambridge, Cambridge University Press, 2000.

Cooper, F. *Colonialism in Question: Theory, Knowledge, History.* Berkeley: University of California Press, 2005.

Corcos, D. "The Jews of Morocco Under the Marinides." *The Jewish Quarterly Review* 54(4), April 1964: 273.

Crocker, D. A. *Ethics of Global Development: Agency, Capability and Deliberative Democracy.* Cambridge: Cambridge University Press, 2008.

Cunningham, D. and Phillips, B. T. "Context for Mobilization: Spatial Settings and Klan Presence in North Carolina, 1964–1966." *American Journal of Sociology* 113(3), 2007: 781–814.

Dahan-Kalev, H. "You're So Pretty-- You Don't Look Moroccan." *Israel Studies* 6(1), Spring 2001: 1–14.

Dahan-Kalev, H. "Zionism, Post Zionism and Fear of Arabness." Presentation at Oxford University Conference Fear, Horror, and Terror Oxford, UK, 2007.

Damis, J. "The Free-School Movement in Morocco, 1919–1970." PhD dissertation, Tufts University, 1970.

Deshen, S. *The Mellah Society: Jewish Community Life in Sherifian Morocco.* Chicago: University of Chicago Press, 1989.

Deshen, S. and Shokeid, M. *Distant Relations: Ethnicity and Politics Among Arabs and North African Jews in Israel.* New York: Praeger Publishers, 1982.

Deshen, S. and Zenner, W. *Jews Among Muslims: Communities in the Pre-colonial Middle East.* New York: New York University Press, 1996.

Dompnier, N. 2001. https://www.lhistoire.fr/le-front-populaire-t-il-voté-les-pleins-pouvoirs-à-pétain

Duara, P. "Historicizing National Identity, or Who Imagines What and When." Unpublished essay, *History from the Nation: Questioning Narratives of Modern China*. Chicago: University of Chicago Press, 1995.

Dunn, R. *Resistance in the Desert: Moroccan Responses to French Imperialism 1881-1912*. London: Croom Helm, 1977.

Durkheim, E. *Division of Labor in Society*, Translated by Steven Lukes. Simon and Schuster, 1893, 2014. Free Press. New York: Imprint of Simon and Schuster.

Dutter, L. "Perceptions of Group Identity and Recent Political Behavior in Northern Ireland." *Political Psychology*, 6(1), 1985: 47–60.

Eickelman, D. F. *Knowledge and Power in Morocco: The Education of a Twentieth-Century Notable*. Princeton: Princeton University Press, 1985.

Elbaz-Luwisch, F. "Narrative Research: Political Issues and Implications." *Teaching and Teacher Education* 13(1), 1997: 75–83.

Eriksen, T. H. "Linguistic Diversity and the Quest for National Identity: The Case of Mauritius." *Ethnic and Racial Studies* 13(1), 1990: 1–26.

Eriksen, T. H. "The Cultural Contexts of Ethnic Differences." *Man* 28(1), 1991a: 127–44.

Eriksen, T. H. "Ethnicity Versus Nationalism." *Journal of Peace Research* 28(3), 1991b: 263–78.

Eriksen, T. H. *Ethnicity and Nationalism*. London: Pluto Press, 2002.

Feinberg, W. "Nationalism in a Comparative Mode." In *The Morality of Nationalism*, edited by R. McKim and J. McMahan, 66–7. Oxford: Oxford University Press, 1997.

Fenton, S. *Ethnicity*. Cambridge: Polity Press, 2010.

Fishman, J. A. "Language and Ethnicity." Presentation at Ethnicity in Eastern Europe conference, University of Washington, June 1976.

Fournier, SC. "Sharing and Unsharing Memories. Life Stories of Jews from Muslim-Arab Countries: Fear, Anger and Discontent Within a Silenced Displacement." Quest. Issues in Contemporary Jewish History. *Journal of Fondazione CDEC*, No. 4, 2012.

Frankfurt, H. *"Taking Ourselves Seriously" and "Getting It Right."* The Tanner Lectures on Human Values, Stanford University, 2004. https://tannerlectures.utah.edu/_documents/a-to-z/f/frankfurt_2005.pdf

Gans, C. *The Limits of Nationalism*. Cambridge: Cambridge University Press, 2003.

Gasper, D. "Sen's Capability Approach and Nussbaum's Capabilities Ethic." *Journal of International Development*, 9(2), 1997: 301–17.

Gellner, E. *Saints of the Atlas*. London: Weidenfeld and Nicolson, 1969.

Gellner, E. *Nations and Nationalism*. Oxford: Blackwell, 1983.

Gelvin, J. L. *Divided Loyalties: Nationalism and Mass Politics in Syria at the Close of Empire*. Berkeley: University of California Press, 1998.

Gershovich, M. *French Military Rule in Morocco: Colonialism and Its Consequences*. Portland, OR: Frank Cass, 2000.

Gillis, J. R. "Memory and Identity: The History of a Relationship." In *Commemorations: The Politics of National Identity*, edited by J. R. Gillis, 3–24. Princeton, NJ: Princeton University Press, 1994.

Gilman, S. "The Frontier as a Model for Jewish History." In *Jewries at the Frontier: Accommodation, Identity, Conflict*, edited by Sander Gilman and Milton Shain, 1–27. Urbana: University of Illinois Press, 1999.

Glover, J. "Nations, Identity, and Conflict." In *The Morality of Nationalism*, edited by R. McKim and J. McMahan, 12–24. Oxford: Oxford University Press, 1997.

Glover, J. *Humanity: A Moral History of the Twentieth Century*. New Haven: Yale University Press, 2001.

Goodin, R. and Klingemann, H. *A New Handbook of Political Science*. New York: Oxford University Press, 1996.

Gottreich, E. *The Mellah of Marrakech: Jewish and Muslim Space in Morocco's Red City*. Bloomington: Indiana University Press, 2007.

Gottreich, E. B. and Schroeter, D. J. (eds.) *Jewish Culture and Society in North Africa*. Bloomington: Indiana University Press, 2010.

Gottreich, E. B. *Jewish Morocco: A History from Pre-Islamic to Post-Colonial Times*. London: I.B. Tauris, 2020.

Gramsci, A. *Selections from the Prison Notebooks*. Turnhout: International Publishers, 1971.

Grosrichard, R. "Shoah, une exception marocaine?" *Best of Zamane*, January, 2013, 58–61.

Gurr, T. R. *Minorities at Risk: A Global View of Ethnopolitical Conflicts*. Washington: United States Institute of Peace Press, 1993.

Gurr, T. R. "On the Political Consequences of Scarcity and Economic Decline." *International Studies Quarterly* 29(1), 1985: 51–75.

Gurr, T. R. *Peoples Against States: Ethnopolitical Conflict and the Changing World System*. Cambridge: Blackwell Publishers, 1994.

Gurr, T. R. "Nonviolence in Ethnopolitics: Strategies for the Attainment of Group Rights and Autonomy." *Political Science and Politics* 33(2), 2000: 155–60.

Gurr, T. R. and Harff, B. *Ethnic Conflict in World Politics*. Oxford: Westview Press, 2004.

Halbwachs, M. *Les cadres sociaux de la mémoire*. Paris: F. Alcan, 1925.

Halbwachs, M. *On Collective Memory*. Translated and edited by L. A. Coser. Chicago, IL: University of Chicago Press, 1992.

Halbwachs, M. *La Memoire Collective*, 2nd ed. Paris: Albin Michel, 1997.

Hall, S. "Cultural Identity and Diaspora." In *Diaspora and Visual Culture: Representing Africans and Jews*, edited by N. Mirzoeff, 21–33. London and New York: Routledge, 2003.

Halstead, J. *Rebirth of a Nation: The Origins and Rise of Moroccan Nationalism*. Cambridge, MA: Center for Middle Eastern Studies, Harvard University Press, 1967.

Hanneman, A. "Independence and Group Rights in the Baltics: A Double Minority Problem." *Journal of International Law* 35, 1995: 1–44.

Hannum, H. "Contemporary Developments in the International Protection of the Rights of Minorities." *Journal of International Law* 66, 1991: 1431–48.

Hannum, H. "Rethinking Self-Determination." *Journal of International Law* 34, 1994: 1–70.

Hart, D. M. *The Aith Waryushun of the Moroccan Rif: An Ethnography and History*. Texas: University of Arizona Press, 1976.
Hartman, G. "Learning from Survivors: The Yale Testimony Project." In *The Longest Shadow: In the Aftermath of the Holocaust*, edited by G. Hartman. Bloomington: Indiana University Press, 1996.
Hastings, A. *The Construction of Nationhood: Ethnicity, Religion and Nationalism*. Cambridge: Cambridge University Press, 1997.
Hatimi, M. "al-jama'at al-yahudiyya al-Maghrebiyya wa al-khiyar al-sa 'b bayna nida"' al- sahyuniyya wa rihan al-Maghreb al-mustaqil 1947–1961." PhD thesis, University Sidi Muhammad ben Abdallah, 2007.
Hatimi, M. "Le Sionisme au Mellah." *Zamane* 44, May 2013: 48–9.
Herder, J. G. *Ideas: Outlines of a Philosophy of History of Man*. New York: Bergmann, 1966.
Herder, J. G. *Another Philosophy of History*. Indianapolis: Hackett, 2004.
Herzl, T. *Altneuland: Old-New Land: Novel*. Haifa: Haifa Publishing Company, 1896.
Hever, H. "Location, Not Identity: The Politics of Revelation in Ronit Matalon's The One Facing Us." *Prooftexts* 30, 2010: 321–39.
Hirsch, M. *Family Frames: Photography, Narrative and Postmemory*. Cambridge, MA: MIT Press, 1997.
Hirsch, M. "The Generation of Postmemory." *Poetics Today* 29(1), 2008: 103–28.
Hirsch, M. and Leo Spitzer. "The Witness in the Archive: Holocaust Studies/Memory Studies." *Memory Studies* 2 (2), May 2009: 151–70.
Hirschberg, H. Z. *A History of the Jews in North Africa, Volume 1, From Antiquity to the Sixteenth Century*. Leiden: Brill, 1974.
Hobsbawm, E. and Ranger, T. (eds.) *The Invention of Tradition*. Cambridge: Cambridge University Press, 1983.
Hobsbawm, E. *Nations and Nationalism Since 1780: Programme, Myth, Reality*. Cambridge: Cambridge University Press, 1992.
Hochberg, G. *Permanent Immigration: Jacqueline Kahanoff, Ronit Matalon, and the Impetus of Levantinism*. Durham: Duke University Press, 2004.
Hoinsington, W. "Cities in Revolt: The Berber Dahir (1930) and France's Urban Strategy in Morocco." *Journal of Contemporary History* 13(3), July 1978: 433–48.
Hoisington, W. *The Casablanca Connection: French Colonial Policy, 1936–1943*. Chapel Hill: University of North Carolina, 1984.
Hoisington, W. *Lyautey and the French Conquest of Morocco*. New York: St. Martin's Press, 1995.
Holden, S. E. "Muslim and Jewish Interaction in Moroccan Meat Markets, 1873-1912." In *Jewish Culture and Society in North Africa*, edited by E. B. Gottreich and D. J. Schroeter, 150–64. Bloomington: Indiana University Press, 2010.
Honneth, A. *The Struggle for Recognition: The Moral Grammar of Social Conflicts*. Cambridge: MIT Press, 1995a.
Honneth, A. *The Fragmented World of the Social: Essays in Social and Political Philosophy*. Albany, NY: SUNY, 1995b.

Hopkins, L. and McAuliffe, C. "Split Allegiances: Cultural Muslims and the Tensions Between Religious and National Identity in Multicultural Societies." *Studies in Ethnicity and Nationalism* 10(1), 2010: 38–58.
Horowitz, D. *Ethnic Groups in Conflict*. Berkeley: University of California Press, 2000.
Hughey, M. W. (ed.). *New Tribalisms: The Resurgence of Race and Ethnicity*. London: Macmillan, 1998.
Hutchinson, J. *Nations as Zones of Conflict*. London: SAGE Publications, 2005.
Hutchinson, J. "Diaspora Dilemmas and Shifting Allegiances: The Irish in London Between Nationalism, Catholicism, and Labourism (1900–22)." *Studies in Ethnicity and Nationalism* 10(1), 2010: 107–25.
Hutchinson, J. and Smith, A. D. (eds.). *Nationalism*. Oxford: Oxford University Press, 1994.
Irwin-Zarecka, I. *Frames of Remembrance*. Piscataway, NJ: Transaction, 1994.
Jabotinsky, V. "The Iron Wall" (O Zheleznoi Stene) in Rassvyet, November 4, 1923. http://www.mideastweb.org/ironwall.htm. Accessed December 16, 2014
Jabotinsky, Z. *The Arabesque Fashion*. Al Sifrut Veomanut, 1927, Tel Aviv.
Jabotinsky, Z. "Sipur Yamay" (The Story of My Times) in Autobiographia. Tel Aviv, Jerusalem, 1936.
Jenkins, R. *Rethinking Ethnicity: Arguments and Explorations*. London, Sage, 2008.
Johnson, K. R. "The Struggle for Civil Rights: The Need for, and Impediments to, Political Coalitions Among and Within Minority Groups." *Louisiana Law Review* 63(759), 2003: 1–28.
Joffé, E. G. H. "The Moroccan Nationalist Movement: Istiqlal, the Sultan, and the Country." *The Journal of African History* 26(4), 1985: 289–307.
Joffé, E. G. H. "Nationalism and the Bled: The Jbala from the Rif War to the Istiqlal." *Journal of North African Studies* 19(4), September 2014: 475–89.
Julien, C. A. *L'Afrique du Nord en March, Nationalismes Musulmans et Souveraineté Française*. Paris: René Julliard, 1952.
Julien, C. A. *Le Maroc face aux impérialismes 1415–1956*. Paris: Editions J.A, 1978.
Kably, M. *Histoire du Maroc: reactualisation et synthese*. Rabat: Edition de l'Institute Royal pour la Recherche sur l'Histoire du Maroc, 2011.
Kalmar, I. D. and Penslar, D. *Orientalism and the Jews of the Mediterranean*. Waltham: Brandeis University Press, 2005.
Kaminer, R. *The Politics of Protest: The Israeli Peace Movement and the Palestinian Intifada*. Brighton: Sussex Academic Press, 1995.
Karsh, E. *Israel: The First Hundred Years, Volume III. Israeli Politics and Society Since 1948: Problems of Collective Identity*. New York: Frank Cass Publishers, 2002.
Katz, J. G. "Les Temps Héroïques The Alliance Israélite Universelle in Marrakesh on the Eve of the French Protectorate." In *Jewish Culture and Society in North Africa*, edited by E. B. Gottreich and D. J. Schroeter, 282–96. Bloomington: Indiana University Press, 2010.
Kaufmann, E. *Rethinking Ethnicity: Majority Groups and Dominant Minorities*. London: Routledge, 2004.

Kedourie, E. *Nationalism*. Oxford: Blackwell, 1993.
Kenbib, M. "Juifs et musulmans au Maroc, 1859-1948. Contribution a l'histoire des relations inter-communautaires en terre d'Islam." *Annales* 52(1), 1997: 194–6.
Kenbib, M. "Muslim-Jewish Relations in Contemporary Morocco." In *Jewish Culture and Society in North Africa*, edited by E. B. Gottreich and D. J. Schroeter, 26–7. Bloomington: Indiana University Press, 2010.
Kenbib, M. "Moroccan Jews and the Vichy Regime, 1940–42." *Journal of North African Studies* 19(4), September 2014: 540–53.
Kenneally, C. *Invisible History of the Human Race*. New York: Viking Adult, 2014.
King, R. *Orientalism and Religion: Postcolonial Theory, India and 'The Mystic East'*. London: Routledge, 1999.
Kosansky, O. "The Real Morocco Itself: Jewish Saint Pilgrimage, Hybridity, and the Idea of the Moroccan Nation." In *Jewish Culture and Society in North Africa*, edited by E. B. Gottreich and D. J. Schroeter, 346–9. Bloomington: Indiana University Press, 2010.
Kyle, K. "Politics, Ethnicity and the Irish Troubles." *Contemporary British History*, 12(4), 1998: 177–83.
Lagnado, L. *The Man in the White Sharkskin Suit: A Jewish Family's Exodus from Old Cairo to the New World*. New York: Harper Perennial, 2007.
Landau, R. *Moroccan Drama: 1900-1955*. San Francisco, CA: The American Academy of Asian Studies, 1956.
Larhmaid, A. "Jewish Identity and Landownership in the Sous Region of Morocco." In *Jewish Culture and Society in North Africa*, edited by E. B. Gottreich and D. J. Schroeter, 59–69. Bloomington: Indiana University Press, 2010.
Larkin, C. *Memory and Conflict in Lebanon: Remembering and Forgetting the Past*. New York: Routledge, 2011.
Laskier, M. *The Alliance Israelite Universelle and the Jewish Communities of Morocco 1862-1962*. Albany: SUNY Press, 1983.
Laskier, M. "The Instability of Moroccan Jewry and the Moroccan Press in the First Decade After Independence." *Jewish History* 1(1), 1986: 41–2.
Laskier, M. M., Reguer, S., Simon, R. S., and Stillman, N. *The Jews of the Middle East and North Africa in Modern Times*. New York: Columbia University Press, 2003.
Lawrence, A. "Rethinking Moroccan Nationalism, 1930–44." *Journal of North African Studies* 17(3), 2012: 475–90.
Leach, C. W. and Williams, W. R. "Group Identity and Conflicting Expectations of the Future in Northern Ireland." *Political Psychology* 20(4), 1999: 875–96.
Lewis, B. "The Question of Orientalism" In The New York Review of Books, June 24, 1982. https://www.amherst.edu/media/view/307584/original/The+Question+of+Orientalism+by+Bernard+Lewis+%7C+The+New+York+Review+of+Books.pdf
Lewis, B. *From Babel to Dragomans: Interpreting the Middle East*. Oxford: Oxford University Press, 2004.

Levisse-Touze, C. "Les Camps d'internement en Afrique du Nord pendant la seconde guerre mondiale." In *Melanges Charles-Robert Ageron*, edited by Charles-Robert Ageron and Abdeljelil Temimi, 2 vols, 601–5. Zaghouan, Tunisia: Fondation Temimi pour la recherche scientifique et l'informaiton, 1996.

Levisse-Touze, C. *L'Afrique du Nord dans la guerre, 1939–1945*. Paris: A. Michel, 1998.

Levy, A. "Center and Diaspora: Jews Late-Twentieth-Century Morocco." *City and Society* 13(2), 2001: 245–70.

Levy, D. and Sznaider, Natan. *Holocaust and Memory in the Global Age*. Philadelphia: Temple University Press, 2006.

Levy, S. *Essais d'histoire & de civilisation judeo-marocaines*. Rabat: Centre Tarik ibn Zyad, 2001.

Levy, S. *Jews of Morocco or Extraterrestrials? Fondation du Patrimoine Culturel Judeo-Marocain*. Casablanca: Jewish Museum of Casablanca, 2006.

Lichtenberg, J. "Nationalism, for and (Mainly) Against," in *The Morality of Nationalism*, edited by Robert McKim and Jeff McMahan, 160–2. New York: Oxford University Press, 1997.

Locke J. "Of Identity and Diversity." In *Essay Concerning Human Understanding*. Berkeley: University of California Press, 1964.

Lowrance, S. "Identity, Grievances, and Political Action: Recent Evidence from the Palestinian Community in Israel." *International Political Science Review* 27(2), 2006: 167–90.

Lugan, B. *Histoire du Maroc des origines à nos jours*. Paris: Perrin, 2000.

Lury, C. *Prosthetic Culture: Photography, Memory, Identity*. London: Routledge, 1998.

Maalouf, A. *In the Name of Identity: Violence and the Need to Belong*. New York: Penguin Books, 2003.

Maghraoui, D. "The Goumiers in the Second World War: History and Colonial Representation." *Journal of North African Studies* 10(4), September 2014: 571–86.

Makdisi, U. S. and P. A. Silverstein (eds.). *Memory and Violence in the Middle East and North Africa*. Bloomington, IN: Indiana University Press, 2006.

Margalit, A. and Joseph Raz, "National Self-Determination." *Journal of Philosophy* 87, 1990: 439–48.

Margalit, A. "The Moral Psychology of Nationalism." In *The Morality of Nationalism*, edited by R. McKim and J. McMahan, 83–5. Oxford: Oxford University Press, 1997.

Margalit, A. *The Ethics of Memory*. Boston: Harvard University Press, 2004.

Massad, J. "Zionism's Internal Others: Israel and the Oriental Jews." *Journal of Palestine Studies* 25(4), 1996: 53–68.

Matalon, R. *My Father at Age Seventy-Nine, Kro Uchtov*. Tel Aviv: Hakibbutz Hameuchad, 2001.

McDougall, J. (ed.). *Nation, Society, and Culture in North Africa*. London: Frank Cass & Co. Ltd., 2003.

McGarry, J. and O'Leary, B. *The Politics of Ethnic Conflict Regulation*. London: Routledge, 1993.

McKim, R. and McMahan, J. (eds.). *The Morality of Nationalism*. Oxford: Oxford University Press, 1997.

Meadwell, H. "Nationalism chez Gellner." *Nations and Nationalism* 18(4), 2012: 563–82.

Meiland, J. W. "What Ought We to Believe? Or the Ethics of Belief Revisited." *American Philosophical Quarterly* 17(1), 1980: 15–24.

Meshal, R. A. "The State, the Community and the Individual; Local Custom and the Construction of Orthodoxy in the Sijills of Ottoman-Cairo, 1558–1646." PhD thesis, Institute of Islamic Studies, McGill University, 2006.

Mikesell, M. and Murphy, A. "A Framework for Comparative Study of Minority-Group Aspirations." *Annals of the Association of American Geographers* 81(4), 1991: 581–604.

Miller, S. G. "Dhimma Reconsidered: Jews, Taxes, and Royal Authority in Nineteenth-Century Tangier." In *In the Shadow of the Sultan: Culture, Power, and Politics in Morocco*, edited by Rahma Bourqia and Susan G. Miller, 103–26. Cambridge, MA: Harvard University Press, 1999.

Miller, S. G. "Apportioning Sacred Space in a Moroccan City: The Case of Tangier, 1860–1912." *City and Society* 13(1), 2001.

Miller, S. G. *A History of Modern Morocco*. Cambridge: Cambridge University Press, 2013.

Miller, S. G. "Filling a Historical Parenthesis: An Introduction to 'Morocco from World War II to Independence'." *Journal of North African Studies* 19(4), September 2014: 461–74.

Mitchell, H. "The Development of Nationalism in French Morocco." *Phylon (1940-1956)* 16(4), 1955: 427–34.

Misztal, B. A. *Theories of Social Remembering*. Maidenhead and Philadelphia, PA: Open University Press, 2003.

Monjib, M. "Souvenirs de l'antijudaisme." *Zamane* 44, May 2013: 46–7.

Moore, C. H. *Politics in North Africa: Algeria, Morocco, and Tunisia*. New York: Little Brown and Company, 1970.

Moore, M. (ed.). *National Self-Determination and Secession*. Oxford: Oxford University Press, 1998.

Moreau, O. "Echoes of National Liberation: Turkey Viewed from the Maghreb in the 1920s." In *Nation, Society and Culture in North Africa*, edited by James McDougall, 58–70. London: Frank Cass, 2003.

Montagne, R. *Les Berberes et l.e Makhzen dans le Sud du Maroc*. Paris: Larose, 1930.

Nasser, G. A. "Shamal Afriqiya Biladuna" ["North Africa Is Our Country"]. In Liberation Rally Culture and Publishing Council, Shamal Afriqiya fi-l-Madi wa-l-Hadir wa-l- Mustaqbal ['North Africa in the Past, Present and Future'], Ikhtarna Lak, Cairo: Dar al-Ma'arif, 1954.

Nathanson, S. "Nationalism and the Limits of Global Humanism." In *The Morality of Nationalism*, edited by Robert McKim and Jeff McMahan, 176–90. Oxford: Oxford University Press, 1997.

Nevo, E. *Neuland*. London: Chatto and Windus, 2014.
Nicholson, G. *Plato's Phaedrus: The Philosophy of Love*. West Lafayette: Purdue University Press, 1999.
Nora, P. "Between Memory and History: les Lieux de Memoire." *Representations* 26, 1989: 7–24.
Nora, P. *Realms of Memory: The Construction of the French Past*. Edited by Lawrence D. Kritzman and translated by Arthur Goldhammer, 3 vols. New York: Columbia University Press, 1998.
Nussbaum, M. "Nature, Functioning and Capability: Aristotle on Political Distribution." *Oxford Studies in Ancient Philosophy* 6, 1988: 145–84.
Nussbaum, M. " Human Functioning and Social Justice. In Defense of Aristotelian Essentialism." *Political Theory* 20(2), 1992: 202–46.
Nussbaum, M. *Women and Human Development: The Capabilities Approach*. Cambridge: Cambridge University Press, 2000.
Nussbaum, M. "Capabilities as Fundamental Entitlements: Sen and Social Justice." *Feminist Economics* 9(2/3), 2003: 33–59.
Nussbaum, M. "Well-Being, Contracts and Capabilities." In *Rethinking Well-Being*, edited by Lenore Manderson, 27–44. Perth: API Network, 2005.
Nussbaum, M. *Frontiers of Justice: Disability, Nationality, Species Membership*. Cambridge, MA: Harvard University Press, 2006.
Nussbaum, M. *Upheavals of Thought: The Intelligence of Emotions*. Cambridge: Cambridge University Press, 2008.
Olick, J. K. and J. Robbins. "Social Memory Studies: From "Collective Memory" to the Historical Sociology of Mnemonic Practices." *Annual Review of Sociology* 24, 1998: 105–40.
Olick, J. K. "Collective Memory: The Two Cultures." *Sociological Theory* 17(3), 1999: 333–48.
Olick, J. K. *States of Memory: Continuities, Conflicts, and Transformations in National Retrospection*. Durham, NC and London: Duke University Press, 2003.
Orwell, G. *Marrakech*. London: New Writing, 1939.
Orwell, G. *Nineteen Eighty-Four*. Penguin Classics, 2013 [1949].
Owen, R. "A Salute to Sami Zubaida's Influence." *Economy and Society* 41(4), 2012: 580–4.
Özkirimli, U. *Theories of Nationalism: A Critical Introduction*. Basingstoke: Macmillan, 2000.
Özkirimli U. "The Nation as an Artichoke? A Critique of Ethnosymbolist Interpretations of Nationalism." *Nations and Nationalism* 9(3), 2003: 339–55.
Pennell, C. R. *Morocco Since 1830: A History*. New York: New York University Press, 2000.
Pennell, R. *A Country with a Government and a Flag: The Rif War in Morocco*. Wisbech: Menas Press, 1986.
Plato. *Phaedrus*. Translated by Paul Woodruff and Alexander Nehamas. Hackett Publishing Company, Inc. 1956, 1995.

Portelli, A. "On the Particularities of Oral History." *A Journal of Social Historians*, 12, Autumn 1981: 45–60.
Pratt, M. L. *Imperial Eyes: Travel Writing and Transculturation*. London and New York: Routledge, 1992.
Quah, S. and Sales, A. *The International Handbook of Sociology*. Thousand Oaks: SAGE Publications, 2000.
Radstone, S. and Schwarz, B. (eds.). *Memory: Histories, Theories, Debates*. New York: Fordham University Press, 2010.
Rawls, J. *A Theory of Justice*. Cambridge, MA: Harvard University Press, 1971.
Rawls, J. *Justice as Fairness: A Restatement*. Cambridge, MA: Harvard University Press, 2001.
Rézette, R. *Les parties politiques marocains*. Paris: Librarie Armand Colin, 1955.
Ricoeur, P. *Time and Narrative*. Chicago: University of Chicago Press, 1984.
Ricoeur, P. *Memory, History, Forgetting*. Chicago: University of Chicago Press, 2004.
Rivet, D. *Le Maghreb a l'epreuve de la colonization*. Paris: Hachettes, 2002.
Robeyns, I. "The Capability Approach: A Theoretical Survey." *Journal of Human Development* 6(1), 2005: 93–114.
Robeyns, I. "The Capability Approach." *The Stanford Encyclopedia of Philosophy*, Summer 2011 Edition. https://stanford.library.sydney.edu.au/archives/sum2011/entries/capability-approach/
Rousseau, J. J. "Discourse on Political Economy," 111–38, and "The Social Contract," 141–227. In *Basic Political Writings*, translated by Donald A. Cress, 1st ed. Cambridge, MA: Hackett Publishing, 1987.
Rousseau, J. J. *Discourse on the Origin and Foundation of Inequality Among Men*. Bedford Cultural Editions Series, 2010.
Said, E. W. *Orientalism: Western Conceptions of the Orient*. New York: Random House, Inc, 1978.
Saith, R. "Capabilities: The Concept and Its Operationalisation." Queen Elizabeth House, University of Oxford. Working Paper Series- QEHWPS66, 2001.
Satloff, R. *Among the Righteous: Lost Stories from the Holocaust's Long Reach into Arab Lands*. New York: Public Affairs, 2006.
Schacter, D. L. "The Seven Sins of Memory: Perspectives from Functional Neuroimaging." In *Memory, Consciousness and the Brain*, edited by Endel Tulving, 119–37. London: Psychology Press, 2000.
Schildkrout, E. "The Ideology of Regionalism in Ghana." In *Strangers in African Societies*, edited by William A. Shack and Elliott P. Skinner. Berkeley and Los Angeles: University of California Press, 1979.
Schreier, J. *Arabs of Jewish Faith, the Civilizing Mission in Colonial Algeria*. New Brunswick: Rutgers University Press, 2010.
Schroeter, D. *Merchants of Essaouria: Urban Society and Imperialism in Southwestern Morocco, 1844–1886*. Cambridge: Cambridge University Press, 1988.

Schroeter, D. "The Jewish Quarter and the Moroccan City." In *New Horizons in Sephardic Studies*, edited by Y. Stilmman and G. Zukcer, 67–81. Albany: SUNY Press, 1993.

Schroeter, D. "Orientalism and the Jews of the Mediterranean." *Journal of Mediterranean Studies* 4(2), 1994: 183–96.

Schroeter, D. *The Sultan's Jew: Morocco and the Sephardi World*. Stanford: Stanford University Press, 2002.

Schroeter, D. and Chetrit, J. "The Transformation of the Jewish Community of Essaouira (Mogador) in the Nineteenth and Twentieth Centuries." In *Sephardi and Middle Eastern Jewries, History and Culture in the Modern Era*, edited by H. A. Goldberg, 99–118. Bloomington: Indiana University Press, 1996.

Schroeter, D. and Chetrit, J. "Emancipation and Its Discontents: Jews at the Formative Period of Colonial Rule in Morocco." *Jewish Social Studies: History, Culture, Society*, 13(1), 2006: 170–206.

Schudson, M. "Lives, Laws and Language: Commemorative Versus Non-commemorative Forms of Effective Public Memory." *The Communication Review* 2(1), 1997: 3–17.

Schwartz, B. "The Social Context of Commemoration: A Study in Collective Memory." *Social Forces* 61(2), 1982: 374–402.

Schwarz, E. and Johan C. Te Velde. "Jewish Agricultural Settlement in Argentina: The ICA Experiment." *The Hispanic American Historical Review* 19(20) 1939: 185–203.

Scott, J. C. *Weapons of the Weak: Everyday Forms of Peasant Resistance*. New Haven: Yale University Press, 2008.

Sedmak, C. "Spiritual Infrastructure: Memory and Moral Resources." *Journal of Israel Affairs* 16(4), 2010: 510–34.

Segalla, S. *The Moroccan Soul: French Education, Colonial Ethnology, and Muslim Resistance, 1912–1956*. Lincoln: University of Nebraska Press, 2009.

Sen, A. "Equality of What?" In *Tanner Lectures on Human Values*, edited by McMurrin. Cambridge: Cambridge University Press, 1980.

Sen, A. "Rights and Capabilities." In *Resources, Values and Development*. Cambridge, MA: Harvard University Press, 1984.

Sen, A. "Well-Being, Agency and Freedom: The Dewey Lectures 1984." *Journal of Philosophy* 82(4), 1985: 169–221.

Sen, A. *Inequality Re-examined*. Oxford: Clarendon Press, 1992.

Sen, A. "Capability and Well-Being." In *The Quality of Life*, edited by M. Nussbaum and A. Sen, 30–53. Oxford: Clarendon Press, 1993.

Sen, A. *Development as Freedom*. New York: Knopf, 1999.

Sen, A. "Human Rights and Capabilities." *Journal of Human Development* 6(2), 2005: 151–66.

Sen, A. *Identity and Violence: The Illusion of Destiny*. London: Penguin Books Ltd., 2006.

Sen, A. *The Idea of Justice*. London: Allen Lane, 2009.

Shamir, S. *The Jews of Egypt: A Mediterranean Society in Modern Times.* Boulder: Westview Press, 1987.
Shenhav, Y. *The Arab Jews: A Postcolonial Reading of Nationalism, Religion, and Ethnicity.* Stanford: Stanford University Press, 2006.
Shenhav, S. R. "Political Narratives and Political Reality." *International Political Science Review* 27(3), 2006: 245–62.
Slouschz, N. *Travels in North Africa.* Philadelphia: The Jewish Publication Society of America, 1927.
Smith, A. D. *The Ethnic Revival in the Modern World.* Cambridge: Cambridge University Press, 1981.
Smith, A. D. *Theories of Nationalism.* New York: Holmes & Meier, 1983.
Smith, A. D. *The Ethnic Origins of Nations.* Oxford: Basil Blackwell, 1986.
Smith, A. D. *National Identity.* Harmondsworth: Penguin, 1991.
Smith A. D. "Gastronomy or Geology? The Role of Nationalism in the Reconstruction of Nations." *Nations and Nationalism* 1(1), 1995: 3–23.
Smith, A. D. *Nationalism and Modernism.* London: Routledge, 1998.
Smith, A. D. *Nationalism.* Cambridge: Polity Press, 2001.
Smith A. D. "The Poverty of Anti-nationalist Modernism." *Nations and Nationalism* 9(3), 2003: 357–70.
Smith, A. D. "The Land and Its People: Reflections on Artistic Identification in an Age of Nations and Nationalism." *Nations and Nationalism* 19(1), 2013: 87–106.
Snir, R. "The Zionist Vision and the Arabic Literature of Iraqi Jews: 'A Caravan from the Village' by Shalom Darwish." In *Zion and Zionism Among Sephardi and Oriental Jews*, edited by W. Z. Harvey and W. Zeev Harvey, 539–60. Jerusalem: Misgav Yerushalayim, 2002.
Somekh, S. *Baghdad, Yesterday: The Making of an Arab Jew* (2004), Jerusalem 2007.
Somers, M. R. "The Narrative Constitution of Identity: A Relational and Network Approach." *Theory and Society* 23, no. 5 (1994).
Somer, M. "Failures of the Discourse of Ethnicity: Turkey, Kurds, and the Emerging Iraq." *Security Dialogue* 36, 2005: 103–28.
Sontag, S. *Regarding the Pain of Others.* New York: Farrar, Straus and Giroux, 2003.
Spence, D. P. *Narrative Truth and Historical Truth: Meaning and Interpretation in Psychoanalysis.* New York: Norton, 1982.
Stephens, J. *Retelling Stories, Framing Culture: Traditional Story and Metanarratives in Children's Literature.* London: Routledge, 1998.
Stora, B. "Maroc, le tratement des histoires proches." *Journal name Esprit*, 266/267, August–September 2000: 88–102.
Styan, D. "Introduction: Sami Zubaida, Modernity, Politics and the Middle East." *Economy and Society* 41(4), 2012: 485–500.
Susin, L. Z. "A Critique of the Identity Paradigm." In *Creating Identity*, edited by H. Haring M. Mieth, and D. Junker-Kenny. London: SCM Press, 2000.
Swirski, S. *Israel: The Oriental Majority.* London: Zed Books, 1989.

Tajfel, H. *Human Groups and Social Categories*. Cambridge: Cambridge University Press, 1981.
Taylor, A. R. "Zionism and Jewish History." *Journal of Palestine Studies* 1(2), 1972: 35–51.
Taylor, C. *Sources of the Self: The Making of the Modern Identity*. Cambridge: Cambridge University Press, 1989.
Taylor, C. *Multiculturalism and the Politics of Recognition*. Princeton: Princeton University Press, 1994.
Taylor, C. "Nationalism and Modernity." In *Morality of Nationalism*, edited by R. McKim and J. McMahan, 32–45. Oxford: Oxford University Press, 1997.
Tessler, M. A. "The Identity of Religious Minorities in Non-Secular States: Jews in Tunisia and Morocco and Arabs in Israel." *Comparative Studies in Society and History* 20(3), 1978: 359.
Thomson, S. "Developing a Multiethnic Ethos: How Colonial Legacies, National Policies, and Local Histories Converged in a Gambian Village Charter." *Studies in Ethnicity and Nationalism* 12(2), 2012: 286–308.
Tibi, B. "Islam and European Ideologies." In *Nationalism*, edited by J. Hutchinson and A. D. Smith. Oxford: Oxford University Press, 1994.
Tonnesson, S. and Antlov, H. "Asia in Theories of Nationalism and National Identity." In *Nationalism*, edited by J. Hutchinson and A. D. Smith. Oxford: Oxford University Press, 1994.
Tololyan, K. "Rethinking Diaspora(s): Stateless Power in the Transnational Moment." *Diaspora* 5, 1996: 3–36.
Tourabi, A. "Judaisme Marocain, une Présence Millénaire." *Zamane* 44, May 2013: 40–1.
Trevisan Semi, E. "Shared Memories and Oblivion: Is Israeli Jews' Nostalgia for Morocco Shared by the Muslims in Morocco?" *Quest*. Issues in Contemporary Jewish History. *Journal of Fondazione CDEC*, No. 4 November 2012.
Trouillot, M. R. *Silencing the Past: Power and the Production of History*. Boston, MA: Beacon Press, 1997.
Tsur, Y. "The Religious Factor in the Encounter Between Zionism and the Rural Atlas Jews." In *Zionism and Religion*, edited by Sh. Almog, J. Reinharz, and A. Shapira. Hanover and London: Brandeis University Press, 1998.
Tsur, Y. *Torn Community: Moroccan Jews and Nationalism, 1943-1954*. Tel Aviv: 'Am 'Oved Publishing. (Hebrew. English Translation by Osnat Krupnik Maas, 2013.), 2001.
Useem, B. "Breakdown Theories of Collective Action." *Annual Review of Sociology* 24, 1998: 215–38.
Varisco, D. M. "Reading Against Culture in Edward Said's Culture and Imperialism." *Culture, Theory, and Critique* 45(2), 2004: 93–112.
Varisco, D. M. "Edward Said and the Culture Behind Orientalism." *Expositions* 7 (2), 2013: 52–4.

Veyne, P. *Writing History: Essay on Epistemology*. Manchester: Manchester University Press, 1984.

Vignoles, V. L., Schwartz, S. J., and Luyckx, K. "Introduction: Toward an Integrative View of Identity" In *Handbook of Identity Theory and Research*. New York: Springer, 2012.

Volf, M. "Love's Memory: The Role of Memory in Contemporary Culture." and "Love's Memory: Redemptive Remembering." Presentation to Princeton Theological Seminary Institute for Youth Ministry, 2002. http://www.ptsem.edu/iym/research/lectures/downloads/2002/1volf.pdf (accessed October 29, 2014).

Volf, M. *The End of Memory: Remembering Rightly in a Violent World*. Grand Rapids, MI: William B. Eerdmans Publishing Company, 2006.

Wagenhofer, S. "Contested Narratives: Contemporary Debates on Mohammed V and the Moroccan Jews Under the Vichy Regime." *Quest*. Issues in Contemporary Jewish History. *Journal of Fondazione CDEC*. N. 4, November 2012.

Walsh, V. "Smith After Sen." *Review of Political Economy* 12(1), 2000: 5–25.

Waterbury, J. *Commander of the Faithful: The Moroccan Political Elite - a Study in Segmented Politics*. London: Weidenfeld and Nicolson, 1970.

Weber, M. *Economy and Society*. Berkeley: University of California Press, 1978.

Weller, M. *Autonomy, Self-Governance and Conflict Resolution: Innovative Approaches to Institutional Design in Divided Societies*. New York: Routledge, 2008.

Werbner, R. (ed.). *Memory and the Postcolony: African Anthropology and the Critique of Power*. London: Zed Books, 1998.

Wiesel, E. *From the Kingdom of Memory: Reminiscences*. New York: Summit Books, 1990.

Winter, J. "The Generation of Memory: Reflections on the Memory Boom in Contemporary Historical Studies." *Bulletin of the German Historical Institute*, 27, 2000: 69–92.

Wyrtzen, J. "Constructing Morocco: Colonial Struggle to Define the Nation, 1912–1956." PhD dissertation, Georgetown University, Washington, DC, 2009.

Wyrtzen, J. *Making Morocco: Colonial Intervention and the Politics of Identity*. Ithaca: Cornell University Press, 2015.

Yack, B. *Nationalism and the Moral Psychology of Community*. Chicago: University of Chicago Press, 2012.

Ye'or, B. *The Dhimmi: Jews and Christians Under Islam*. Fairleigh: Dickinson University Press, 1985.

Yehuda, Z. "The Place of Aliyah in Moroccan Jewry's Conception of Zionism." *Studies in Zionism* 6(2), 1985: 199–210.

Yerushalmi, Y. H. *Zakhor: Jewish History and Jewish Memory*. Seattle: University of Washington Press, 1996 [1982].

Zafrani, H. *Two Thousand Years of Jewish Life in Morocco*. Hoboken: Ktav Pub. House, 2002.

Zerubavel, Y. *Recovered Roots: Collective Memory and the Making of Israeli National Tradition*. Chicago: University of Chicago Press, 1995.

Zisenwine, D. *The Emergence of Nationalist Politics in Morocco: The Rise of the Independence Party and the Struggle Against Colonialism After World War II*. London and New York: Tauris Academic Studies, 2010.

Zubaida, S. *Islam, the People and the State: Political Ideas and Movements in the Middle East*. London: I.B. Tauris & Co. Ltd, 2009.

Zubaida, S. *Beyond Islam: A New Understanding of the Middle East*. London: I.B. Tauris, 2011.

Zubaida, Sami. "The Quest for Cultural Authenticity and the Politics of Identity." Lecture at the British Society for Middle Eastern Studies Annual Lecture, London School of Economics, London, UK, February 5, 2014.

Zurn, C. F. "Recognition, Redistribution, and Democracy: Dilemmas of Honneth's Critical Social Theory." *European Journal of Philosophy* 13(1), 2005: 89–126.

Periodicals and Colonial Archives

National Library of the Kingdom of Morocco, Rabat

"'A nos lectures," *L'Action du Peuple*, No. 1, August 4, 1933.
El Ouezzani, M. "La Politique berbère." *L'Action du Peuple*, August 18, 1933, 2.
El-Kholti, Mohammed. "Les israélites et nous." *L'Action du Peuple*, August 18, 1933, 4.
"L'amitié Judeo-Musulmane." *L'Action du Peuple*, September 1, 1933, 1.
Bendayan, I. "Lettre ouverte à M. Kholti." *L'Action du Peuple*, September 8, 1933.
El-Kholti, "Le rôle de la Jeunesse Israélite dans l'évolution marocaine." *L'Action du Peuple*, January 26, 1934.
El-Kholti, M. "Sionisme et patriotisme marocain." *L'Action du Peuple*, March 2, 1934.
Bouhlal, A. "En marge du meeting de la L.I.C.A." *L'Action du Peuple*, May 6, 1937, 3.
El-Mesquine. "Les Juifs et Nous." *L'Action du Peuple*, June 17, 1937, 5.
Sammoun, A. "Pour l'entente judéo-arabe au Maroc." L'Action du Peuple, July 1, 1937.
El-Mesquine, "L'entente islamo-judaïque ne peut se fair que dans le cadre nationale?" *L'Action du Peuple*, July 15, 1937, 3.

Hassan Archive of the Royal Palace, Rabat

"La Politique musulmane et l'Afrique du Nord." *La Nation Arabe*, No. 3, V Année, Janvier- Février 1935, 184.
"Notre ouvrage "Le nouveau monde musulman" est interdit au Maroc." *La Nation Arabe*, No. 3, V Année, Janvier-Février 1935, 186.
"L'oppression française au Maroc." *La Nation Arabe*, No. 3, V Année, Janvier-Février 1935, 201.
"Ce n'est pas par l'assimilation mais par la justice et l'égalité que la France peut réussir dans le Nord de l'Afrique." *La Nation Arabe*, No. 4, V Année, Mars–Avril 1935, 262.

"Le nouveau part national en Palestine." *La Nation Arabe*, No. 5, V Année, Mai–Juin 1935, 292.

"Annexes au Plan de Réformes Marocaines." *La Nation Arabe*, No. 5, V Année, Mai–Juin 1935, 316.

"Le Nord de l'Afrique." *La Nation Arabe*, No. 5, V Année, Mai–Juin 1935, 339.

"Le Congrès Sioniste." *La Nation Arabe*, No. 6, V Année, Juillet–Septembre 1935, 386.

"Pourquoi les Arabes ne sont pas Chrétiens." *La Nation Arabe*, No. 7, V Année, Octobre- Novembre 1935, 431.

"Le Maroc proteste." *La Nation Arabe*, No. 7, V Année, Octobre–Novembre 1935, 443.

"L'influence des Juifs et la crise morale en Angleterre." *La Nation Arabe*, No. 8, V Année, Janvier–Avril 1936, 475.

"Les minorités religieuses." *La Nation Arabe*, No. 8, V Année, Janvier–Avril 1936, 520.

"Pourquoi l'entente est impossible avec les Juifs." *La Nation Arabe*, No. 9, V Année, Mai–Août 1936, 567.

"La Société des Nations est responsible des troubles en Palestine." *La Nation Arabe*, No. 9, V Année, Mai–Août 1936, 572.

"Les Juifs ont tout calculé sauf la présence des Arabes en Palestine." *La Nation Arabe*, No. 9, V Année, Mai–Août 1936, 604.

"Au Congrès Juif Mondial; une voix arabe." *La Nation Arabe*, No. 9, V Année, Mai–Août 1936, 613.

King Abdul-Aziz Al Saoud Foundation for Islamic Studies and Human Sciences, Casablanca.

"Pour la sécurité de l'oeuvre française faut-il garder les marocains dans l'ignorance?" Maghreb, 1932.

"Le scandale Abdellah ben Mohammed." *Maghreb*, December 1932, 17–19.

Al-Maghrebi, "Les aspirations du 'Maghreb." *Maghreb*, July 1932.

"Consequences du dahir berbère." *Maghreb*, October 1932, 6–7.

Tract Following an Arabic Pamphlet. El Ouezzani. *Maghreb*, November 1932, 40. Cited in Wyrtzen, J. p. 153.

Abdillah, A. " Comment le protectorat respècte notre langue?" *Maghreb*, January 1933, 30–32.

"En Marge du dahir berbère." *Maghreb*, February 1933, 36.

Belafrej, A. "Et maintenant?" *Maghreb*, No. 11, June 1933, 50–1.

El Ouezzani, M. "La politique berbère et le statut du Maroc." *Maghreb*, No. 11, June 1933, 20–6.

El Ouezzani, M. "20eme anniversaire de la politique berbère (1914–1934)." *Maghreb*, June 1934, 10.

Longuet, Robert-Jean. *Maghreb: Revue Mensuelle de Documentation Économique et Sociale*. Décembre 1932, No. 6, 1–2.

Longuet, Robert-Jean, "La Liberté? De Conscience au Maroc. Le scandale Abdellah ben Mohammed." *Maghreb: Revue Mensuelle de Documentation Économique et Sociale.* Décembre 1932, No. 6, 17–19.

"Réponse à Monsieur Carette Vouvet. Pour la France et le Maroc contre le dahir berbère." *Maghreb: Revue Mensuelle de Documentation Économique et Sociale.* Décembre 1932, No. 6, 30–2.

Sixte-Quenin. "Le dahir berbère." *Maghreb: Revue Mensuelle de Documentation Économique et Sociale.* Décembre 1932, No. 7, 5–6.

El Beidaoui, Mohammed. "La colonisation… à longue échéance." *Maghreb: Revue Mensuelle de Documentation Économique et Sociale.* Décembre 1932, No. 8, 32.

Abou Abdillah. "Comment le protectorat respecte notre langue." *Maghreb: Revue Mensuelle de Documentation Économique et Sociale.* Janvier 1933, No. 9, 30–2.

El Ouezzani, Mohammed. "Le problème de l'enseignement au Maroc." *Maghreb: Revue Mensuelle de Documentation Économique et Sociale.* Janvier 1933, No. 10, 23–7.

Longuet, Jean. "Député de la Seine, Vice-Président de la Commission des Affaires Étrangères." *Maghreb: Revue Mensuelle de Documentation Économique et Sociale.* Mai–Juin 1933, No. 11, 1–2.

Monnet, Georges. "L'Émancipation des Peuples doit être notre but dans les colonies." *Maghreb: Revue Mensuelle de Documentation Économique et Sociale.* Mai–Juin 1933, No. 11, 3–6.

El Ouezzani, Mohammed. "La politique berbère et le statut au Maroc." *Maghreb: Revue Mensuelle de Documentation Économique et Sociale.* Mai–Juin 1933, No. 11, 20–6.

Belafrej, Ahmed. "Et maintenant?" *Maghreb: Revue Mensuelle de Documentation Économique et Sociale.* Mai–Juin 1933, No. 11, 50–1.

El Ouezzani, Mohammed. "Le Protectorat." *Maghreb: Revue Mensuelle de Documentation Économique et Sociale.* Mai–Juin 1933, No. 12, 16–23.

Arieh, Gor. "L'Islam et les Juifs." *Maghreb: Revue Mensuelle de Documentation Économique et Sociale.* Mai–Juin 1933, No. 12, 47–8.

Benjelloun, Abdelmajid. "Le part pris par le mouvement nationaliste marocain de la zone d'influence espagnole dans le processus de libération du Maroc." *Revue d'Histoire Maghrebine*, 43–4, Novembre 1986, 5–42.

Bouyahia, Salam. "Les relations syndicales maghrébines et rôle des travailleurs pour l'unité du Maghreb Arabe (1946–1959)." *Revue d'Histoire Maghrébine*, No. 43–44, Novembre 1986 part 2, 5–96.

Foundation for Moroccan Jewish Heritage, Casablanca.

Cohen, A. "Appel a la Population Israelite du Maroc." *Fez*, 1933.
Sammoun, A. "L'Amitié Judéo-Musulmane." *L'Avenir Illustre*, Février 28, 1937, 4.

Ministère des Affaires Etrangères. Archives diplomatiques, Nantes.

MAE-Nantes, Cabinet Diplomatique, Carton 668, Dossier 1. Letter from Ministry of Foreign Affairs to General Lyautey, Commissioner Resident General of the Republic of France, "Recrutement de volontaires Israélites."

MAE-Nantes, Cabinet Diplomatique, Carton 668, Dossier 1, Letter from Col. Berriau, Head of Intelligence Service, to Adjunct Secretary General of the Protectorate, Cabinet Diplomatique (November 24, 1918).

MAE-Nantes, Direction de l'Interieur (DI), Questions Juives, Dossier 1.

MAE-Nantes, Series Maroc, Cabinet Diplomatique, Carton 670, Dossier General. Note from Director of Sharifian Affairs, State Section (May 28, 1937).

MAE-Nantes, Series Maroc, Cabinet Diplomatique, Carton 670, Dossier General. Letter from M. Avonde-Froment, Consul General of France in Tangier to Résident Général Hogues (July 4, 1938).

MAE-Nantes, Series Maroc, Cabinet Diplomatique, Carton 670, Dossier General. Note from head of Financial Property Conservation Service, "D'évolution de la succession de M. Achille Taieb, Israélite d'origine tunisienne, naturalise français." (November 13, 1940).

MAE-Nantes, Series Maroc, Direction de l'Interieur (DI), Carton 111. Letter from Col Chevroton, Head of the Meknès Region to the Director of Political Affairs (November 15, 1944).

MAE-Nantes, Series Maroc, Cabinet Diplomatique, Carton 668, Dossier 1, Letter No. 1667 from Chief of Municipal Services in Safi to Résident Général Lyautey.

MAE-Nantes, Series Maroc, Cabinet Diplomatique, Carton 670, Dossier General, "Etude sur le Sionisme au Maroc." (April 3, 1945), 8–9.

MAE-Nantes, Series Maroc, Cabinet Diplomatique, Carton 668, Dossier 2, Letter from Chief Inspector for Jewish Institutions in Morocco, Yahya Zagury, to Head of Diplomatic Office, "Quêtes effectues en Afrique du Nord au profit de communautés palestiniennes."

MAE-Nantes, Series Maroc, Cabinet Diplomatique, Carton 668, Dossier 2, Letter from Résident Général Lyautey to Minister of Foreign Affairs, "Questions Israélites. Les Juifs Marocains et le Sionisme." (September 17, 1919).

MAE-Nantes, Series Maroc, Cabinet Diplomatique, Carton 668, Dossier 2, Letter from Résident Général Lyautey to Zionist Organization of London (June 26, 1926).

MAE-Nantes, Series Maroc, Cabinet Diplomatique, Carton 668, Dossier 2, Note de Renseignement, "Propagande Sioniste." (May 7, 1930).

MAE-Nantes, Series Maroc, Cabinet Diplomatique, Carton 668, Dossier 2, Letter from Counselor to the Sharifian Government to the Head of the Diplomatic Office in Rabat, "Objet: Propagande sioniste au Maroc."

MAE-Nantes, Series Maroc, Cabinet Diplomatique, Carton 668, Dossier 2, Letter from Résident Général Noguès to Minister of Foreign Affairs, "A/S Front national juif en Palestine." (November 6, 1936).

MAE-Nantes, Direction de l'Interieur (DI), Questions juives, Dossier 24, Report from Civil Controller, Region of Rabat, to Director of Political Affairs, No. 605, "A/S Tracts anti-juifs," (August 7, 1936).

MAE-Nantes, Direction de l'Interieur (DI), Questions juives, Dossier 24, Report from Résident Général Lauzanne, Region of Taza, to Director of Indigenous Affairs, (May 25, 1938).

MAE-Nantes, Direction de l'Interieur (DI), Dossier 24, Renseignements No. 559 (May 18, 1938).

MAE-Nantes, Series Maroc, Cabinet Diplomatique, Carton 29.

MAE-Nantes, Series Maroc, Cabinet Diplomatique, Carton 670. Note de renseignements: Politique anti-allemande (December 30, 1938).

MAE-Nantes, Series Maroc, Direction de l'Interieur (DI), Carton 111. Circulary letter from Ministry of National Defense, of War, and Foreign Affairs on the subject of "Indigènes Israélites nord-africains." (October 25, 1939).

MAE-Nantes, Direction de l'Interieur (DI), Statut des Juifs, Dossier 5, Notes de Renseignements, No. 217, and No. 432.

MAE-Nantes, Direction de l'Interieur (DI), Statut des Juifs, Dossier 5. Circulary letter from Direction de la Santé Publique et de la jeunesse (June 16, 1941), "Hôspitalisation des Juifs algeriens."

MAE-Nantes, Series Maroc, Direction de l'Interieur (DI), Statut des Juifs, Dossier 5-6. Circulaire Viziriel No. 372 (April 1, 1941).

MAE-Nantes, Series Maroc, Direction de l'Interieur (DI), Dossier 6, Statut des Juifs pendant la Seconde Guèrre Mondiale (August 1940– May 1945).

MAE-Nantes, Series Maroc, Direction de l'Interieur (DI), Statut des Juifs, Dossier 6. Instruction Résidentielle (November 15, 1941), Pour l'examen des demandes de dérogation résultant de la législation en vigueur sur les Juifs.

MAE-Nantes, Series Maroc, Direction de l'Interieur (DI), Statut des Juifs, Dossier 6. Circulary No. 7 from Director of Public Security Services, Cordier, to Secretary General of the Protectorate (April 20, 1942).

MAE-Nantes, Series Maroc, Direction de l'Interieur (DI), Statut des Juifs, Dossier 5-6. Letter from Director of Public Instruction to Secretary General of the Protectorate. "Objet: A/S de Mme Poizot." (February 9, 1943).

MAE-Nantes, Direction de l'Interieur (DI), Statut des Juifs, Dossier 5-6. Direction des Affaires Politiques, Note au sujet de l'habitat juif dans les villes européens (July 5, 1941).

MAE-Nantes, Direction de l'Interieur (DI), Statut des Juifs, Dossier 5-6. A/S recasement de certains Juifs dans les mellahs (September 14, 1941).

MAE-Nantes, Direction de l'Interieur (DI), Statut des Juifs, Dossier 5-6. Letter from Director of Political Affairs to Secretary General of the Protectorate, "Objet: Statut des Juifs: Extension au Maroc de la législation métropolitaine postérieure en 2 juin 1941." (May 9, 1942).

MAE-Nantes, Series Maroc, Cabinet Diplomatique, Carton 670, Dossier General, Etude sur le Sionisme au Maroc (April 3, 1945).

MAE-Nantes, Series Maroc, Direction des Affaires Cherifiènnes (DAC), Carton 323, Emeutes à Sefrou (August 3, 1944).

MAE-Nantes, Series Maroc, Direction de l'Interieur (DI), Dossiers 24, Report from General de Division Suffren, Chef de la Region de Fès, to Director of Political Affairs, regarding "Incident du 30 juillet à Sefrou." (September 4, 1944).

MAE-Nantes, Direction de l'Interieur (DI), Questions juives, Dosser 2 (1944–48), "Note de Direction des Affaires Politique: Au sujet de la réorganisation des comités des communautés Israélites (November 30, 1944).

MAE-Nantes, Direction de l'Interieur (DI), Questions juives, Dossier 2. Letter from Dr. Leon Kubowitzki, Secretary General of World Jewish Congress to Henri Bonnet, French Ambassador to the United States (July 11, 1947).

MAE-Nantes, Series Maroc, Direction de l'Interieur (DI), Questions juives, Dossier 26, Telegram from Delegue Residence Generale, Lacoste, to Diplomatie, Paris, 464–72 (June 3, 1948).

MAE-Nantes, Direction de l'Interieur (DI), Question juives, Dossier 26, Clipping from Ar- Ra'I Al–'Amm (May 12, 1948).

MAE-Nantes, Series Maroc, Direction de l'Interieur (DI), Questions juives, Dosser 26, Report from Civil Controller of Oujda to Résident Général (June 19, 1948).

MAE-Nantes, Series Maroc, Direction des Affaires Cherifiènnes (DAC), Carton 325, Note No. 188 of the Cabinet Diplomatique, Juifs marocains en Israël (June 23, 1952).

Service Historique de la Defense- Fond de l'Armée de Terre, Chateau de Vincennes.

SHD-AT. Carton 3H 305. Extrait du rapport du directeur de l'office du Protectorat de la République Française au Maroc. A/S de la participation du Maroc à l'Exposition Coloniale Internationale de Paris de 1931.

SHD-AT, Carton 3H 247, Office de Liaison, Rabat. Renseignement, A/S manifestation anti- française en Lybie à l'occasion du dahir du 16 mai 1930 du Sultan du Maroc.

SHD-AT, Carton 3H 247. Office de Liaison, Rabat, Renseignement: A/S Agitation Musulmane-Israélite. (May 15, 1933).

SHD-AT, Carton 3H 247. Office de Liaison, Rabat. Renseignement: Protestations d'éléments destouriens du Caire a/s de l'indépendence religieuse accordée aux berbères du Maroc (November 27, 1930).

SHD-AT, Carton 3H 247, Office de Liaison, Rabat, Renseignement, Sujet: agitation de l'Association Universelle de la Jeunesse Musulmane à l'occasion du Dahir du Sultan du Maroc sur les tribus berbères (November 10, 1930).

Centre des Archives d'Outre Mer (AOM), Aix-en-Provence.

AOM 27H5 Review de la Prèsse musulmane (Ministère des Colonies), Nos. 1415–9/EMA Paris.

AOM 27H6 Review de la Prèsse musulmane (Ministère des Colonies), Nos. 2816–2/EMA (27 Mars 1941), Paris.

Index

Alliance Israélite Universelle (AIU) 3, 53, 62–5, 71, 73, 82–3, 123–5, 132, 141, 167
Amazigh 3, 117, 143, *see also* Berber
Anfa Conference 68

Balfour Declaration 76
belonging (groups of) 16, 105, *see also* theory of recognition
Berber 65, 97, 108, 143, *see also* Amazigh
    Dahir 59, 88, 90, 96, 98, 102, 109
blad al-Makzhan/blad al-siba 3, 58, 89, 96–7, 99, 102, 108, 110, 116, 126

capability approach 16, 146–9, *see also* memory capability
Crémieux Decree 60–1, 66–7, 127, 141, 164

dhimmi 49–50, 69, 86

ethics (of remembering) 32

Gallicization 92

Hibbat-Sion 82
Hibra 131

identity (theories of) 16, 19–24, 29, 33, 43, 58
    collective 36
    cultural construct 24, 131
    dynamism 21, 43, 105, 129, 138, 141
    ethnic 39–41
    fluidity 21, 29, 129, 138
    pluralism 20, 29, 33, 122, 129, 141
Istiqlal 70, 94, 107, 111–14

megorashim 51

mellah 130–1, 137
memory 30–7, 144–53, 156
    cultural memory 37
memory capability 2, 11, 36, 146, 153–7, *see also* capability approach
Mizrahi 17, 73
Moroccan Action Committee (CAM) 101–2
Moroccan Communist Party 113, 134
Museum of Moroccan Judaism 2

narrative 142, 149
nationalism 24–46
    adaptive ethno-symbolism 12
    ethno-symbolism 25
    modernism 25–7
    perennialism 25
    postmodernism 28
    primordialists 25

Operation Torch 68, 127
orientalism 70–2

parenthesis theory 4, 5
Political Zionism 46, 60, 69–70, 73–86, 106, 117, 128–9, 134, 141, 161

Rif War 97

Salafiyya movement 91
solar system approach 3, 162
Statut des Juifs 66, 133

Tangier speech 88, 114–15
theory of recognition 19, *see also* belonging
toshavim 51
Treaty of Fez 56, 64, 89

Zamane 1, 69

www.ingramcontent.com/pod-product-compliance
Lightning Source LLC
Chambersburg PA
CBHW072108010526
44111CB00037B/2027